THEOLOGY AND SANCTITY

THEOLOGY AND SANCTITY

ROMANUS CESSARIO, OP

Edited by Cajetan Cuddy, OP

SAPIENTIA PRESS
of Ave Maria University

Sapientia Press
of Ave Maria University
5050 Ave Maria Blvd.
Ave Maria, FL 34142
800-537-5487

Distributed by:
The Catholic University of America Press
c/o HFS
P.O. Box 50370
Baltimore, MD 21211
800-537-5487

Printed in the United States of America.

Library of Congress Control Number: 2014939114

ISBN: 978-1-932589-70-2

CONTENTS

FOREWORD

I am grateful to have the opportunity to express my respect for and friendship with Father Romanus Cessario in a foreword to this collection of some of his major essays.

In our age of intellectual specialization, a vision of the whole exceeds the grasp of even highly intelligent persons. Conferences bring together experts who share diverse viewpoints embedded in methodologies that themselves limit the ability to think outside of preordained boxes. Wisdom goes begging. By contrast, habitual contemplation of the foundation of personhood and of the action of God to save humanity discloses a vision of the whole, which is where truth is discovered and enjoyed.

Father Cessario gives us the fruit of such contemplation in these chapters. His guide in attaining the vision presented here is his brother Dominican St. Thomas Aquinas, who is also the common doctor of the whole Church. The Church is always challenged to keep before the faithful the whole truth, in the light of which particular Church teachings make sense.

Reason is capable of wholistic vision, but it is God's grace, strengthened by the gift of faith, that moves the searcher from knowing about God to knowing God as he wants to be known, even as a friend. Faith is therefore both vision and critique. To make use of reason's unaided efforts to come to a vision of the whole, Aquinas had to convert Aristotle's terms of analysis by stretching the meaning of substance and the category of relation to make them serve the doctrines of the Incarnation and the

Blessed Trinity, to elucidate biblical teaching on creation and adoptive sonship.

Sin clouds one's vision. There is in this volume no bizarre musings about "sin mysticism"; there is simply a deep conviction about God's love for all sinners. The dynamics of grace overcome sin and its consequences, but they are powerful only because God first loves us and gives the power to love him in return. Contemplating God's goodness is therefore intrinsic to grasping the truth about ourselves. The love of learning partners with the desire for God.

There are privileged moments when the working of grace becomes clear and when the vision of the whole, the world as God sees it, is more accessible. In the celebration of the sacraments of the Church, which are the actions of the risen Christ, believers enter into "resurrection time." Father Cessario writes beautifully of the way ordained priests open the vista of eternity for the faithful gathered in this world. Each time the Mass is offered, the world changes. Each place in which the Mass is celebrated becomes, for a brief time, the center of the cosmos.

These are essays with clarity of logic and argument, writings that are scrupulous in their accurate use of sources. In short, Father Cessario's contributions are the result of scholarship dedicated to presenting the whole truth, grounded in the conviction that "only the truth has grace."

—Francis Cardinal George, OMI
Archbishop of Chicago

INTRODUCTION

"Only the Truth Has Grace"

In 1972, a year after his ordination, a young Dominican priest submitted a 123-page thesis titled "The Notion of Person as Relation" to the Pontifical Faculty of the Immaculate Conception in Washington, DC, in partial fulfillment of the requirements for the degree of Licentiate in Sacred Theology (STL).[1] After his graduation, his Dominican superiors assigned him to teach theology at Providence College in Providence, RI. Four years later, in 1976, he was sent to the University of Fribourg in Switzerland to pursue doctoral studies under the direction of the renowned Irish theologian Colman E. O'Neill, OP. In 1980, he completed a doctoral dissertation titled "Christian Satisfaction in Aquinas: Towards a Personalist Understanding."[2] The continuity of themes does not escape even the casual reader. Romanus Cessario, OP, has been thinking about the personal and moral implications of *sacra doctrina* for over forty years.

The concluding sentences of his STL thesis read as follows:

> The notion of person as relation not only satisfies the demands of rigorous systematic theology but also fulfills the exigencies of the catechetical task as well. Far more important, it is a service-

1. Romanus Cessario, OP, "The Notion of Person as Relation: A Study in the Concept of Person as Developed within the Tradition of Thomist Trinitarian Theology in the Light of Some Contemporary Approximations of that Definition," STL diss., Pontifical Faculty of the Immaculate Conception, 1972.

2. The dissertation was published as a book in 1982: Romanus Cessario, OP, *Christian Satisfaction in Aquinas: Toward a Personalist Understanding* (Washington, DC: University Press of America, 1982).

> able tool for mystical theology (in the non-esoteric sense of that word) where the knowledge that is sought is not terminated in some concept of God, be it ever so formally perfect, but, as far as is possible in this life, at the very possession of the Three Who subsist in mutual relatedness with Each Other, the Father, the Son and the Holy Spirit.[3]

It is characteristic of contemporary theology students to devote much energy to locating the places in a particular theologian's corpus wherein the theologian manifests growth, development, and change, which is why this excerpt from Father Cessario's earliest theological writing is so arresting. His intent that theological knowledge "not terminate in some concept of God, be it ever so formally perfect," but rather in "the very possession" of he who is Father, Son, and Holy Spirit, stands in essential continuity with the writings his mature thought has produced. For example, the opening sentence of his 1996 volume *Christian Faith and the Theological Life* reads: "To acquire knowledge about God is one thing; to commit oneself to him is another. Though these actions are obviously related, they constitute discrete moments in the development of the Christian life."[4] Without doubt, Father Cessario's understanding of *sacra doctrina* has deepened since 1972. In light of these two passages separated by twenty-two years and service on two theological faculties, however, I suggest that any developments discernable within his writings are not substantial but only accidental in nature. Romanus Cessario was a Thomist in 1972, and he remains a Thomist today, and the influences that guided him during the course of his earliest studies continue to manifest themselves even in his more recent work.[5] For the past four decades, Father Cessario has consistently maintained that only God himself fully satisfies the human desire for knowledge and love.[6] Ideas—even good ideas—about God are insufficient. God alone suffices.[7]

3. Cessario, "Notion of Person as Relation," 96.

4. Romanus Cessario, OP, *Christian Faith and the Theological Life* (Washington, DC: Catholic University of America Press, 1996), 1.

5. For Cessario's own account of his theological and spiritual formation, see "Culture and Contemplation: Catholicism in the Twenty-First Century" (chap. 13, this volume).

6. "Because only God can fulfill the expectations of the human heart, moral realism measures human actions in accord with how completely they draw the person to union with the living God." Romanus Cessario, OP, *Introduction to Moral Theology*, rev. ed. (Washington, DC: Catholic University of America Press, 2013), 48.

7. "Because knowledge in faith initiates a relationship between the one who believes and

Because truth and love ultimately terminate in God himself, theology and sanctity do not admit to any separation within the human person. God calls the whole human person to beatific communion, and his saving grace enacts nothing short of complete personal transformation and perfection in Christ. "Moral realism unequivocally rejects all forms of anthropological dualism. Christian life does not simply embody a spiritual ideal."[8] Father Cessario has devoted his life to the exposition and application of the moral realism of St. Thomas Aquinas. St. Thomas was not an idealist. He was interested in being as it is actually found in reality. The concrete, the individual, and the particular mattered a great deal to St. Thomas, and he did not fear the complications that necessarily accompany a being's composite existence. Likewise, Thomistic moral realism does not foster any insecurity regarding moral truth even in the shadows of human complexity, weakness, and sin. Indeed, the truth about human perfection carries saving implications for the human person, regardless of the gravity of his moral situation: "In the work of evangelization, there exists no room for compromise on what the grace of Christ can accomplish in anyone, no matter what his or her state or condition may be."[9] The truth of God's love suffers no extrinsic limitations or restrictions. Moral truth triumphs over personal sin.

THEOLOGY, SANCTITY, AND THE TRUTH OF GOD'S LOVE

It is a great honor for me to assemble, edit, and arrange the chapters that together form *Theology and Sanctity*. All of the chapters in this volume originally appeared as independent essays in various theological

---

the very Persons of the blessed Trinity, the virtue of faith is properly referred to as a 'supernatural virtue.' Affirming clearly the supernatural character of faith, theologians maintain that the proper object of knowledge in faith is nothing short of God who is the First Truth" (Cessario, *Christian Faith*, 51).

8. Romanus Cessario, OP, *The Moral Virtues and Theological Ethics*, 2nd ed. (Notre Dame, IN: University of Notre Dame Press, 2009), 65. Thus even "the concupiscible and irascible sense appetites, which, in themselves comprise the emotional life of the human person, possess the capacity for true virtuous formation ordered to the authentic finalities of both nature and grace" (ibid.). This account of the virtues, of course, is distinctively Thomistic (cf. ibid., 63–66).

9. Ibid., 66.

publications. The earliest essay included in this volume, "On Bad Actions, Good Intentions, and the Loving God" (chap. 9), was published in 1997. The most recent piece, "Culture and Contemplation: Catholicism in the Twenty-First Century" (chap. 13), appeared in 2013. Nonetheless, although the following chapters were originally composed as independent theological works, they have been carefully selected and arranged to form a coherent, integral whole.

I have written headnotes to help facilitate the volume's immediate usefulness. Each chapter's introduction summarizes its content and identifies its continuity with the chapters that precede and follow it. Additionally, each chapter has received minor editorial adjustments, mostly within the footnotes for conformity of style.

The chapters are all structured around—and consider under different aspects—the two essential principles that inform all of Father Cessario's theology: (1) God loves us because of his goodness, not because of our goodness; and (2) only the truth has grace. In short, the truth of God's love serves as the unifying theme that integrates each of this volume's chapters. Of course, these two elements are not original to Father Cessario: they shape the thought of St. Thomas himself. Nonetheless, Father Cessario's distinctive ability to educe the practical and spiritual implications of Thomistic doctrine for our modern period provides contemporary students, professors, seminarians, and priests with a unique aid for sacred study, holy teaching, Christian life, and pastoral ministry.

During a sermon preached before university students, St. Thomas once said, "as a father has brought you forth physically, a *magister* brings you forth spiritually."[10] This analogy between the physical generation of natural paternity and the spiritual generation of the teacher of sacred truth is matter for fruitful contemplation. The father and the *magister* both engender a principle of life. *Sacra doctrina* imparts living truth. The authentic doctrine of St. Thomas Aquinas enkindles a vitality that exceeds mere intellectual stimulation. Indeed, Thomism remains perennial in the life of the Catholic Church because it is properly ordered

10. Thomas Aquinas, "Sermon 08: *Puer Jesus*—Sermon on the First Sunday after Epiphany," in *Thomas Aquinas: The Academic Sermons*, trans. Mark-Robin Hoogland, CP (Washington, DC: Catholic University of America Press, 2010), 102 (3.2.1). Emphasis original.

toward nothing less than the sanctifying transformation of persons.[11] Flowing from the Thomist tradition, each of the following chapters is a work of *holy teaching*—teaching founded upon divine truth and ordered toward the salvation of souls.[12] Theology and sanctity are inseparable realities, because only the truth has grace.

I thank Roger Nutt of Ave Maria University for the kind invitation to edit and assemble the essays in this volume. I also thank Ashleigh McKown for her patient kindness, editorial aid, and literary skill. Additionally, I want to acknowledge the invaluable assistance of my Dominican brother Sebastian White, OP, who provided generous assistance with some of the more tedious chores a project of this kind requires.

Finally, I would like to thank Romanus Cessario himself. Father Cessario was the first priest to explain to me the truth about God's love, and it was from him that I first learned that only the truth has grace. Thank you, dear father and brother in St. Dominic and the Holy Preaching.

—Cajetan Cuddy, OP
April 1, 2014

11. See Romanus Cessario, OP, *A Short History of Thomism* (Washington, DC: Catholic University of America Press, 2005); and Cajetan Cuddy, OP, and Romanus Cessario, OP, "Witness to Faith: George Weigel, Blessed John Paul II, and the Theological Life," *Nova et Vetera* 10, no. 1 (2012): 1–13.

12. See Victor White, OP, *Holy Teaching: The Idea of Theology According to St. Thomas Aquinas* (London: Blackfriars, 1958).

THEOLOGY AND SANCTITY

CHAPTER 1

THE GRACE ST. DOMINIC BRINGS TO THE WORLD

A Fresh Look at Dominican Spirituality

This chapter introduces the overarching themes present within *Theology and Sanctity*. As I noted in my introduction, Father Cessario is a Dominican priest, and the reality of his religious and sacramental identity informs all of his thought and writing. Here we discover the distinct "form" of Dominican life—*forma vitae*—that characterizes his teaching and preaching. This form originates from a personal source, the Order's founder: "The Dominican form of life flows from the grace St. Dominic introduces into the world." Marked with the evangelical impress of its Holy Father (the *vir evangelicus*), the Order of Preachers "is known to have been established, from the beginning, for preaching and the salvation of souls, specifically." When we consider the uniquely evangelical character of his life and mission, we recognize that St. Dominic "enjoys a strong claim to holding the copyright on the expression" known as "new evangelization."

Because of the nature of this special grace, Dominicans "pause before applying the term 'spirituality' to their graced form of life." This hesitation stems from the Thomistic conviction that there is nothing

Originally published as "The Grace Saint Dominic Brings to the World: A Fresh Look at Dominican Spirituality," *Logos* 15, no. 2 (2012): 1–17. Reprinted by permission.

essentially programmatic about the saving movements of divine grace. One encounters the Dominican form of life not in the calculative or in the abstract, but in the concrete, sanctifying rhythms of the Order's "regular observance." Father Cessario explains that "those who maintain a life of prayer, study, and recollection inevitably are the same friars who find the time to accomplish the most notable achievements for the salvation of souls." This sanctifying unity of contemplation and evangelization lies at the heart of both theology and sanctity.

The phrase "Dominican spirituality" has entered only lately into common usage within the Dominican Order. Neither St. Dominic (ca. 1172–1221) nor the early Dominican saints, including Thomas Aquinas (1224/25–74) and Catherine of Siena (1347–80), would have recognized the expression. These holy ones of course would have known and observed the practices that today one includes under the heading of "Dominican spirituality." But they would have understood these basic pieces of Dominican life as indispensable constituents of that regular form of life that, since the first decades of the thirteenth century, Dominicans have fostered and sustained. They would have accepted these practices, in other words, as composing the rhythm of Dominican life, though not as expressing the unique features of a classifiable Dominican spirituality.

Although the distinction initially may strike one as trifling, it is one thing to animate a form of life that embodies a divine grace and another to observe the axioms of a spirituality, even of a school whose authenticity the Church recognizes. The Dominican scholar Thomas Gilby says that form refers to "the inner shaping principle of a thing."[1] Like the natural forms that exist in creation, or even like the aesthetic forms that artists impose on their materials, form implies that something possesses an identifiable stability. We easily distinguish pineapples from panda bears and the music of George Frideric Handel from that of Harry Connick Jr. In a word, form indicates what makes someone or something

1. Thomas Gilby, OP, *God's Will and Providence*, vol. 5 (Ia. 19–26), *St. Thomas Aquinas, Summa Theologiae* (New York: McGraw-Hill, 1967), 193.

to be what he, she, or it is. Dominican form gives shape to a distinctive way of life within the Church. An official document of the Order of Preachers in fact employs the phrase *forma vitae*, the form of the Order's life.[2] Were Dominicans to speak about their "spirituality," they would necessarily mean the expression "Dominican spirituality," the distinctive form of life that distinguishes them from members of other religious institutes. They would at the same time describe the inner shaping principle that those who are drawn to espouse Dominican life desire to embrace, to make their own, and to give themselves to, all under the impulse of a freely given grace that we call a "vocation."

The Dominican form of life flows from the grace St. Dominic introduces into the world. It is a marvelous thing to ponder that one specific grace, originally embodied in the Castilian priest Dominic of Caleruega, today unites Dominican priests and cooperator brothers all over the world. This same grace also places today's Dominicans in a direct lineage with those men who for almost eight hundred years have worn the black-and-white habit of Dominic's Order. The Dominican form received its official recognition from the Roman Pontiff Honorius III (d. 1227) on December 22, 1216. Although his predecessor, the illustrious Pope Innocent III (d. July 1216), had confirmed Dominic in his project, Pope Honorius's bull, a document that miraculously survived the fury of the French Revolution and today is housed in the French provincial archives of the Haute-Garonne, accounts for the much-anticipated eighth centenary jubilee of the Order to be celebrated in 2016.[3] The inspiration for speaking of a grace that stands at the heart of a Dominican vocation comes from words that Honorius III addressed to Dominic in January 1221, some six months before the saint's death. These words have found their way into the *Constitutio Fundamentalis*, a text of recent composition

2. *Constitutio Fundamentalis*, §VIII: "Propositium fundamentale Ordinis et forma vitae ab ipso profluens momentum suum quocumque Ecclesiae tempore servant." See also §VI: "Forma Ordinis, ut est societas religiosa, ex eius missione et communione fraterna oritur." Unfortunately, the official English version translates (less technically) the Latin *forma* as "nature." This English version is the one authorized by Timothy Radcliffe (Dublin: Dominican Publications, 1998).

3. M. H. Vicaire, *Histoire de Saint Dominique*, vol. 2, *Au Coeur de l'Église* (Paris: Cerf, 1982), 67.

that serves as a kind of preface to the constitutions and ordinations that today govern Dominican life: "He who never ceases to make his Church fruitful through new offspring," began the pope, "wishes to make these modern times [the thirteenth century] the equal of former days [the first Christian centuries] and to spread the Catholic faith. So he inspired you [Dominicans] with a holy desire to embrace poverty, profess the regular life and commit yourselves to the proclamation of the word of God, preaching everywhere the name of our Lord Jesus Christ."[4] No doubt about it. Pope Honorius III understood that the development of the Dominican Order proceeded from a grace that St. Dominic—and, through his mediation, the first Dominicans—had received from God.

DOMINICAN "SPIRITUALITY"

As a general rule, Dominicans should pause before applying the term "spirituality" to their graced form of life. The reason for this caution lies in the very intricate evolution of the concept of spirituality, especially since the seventeenth century. We learn about this evolution in the authoritative reference for all matters dealing with spirituality, namely, the multivolume *Dictionnaire de Spiritualité*, begun by Jesuit scholars in 1932.[5] In the article that treats both the word and the notion of spirituality, one discovers that the term in its present meaning comes into currency among Catholic authors of the seventeenth century; for example, the renowned French ecclesiastics Jacques-Bénigne Bossuet (1627–1704) and François Fénelon (1651–1715).[6] Arguably, a first use of spirituality in the modern sense of the term occurs earlier in the writings of a Capuchin author, Constantin de Barbanson (1582–1631), whose main work, *Les secrets sentiers de l'amour divin*, first saw the light of day at Cologne in 1623, with many editions in several languages coming into print thereafter.[7] Spirituality

4. *Constitutio Fundamentalis*, §I.

5. *Dictionnaire de spiritualité, ascétique et mystique: Doctrine et histoire* (Paris: Beauchesne, 1932–95).

6. Aimé Solignac, *Dictionnaire de spiritualité ascétique et mystique*, 14:1142.

7. See the review of the Paris 1932 edition by Fernand Van Steenberghen in *Revue néoscolastique de philosophie* 40 (1937): 325.

emerges, then, within the context of the Church's efforts undertaken in Europe after the Council of Trent to provide models of authentic Catholic life for clergy, religious, and laypeople. From the seventeenth century until our own day, spiritualities of all descriptions have multiplied.

The dimensions of spirituality as a growth market may be judged from the sheer volume of the *Dictionnaire de Spiritualité*. This standard reference work contains fifteen volumes with an index (volume 16), published in 1995, that comprises 751 pages. During the modern period, many persons and institutes have devised and promoted distinctive views on the most suitable way for the believer to reach Christian perfection. Oftentimes, battles raged between authors and among different schools of thought, especially in France. One of the most celebrated of these controversies centered on the enigmatic figure of Madame Guyon (1648–1717), a French Catholic laywoman whose penchant for quietism pitted two French bishops, the aforementioned Bossuet and Fénelon, against one another. In his study of this controversy, Ronald Knox titles his chapter "Madame Guyon and the Battle of the Olympians."[8] It is instructive that when Bossuet, who opposed Madame Guyon, used the term *spiritualité*, he ordinarily meant it in a pejorative way; for example, in the phrase *la nouvelle spiritualité*, by which Bossuet meant the practices of the quietists.[9] In 1699, Pope Innocent XII sanctioned Madame Guyon's quietist *pensées*.

To discover the theoretical conception that prompted the explosion of spiritualities, one may usefully consult the four-volume work by the Sulpician author Pierre Pourrat (1871–1957), *La spiritualité chrétienne*, first published in Paris during *les Années folles*. This twentieth-century author from the Society of Saint-Sulpice explains the place spirituality has held in Catholic life since the sixteenth-century Reformation.[10] "Spirituality," Pourrat writes, "is that part of theology which deals with Christian perfection and the ways that lead to it ... [it] is divided into *Ascetic Theology* and *Mystical Theology*."[11] The science of spirituality, as it

8. Ronald A. Knox, *Enthusiasm: A Chapter in the History of Religion* (Westminster, MD: Christian Classics, 1983), chap. 14, 317–55.

9. Solignac, *Dictionnaire de spiritualité ascétique et mystique*, 14:1148.

10. Pierre Pourrat, *La spiritualité chrétienne*, 4 vols. (Paris: J. Gabalda, 1921–30).

11. Pierre Pourrat, *Christian Spirituality*, trans W. H. Mitchell and S. P. Jacques (Westminster, MD: Newman Press, 1953), v.

developed in the modern period, imposed almost imperceptibly a tripartite division upon the one theological science. The members of this division include dogmatic theology, moral theology, and spiritual theology, which, as Pourrat indicates, concerns "Christian perfection." Dominicans, at least inasmuch as they follow Aquinas, cannot admit this Balkanization of theology. Aquinas could not express himself more clearly on the question than he does in *Summa Theologiae* I, q. 1, art. 3: *Dicendum sacram doctrinam unam scientiam esse.* In other words, *sacra doctrina* should be declared a single science.[12] Nonetheless, Pourrat's threefold division of theology reflects the view that the majority of working theologians held from at least the seventeenth century until roughly the period of the Second Vatican Council (1962–65).

During the twentieth century and even earlier, a few Dominicans remembered that one cannot separate the study of Christian perfection from the theses defended in both dogmatic and moral theology.[13] Their voices went largely unheard. After Vatican II, another sort of evolution took place. Today, spirituality so dominates some theological and ministerial landscapes that, for many Christians, enthusiasm for spiritual theology has eclipsed both interest in and concern for dogmatic and moral theology. And it goes without saying that more often than not the classical lessons in ascetic and mystical theologies have been replaced by the aphorisms and axioms of therapeutic psychology and special advocacies. It falls outside the scope of this essay to discuss how Catholic theology found itself entangled in ersatz spiritual exercises such as aroma meditation, the Enneagram, and Reiki. Official efforts to restrain these anomalies often meet with hardcore resistance, however, especially from those people who stand to profit financially from such "programs."

To understand better what distinguishes Dominican life from many later forms of religious life, including those institutes (like the Jesuits and Salesians) that rely on their own spiritualities, it is advisable to return to the circumstances that first prompted the separation of spiritual

12. Thomas Gilby, OP, *Christian Theology*, vol. 1 (Ia. 1), *St. Thomas Aquinas, Summa Theologiae* (New York: McGraw-Hill, 1964), 13.

13. For an account, see Servais Pinckaers, *The Sources of Christian Ethics*, trans. Sister Mary Thomas Noble, OP (Washington, DC: Catholic University of America Press, 1995).

theology from doctrine and morals. The history of the sixteenth-century Catholic Reform remains a complicated one to analyze. The celebrated Dominican historian Father Guy Bedouelle observes that some Catholic reformers shared with the Protestants an impatience with speculative subtleties and a preference for the new humanist studies. The author points, for example, to the sixteenth-century Bishop of Verona Gian Matteo Giberti (1495–1543), who installed a printing press in his episcopal palace to produce patristic and modern texts in Greek.[14] To those who were charged with implementing the reforms of the Council of Trent, it seemed that the Church no longer enjoyed the leisure to indulge in what not a few regarded as the esoteric Latin exercises of late medieval scholastic debate. Something similar occurred after World War I. *Ressourcement* theology of the kind practiced during the mid-twentieth century goes hand in hand with *engagement*—taking on, investing, revitalizing. Recall that the first volume in the series, *Sources chrétiennes*, published in 1942 by Jesuit scholar Jean Daniélou, was Gregory of Nyssa's *The Life of Moses*, a work of practical instructions to a young monk.[15]

In the wake of the Protestant Reform, the agents of the Catholic Reform, mainly priests and bishops, turned their attention to the practical affairs of Catholics living in the world. St. Francis de Sales (1567–1622), the saintly though exiled Bishop of Geneva, is generally credited with composing the first enduring set of counsels for those who sought to live a devout or spiritual life while remaining active in the affairs that the laity are charged to transform: the home, economics, and political order.[16] His *Introduction to the Devout Life*, first published in 1609, remains a recognized classic of modern Catholic spirituality. Salesian spirituality, however, reorganized Catholic living. The one who follows the Salesian model prays in order to sanctify his or her life, whereas the monastic ideal maintained a regular form of life so that the monk or nun (or, later, the friar) would grow in holiness, thus rendering a per-

14. Guy Bedouelle, OP, *The Reform of Catholicism, 1480–1620*, trans. J. K. Farge (Toronto: PIMS, 2008), 62–63.

15. For further commentary, see Romanus Cessario, OP, "An Observation on Robert Lauder's Review of G. A. McCool, S.J.," *Thomist* 56 (1992): 701–10.

16. Bedouelle, *Reform of Catholicism*, 106–9.

son fit to offer God the most excellent expression of prayer and worship. Because the Salesian model offers an alternative to the older monastic forms of life, Salesian devotion and spirituality differ substantially from what animates Dominican life: the Dominican *forma vitae,* that is, the Dominican Order's distinctive form of apostolic life. But St. Francis de Sales has left his stamp on much modern Catholic devotional practice in the Latin Church. What can one conclude? While the solutions devised by the saints of the sixteenth century, including heroes like St. Philip Neri (1515–95), produced many praiseworthy results at a critical moment for the Church, they nonetheless exacted a price on what one might call the classical model of Catholic clerical life, at least that clerical life associated with religious consecration. This thought may seem startling at first, especially recalling that on March 12, 1622, Pope Gregory XV canonized five persons: SS. Ignatius Loyola (1491–1556), Francis Xavier (1506–52), Teresa of Avila (1515–82), Philip Neri—all saints of the Catholic Reform—and the twelfth-century layman and day laborer Isidore the Farmer, who himself in all likelihood had never heard anyone utter the word "spirituality."

As I have said, the form that informs Dominican life follows upon the monastic model of life and not the Salesian conception of spirituality. The Fundamental Constitution stipulates as much: "Sharing the Apostles' mission, we also follow their way of life, in the form devised by St. Dominic (*secundum formam a Sancto Dominico conceptam*). We do our best to live of one accord the common life, observing faithfully the evangelical counsels, fervent in prayer and in the common celebration of the liturgy, especially the Eucharist and the divine office, diligent in study and constant in regular observance (*in regulari observantia perseverantes*).[17] The phrase "regular observance" refers to the everyday discipline that governs life within a Dominican priory. Some of these observances, such as the architectural shape of our convents—classically built around a monastic cloister with the principal rooms, chapel, refectory, and library located off the inner courtyard—and the wearing of the religious habit, strike the eye of the visitor, whereas others, such as silence

17. *Constitutio Fundamentalis,* §IV.

and a spirit of recollection, may take time to notice.[18] Dominicans are not monks, of course. They move around rather than commit to stability of place and they replace manual labor, such as shepherding, jelly making, beekeeping, and so forth, with the arduous work of ongoing study, book reading, essay writing, media publishing, whatever is useful for the salvation of souls.[19] Still, the theological gene that distinguishes the Dominican form of life from those religious institutes that trace their beginnings to the post-Tridentine period—foremost among them, I should add, rank the Jesuits—commits the Dominican to follow the pattern of life that St. Dominic himself lived as a regular Augustinian canon in his native Spain at the cathedral of Osma. It comes as no surprise to discover that, when the Fourth Lateran Council held in 1215 forbade the production of new religious rules and instead counseled that new foundations should adopt one of the existing and approved rules in the Church, Dominic chose the Rule of Augustine. This ancient document still binds those who make profession in the Dominican Order.[20]

THE END AND ELEMENTS OF THE DOMINICAN FORM OF LIFE

The Fundamental Constitution stipulates the elements of the Dominican form of life. The document begins by describing the Order's fundamental purpose: "The Order of Friars Preachers, founded by St. Dominic, 'is known to have been established, from the beginning, for preaching and the salvation of souls, specifically.'"[21] Dominicans exist for preaching and the salvation of souls. "End" dominates the life of the Dominican in the same way that God intends the supernatural end of human life to direct the lives of all who dwell on this earth. All that transpires within a typical Dominican day finds its lodestar in the act of preaching and in an un-

18. For an impressive sampling of the layout of Dominican convents in medieval France, see Georges Rohault de Fleury, *Gallia Dominicana: Les Couvents de St Dominique au Moyen Age*, 2 vols. (Paris: Imprimerie Emile Collot, 1903).

19. See *The Book of the Constitutions and Ordinations of the Brothers of the Order of Preachers*, no. 77, §1.

20. See Vicaire, *Histoire de Saint Dominique*, 39–41.

21. *Constitutio Fundamentalis*, §II.

wavering resolve to save souls. With a calculated arbitrariness, I have arranged certain key elements of the Dominican form of life under each of the two headings that express the Dominican Order's *raison d'être*: First, preaching, which requires prayer, study, and recollection; second, saving souls, which requires holiness of life, zeal, and a touch of genius. I examine each of these six qualities in turn. Before doing so, however, it is important to note that the order of charity (*ordo caritatis*) requires that while Dominicans dedicate themselves to preaching and the salvation of souls, they must at the same time save their own souls. The Dominican form does not supply a utilitarian formula for maximizing evangelical efficiency. Dominican life does not provide a recipe to build a better mousetrap. Rather, the Dominican form is designed to ensure that the one who embraces it himself becomes holy as St. Dominic became a saint by his personal acts of loving God. "Our brothers, therefore," the Fundamental Constitution continues, "as the founder prescribed, 'should everywhere behave uprightly and religiously, as men intent on procuring their own and other people's salvation: they should behave as evangelical men, following in the footsteps of the Saviour, speaking to God or of God, among themselves or with their neighbours.'"[22] With this caveat in mind, I proceed to examine the elements of the Dominican form. These elements sanctify those men who embrace the Order's form, even as Dominican life readies them to work for the salvation of others. Today the Church speaks about the "new evangelization." St. Dominic, I aver, enjoys a strong claim to holding the copyright on the expression.

Preaching

"Since the ministry of the word and of the sacraments of faith is a priestly function, ours is a clerical Order." Thus states the Fundamental Constitution, paragraph VI. Dominicans maintain the basic pattern of clerical life that has existed in the Church for centuries, just as St. Dominic himself received the standard clerical formation that flourished during the late twelfth century. Three considerations follow from the Domini-

22. *Constitutio Fundamentalis*, §II, citing the Primitive Constitutions, dist. II, c. 31.

can commitment to the clerical state and its prerogative of preaching, that is, from Dominicans "having been made cooperators with the episcopal order by priestly ordination."[23]

1. *Prayer*. One of the unfortunate outcomes of the contemporary penchant for marketing spiritualities appears in the commonly held view that prayer serves the personal needs of the one who prays. People develop prayer techniques that help them get through a tough day or a difficult period. Within Catholic theology, scant warrant exists for making prayer this kind of therapeutic or palliative exercise. Because prayer constitutes an act of the virtue of religion, God—not man—becomes the first beneficiary of man's prayer. Aquinas makes this point clearly: "Through prayer man offers reverence to God because he subjects himself to God and professes that God is the source of all that he is and all that he has. Clearly, therefore, prayer is an act of religion."[24] We can infer from this definition of prayer that the Dominican priest first of all embodies the religious man. He stands out as a religious man in the strong sense of the term. For, by his prayer, the Dominican priest subjects himself to Almighty God and acknowledges him as the source of every benefit. It takes strength to pray in this reverential way. The Dominican priest, of course, is expected to pray well. At the same time, he is able to distinguish authentic prayer from prayer that occasions sensible consolations. One reason why the prayer that stands at the heart of the Dominican form of life occurs during the Holy Sacrifice of the Mass and the Divine Office—to which one can also append the recitation of the Rosary—may be found in the official nature of these liturgical actions and in the canonized meditations that accompany the recitation of the Rosary. Other forms of prayer, such as processions and litanies, find their niche within the Dominican form. Whatever mode Dominican prayer adopts—and I recognize that further distinctions need to be made between the official prayer of worship that the Church supplies in the Mass and Divine Office and those other modes of prayer that sustain these liturgical actions—one thing remains undeniably true. Dominican prayer expresses the vir-

23. *Constitutio Fundamentalis*, §V.

24. *ST* II-II, q. 83, a. 3.

tue of religion. In other words, prayer remains something owed to God. Within this context, outsiders should understand why Dominicans take great pains to ensure that the choral office proceeds in a way that honors the Divine Majesty. Choir practice never wastes a Dominican's time.

2. *Study*. Assiduous study follows prayer. What we believe, we also want to understand. We confess that God is a Trinity of Persons. We want to understand, as much as a supernatural mystery allows, what it means that God is Three Persons in One divine nature. We confess that Jesus Christ is God. We want to understand—again, as much as a human person can gain access to the hypostatic union—what it means that there subsist two complete and integral natures, human and divine, in the one divine person of the Word. The list continues. The Dominican investigates within one science all that the Church holds out for our belief. We call this exercise doing theology. Only habitual study enables one to do theology. Experience alone does not. Each article of the Creed and everything else that God has revealed for our salvation draws us into the divine mystery that the articles of faith, the twelve articles of the Creed, express in words. The pure contemplative may pause before these mysteries with a devotion that words cannot express. The Dominican nuns devote themselves to this kind of contemplation as their personal and corporate response to the act of faith. The Dominican priest, however, cannot limit his response to God's Word to contemplation. Instead it falls on his shoulders to present the truths of salvation in a way that those who listen to his preaching can understand what God has revealed about himself and the world. This indisputable fact of Dominican clerical life explains the familiar adage that the Dominican Order takes as a motto: *contemplari et contemplata aliis tradere*—to contemplate, and to give to others the fruit of one's contemplation.[25]

3. *Recollection*. Prayer and study cannot transpire outside of a context of recollection. The Dominican should never discover that he has become a man completely distracted by distractions. Nothing separates

25. For commentary on this distinctive feature of the Dominican life, see M.-M. Labourdette, OP, "L'idéal dominicain," *Revue Thomiste* 92 (1992): 344–54.

a Dominican from the ethos of contemporary life more than the careful practice of personal recollection. In a word, recollection means that the Dominican maintains an inner awareness not only of the presence of God but also of the importance of divine things. The Dominican priest cannot survive long apart from the practice of a recollected life. Interior recollection does not come easy. The Dominican convent is constructed to promote the habitual practice of recollection. Externals matter. So Dominicans observe silence, custody of the eyes, and, apart from the times of recreation, an air of tranquility that disposes the powers of the soul to pursue the noble actions that embracing the Dominican form requires of them: praying and studying. In the novitiate of my day, television was not allowed; of course, in 1964, we had no personal computers or other such electronics. There is no need to point out the threat that the private world of cyberspace poses to maintaining recollection. Even before the specter of pornography and *le monde osé* arises, the Internet occasions a scary challenge to sustaining a life of recollection. Without a conscious effort to maintain one's recollection, however, no one—and surely no Dominican—can give himself over to prayer and study with devotion.

THE DOMINICAN FORM AND THE SALVATION OF SOULS

Next I focus on those elements of the Dominican form, the *forma vitae*, that serve to promote the salvation of souls. If prayer, study, and recollection combine to construct the contemplative side of Dominican life, holiness of life, zeal, and a touch of genius achieve their effects (insofar as these qualities affect others) in the persons to whom a Dominican preaches, especially those whom he encounters personally as a priest.[26] One should not, however, overdraw the distinction between contemplation and action. For it inevitably remains the case that those who maintain a life of prayer, study, and recollection are the same friars who find

26. Important as the right use of mass media remains for the work of preaching—for example, websites and monthly publications such as *Magnificat*—the communication of divine grace through preaching is inseparable from a personal encounter with the sacred person whom the sacraments render apt to serve this mediation.

the time to accomplish the most notable achievements for the salvation of souls. The Fundamental Constitution describes the desired union of contemplation and action in the following words: "The life of the order comprises a synthesis of these elements [the pieces of the Dominican form], inseparably interconnected, harmoniously balanced and mutually enriching. It is an apostolic life in the full sense of the word, from which preaching and teaching ought to issue from an abundance of contemplation."[27] Given this high challenge, nothing matches the adventure of pursuing and completing a Dominican vocation.

The salvation of souls reflects the cry that issued so frequently from the heart of St. Dominic, his *cri de coeur*. A first Latin phrase taught to Dominicans of yesteryear runs like this: *Nemo potest dare quod non habet*. Novice masters, student masters, and other persons engaged in forming young Dominicans would remind them that a successful apostolic life issues only from within, from within the heart of a holy Dominican. For, as the Latin phrase declares, no one can give what he does not possess.

Holiness of Life

The Dominican commits himself to the embrace of sanctity. As already mentioned, holiness of life needs no further justification to pursue than the injunction Christ delivers at the end of the Sermon on the Mount: "Be perfect, just as your heavenly Father is perfect" (Mt 5:48). The Dominican, as Aquinas reminds us, aims not only to shine but also to illumine.[28] But the Dominican pursues holiness of life in a way that separates him from the modern preference for voluntarism. Holiness for a Dominican—believe it or not—first of all involves the intellect. Dominican holiness flows from the virtue of prudence. Prudence shapes the practical intelligence. To give only one example: before one can will effectively to be temperate with the pleasures of food, drink, or sex, a man first needs to distinguish between the shameful and the noble, the honorable and the vile. In another place, I have discussed with reference

27. *Constitutio Fundamentalis*, §IV.
28. See *ST* II-II, q. 188, art. 6.

to certain historical details the intellectual character of Dominican holiness.[29] For now, permit me to borrow an observation from a respected theological commentator: "St. Thomas," writes this author, "would not approve a facile use of the phrase 'the will of God' as comfort either to superiors or subjects; within the limits of their relationship (art. [2a2ae 104] 4–5) both are assured that it is God's will that the one command and the other obey; there is no such guarantee that the content of the command is God's will."[30]

It is fairly well known that the ancient Dominican form of profession includes only one vow. The *Summa Theologiae* of Aquinas supplies the theological grounds for this manner of religious consecration. Aquinas explains that "the vow of obedience includes the other vows, [though] not vice versa. For although a religious is bound by vow to observe continence and poverty, these are also included under obedience, which embraces many other things besides continence and poverty."[31] The Fundamental Constitution explains a further purpose for professing only obedience: "we consecrate ourselves entirely to God by profession, thus becoming members of [the] Order and dedicated in a new way to the universal Church."[32] Dominican profession commits the member of the Order to common life, obedience to legitimate superiors, chastity, and poverty. The Dominican distinctively lives out these practices and virtues within the context of what is called regular observance, as I have already mentioned in distinguishing partisans of spiritualities from observants of a life form (*forma vitae*).

Zeal

To remark on zeal within the context of discussing the Dominican life leads the studious inquirer back to the figure of St. Dominic. The best

29. See Romanus Cessario, "Molina and Aquinas," in *A Companion to Luis de Molina*, ed. Mathias Kaufmann and Alexander Aichele (Leiden: Brill, 2014), 291–323.

30. T. C. O'Brien, *Virtues of Justice in the Human Community*, vol. 41 (2a2ae. 101–22), *St. Thomas Aquinas, Summa Theologiae* (New York: McGraw-Hill, 1972), 49.

31. *ST* II-II, q. 186, a. 8.

32. *Constitutio Fundamentalis*, §III.

way to measure the zeal that Dominic generates in those who embrace the form of life that he bequeathed to his Order is to pick up the *Catalogus Hagiographicus Ordinis Praedicatorum*, newly edited in 2001 by Father Innocent Venchi, OP.[33] There one discovers that the Dominican Order rejoices in many, many saints and blesseds. To limit our consideration to the friars, these recognized holy ones include some popes, more archbishops and bishops, countless priests, and not a few cooperator brothers, of whom one paradoxically enjoys more renown worldwide than do the popes and martyrs and many of the great theologians. He of course is the seventeenth-century Peruvian son of a Spanish gentleman and Panamanian woman of color, St. Martin de Porres (1579–1639). To develop the zeal that remains proper to the sons of Dominic, read the lives of the saints and blesseds. They stun the imagination. They attract by their diversity. They illuminate the potentialities resident in what Dominicans from the beginning have referred to as the grace of preaching, the *gratia praedicationis*.[34]

A Touch of Genius

Dominicans inherit from St. Dominic his aptitude for confronting the unexpected. The history of St. Dominic presents the attentive reader with the figure of a man who followed his bishop on a routine business trip, discovered Catholic life under large-scale attack from heretical deformations of doctrine, responded to these politically supported heretics on several fronts while at the same time managing to win local approval from the Bishop of Toulouse, then traveled to Rome to obtain official recognition of his projected worldwide Order, and finally oversaw the first attempt in Bologna to organize a priory of his newly legitimized Order. More people probably recognize the *fioretti* of Francis of Assisi than they do the biographical details of St. Dominic. The Poor Man of Assisi displayed charismatic leadership and profound attachment to the

33. Fr. Innocent Venchi, ed., *Catalogus Hagiographicus Ordinis Praedicatorum* (Rome: Postulatio Generalis, 2001).

34. Guy Bedouelle, OP, *Dominic, or the Grace of the Word*, trans. Sister Mary Thomas Noble, OP (San Francisco: Ignatius Press, 1995), 123–28.

imitation of Christ. Dominic exhibited the qualities of a master artist, like the artistic genius who knows by a sort of instinct just how to create a masterpiece. The French priest who reestablished the Dominican Order in Europe after the utter destruction of the French revolutionary and Napoleonic suppressions, Henri-Dominique Lacordaire, offers an example of one of many modern figures who replicate the religious genius of Dominic.

CONCLUSION

Students of philosophy will recognize immediately that to observe a specific form of life implicates Dominicans in the perennial problem of the one and the many. The problem resolves itself, however, to the extent that those who embrace the Dominican form allow it to transform them. To adapt the phrase of one Dominican author, they then all become as one after "the image of St. Dominic."[35] The government of the Order facilitates creating a communion of brothers committed to the same fundamental objectives. Dominican "government is communitarian in a manner peculiar to itself, for superiors ordinarily take office after elections by the brothers and confirmation by a higher superior."[36] One indisputable sign of the genius that attaches to the form of life that St. Dominic inspires rests on the fact that the Order has never suffered permanent divisions. Reforms, yes; divisions, no. No Dominicans of this or that observance exist. No wonder the Fundamental Constitution is bold in affirming that "the Order's fundamental purpose and the way of life which follows from it retain their worth in every age of the Church's existence."[37] In the Latin text, the phrase "way of life" appears as *forma vitae*.

35. Guy Bedouelle, OP, *In the Image of St. Dominic: Nine Portraits of Dominican Life*, trans. Sister Mary Thomas Noble, OP (San Francisco: Ignatius Press, 1994).

36. *Constitutio Fundamentalis*, §VII.

37. *Constitutio Fundamentalis*, §VIII.

CHAPTER 2

LOVE, FRIENDSHIP, AND BEAUTY

This chapter introduces the theme of friendship. St. Thomas teaches that "charity signifies not only the love of God, but also a certain friendship with him" (*ST* II-II, q. 23, a. 1). Building upon his consideration of St. Dominic, Father Cessario suggests that the religious life is an indispensable part of the "new evangelization," saying "the consecrated person stands at the center of this work [i.e., the transformation of culture] as a living icon of the transformed life." Thus only a Trinitarian, "theological hermeneutic guarantees an authentic interpretation of religious and other forms of consecrated life." As *Vita consecrata* says, "the consecrated life proclaims what the Father, through the Son and in the Spirit, brings about by his love, his goodness, and his beauty" (§7).

The importance of religious consecration "as the foundation of mission" is recognized in light of this "Trinitarian triad": love, goodness, and beauty. Each of these three characteristics reflects the truth of God's own divine life and being, and the loving union he establishes among his children. The *communicatio* of benevolent love establishes authentic, true friendship—with God and with neighbor. This loving *communicatio* is founded upon the goodness of the truth.

Originally published as "Love, Friendship, and Beauty," *Logos* 11, no. 4 (2008): 147–63. Reprinted by permission.

"Contemplation forms the foundational activity of friends." Friendship is not an end in itself. "Friendship must be about something." While characteristic of the Christian life in general, the contemplation of divine truth serves as the "unifying principle of friendship" within the bond of religious consecration. Although goodness and beauty are the same in substance, they differ in formality: "the good answers to appetite," while the "the beautiful answers to knowledge" (*ST* I, q. 5, a. 4, ad 1). Hence the contemplation of divine truth and goodness wholly engages the rational capacities of the human person. Contemplation forges the bonds of friendship, theology, and sanctity.

In the 2007 festschrift essay that I offered to Father Matthew Lamb, I made reference to the commission of American prelates that was appointed almost twenty-five years ago to inquire into the sharp decline of vocations to religious life in our country after the Second Vatican Council (1962–65).[1] It was within the context of the Extraordinary Holy Year in honor of the Redemption, on Easter Sunday, April 3, 1983, that Pope John Paul II sent to US bishops a message on this matter. In this letter, the pope expressed "grave concern" over the "the marked decline in recent years in the numbers of young people seeking to enter religious life." To address this grave concern, John Paul, in the spring of 1983, appointed the Quinn Commission. This circumstance forms the proximate background for a document that affords the occasion for this article. It was on May 31, 1983, that the Holy See issued the document whose twenty-fifth anniversary we observed in 2008, titled "Essential Elements in the Church's Teaching on Religious Life as Applied to Institutes Dedicated to Works of the Apostolate." Whereas the findings and the recommendations of the Quinn Commission have come and gone, the work of institutes and organizations that took seriously the recommendations of "Essential Elements" continues to bear fruit.[2]

1. "*Tanquam spiritualis pulchritudinis amatores*: The Consecrated Vocation of Matthew Lamb," in *Wisdom and Holiness, Science and Scholarship: Essays in Honor of Matthew L. Lamb*, ed. Michael Dauphinais and Matthew Levering (Naples, FL: Sapientia Press, 2007), 17–45.

2. The substance of this essay was delivered to a regional meeting of the Institute on Religious Life held in Boston, Massachusetts, in the fall of 2007.

Within this same time frame (1983–2008), John Paul began to speak frequently about a "new evangelization." The original mention of this phrase may date from his first apostolic visit to Poland on June 9, 1979, when John Paul in Nowa Huta vehemently lifted the Cross and, deeply moved, proclaimed, "A new evangelization has begun!" From the early 1980s, the new evangelization became a leitmotiv of the rhetoric that we have come to associate with John Paul's papacy. This history may explain why Pope Benedict XVI chose the *ad limina* visit of the Polish hierarchy in 2005 to express his conviction that the secret of the new evangelization lies in sound collaboration among bishops, priests, religious, and laity.[3] In the teachings of the postconciliar popes, we discover that the new evangelization is intended to enact the sanctification of culture. For John Paul, post-Communist European culture; for Benedict, post-Christian Western culture. Both popes, however, have emphasized the actual urgency of the renewal task, of promoting the new evangelization, even though it must be acknowledged that the Church has always been faced with the daunting challenge to transform the secular culture of a given period.

Take, for example, the church of Santa Maria Novella in Florence. Within the church and the cloister walks, one still sees fading frescoes that depict Dominican priests encouraging early Renaissance Florentines to look beyond the richly material world of the capitalist-humanist period known as the Quattrocento. These Dominican friars urged the citizens of Florence to consider instead the spiritual values of eternal life. Fifteenth-century humanism constituted what one might call a distraction for Christian believers; certain figures of the period give evidence of espousing misplaced values and of pursuing exaggerated directions. By contrast, the new evangelization of the late twentieth and early twenty-first century encounters a culture that has been deformed by the ideologies generated out of the philosophical errors of the modern period. In short, we find ourselves in a more disadvantageous position than did the contemporaries of artists such as Donatello, Fra Angelico, and Botticelli. Today, the Church asks Catholics to persuade a people wed-

3. See "Benedict XVI Tells 'Secret' of New Evangelization," *Zenit*, December 5, 2005. http://www.zenit.org/article-14740?l=english.

ded to technocracy and committed to expediency of the truth that Christ alone reveals to us our high destiny, and that the Church alone provides what is required to pursue this destiny. To put it differently, to a world of technocratic utilitarians, the Church announces the way to the highest wisdom; and to a culture dominated by the allure of the expedient, the Church insists on the life of virtuous excellence.

While bishops and diocesan priests enjoy their specific roles in transforming culture, the consecrated person stands at the center of this work as a living icon of the transformed life. He or she claims by divine right a place on Mount Tabor, the biblically warranted venue of transformation.[4] To discover the source of this mission for consecrated religious, we must return to the beginning of Western monastic history. St. Benedict stands at the origin of the unique contribution that religious persons make to the transformation of culture. For more than 1,500 years, it has been the prerogative of Western monks to show that the great heritage of classical Christian culture recognizes that, on the one hand, learning is necessary if one is to approach God and to express what is discovered about him, while secular literature, on the other hand, must be continually transcended and elevated in the striving to attain eternal life. In his classic study on monastic culture, *The Love of Learning and the Desire for God*, Dom Jean Leclercq speaks about "devotion to heaven" as the dominant disposition that guided the educational work of the medieval monks.[5]

The interpretation of the document issued by the Sacred Congregation for Religious and for Secular Institutes, "Essential Elements in the Church's Teaching on Religious Life," should be undertaken with reference to the later and perhaps weightier 1996 Post-Synodal Exhortation of John Paul, *Vita consecrata*. There we read that "the deepest meaning of the evangelical counsels is revealed when they are viewed in relation to the Holy Trinity."[6] The original model for combining consecration and mission is found within the mystery of the Most Blessed Trinity.

4. *Vita consecrata*, §40: "This is particularly true whenever one descends from the 'mountain' with the Master and sets off on the road which leads from Tabor to Calvary."

5. Jean Leclercq, OSB, *The Love of Learning and the Desire for God: A Study of Monastic Culture*, trans. Catherine Misrahi (New York: Fordham University Press, 1974), chap. 4.

6. *Vita consecrata*, §21.

"Sheer joy is God's," writes St. Thomas Aquinas, "and this demands companionship . . . But creatures cannot be loved above all; they are not attractive enough. Therefore in the divine begetting is there perfect lover and perfect beloved, distinct, but of one nature."[7] In other words, the foundational model for religious apostolic life is discovered in the way that the Father and the Son exist within the divine nature. This means that only a theological hermeneutic guarantees an authentic interpretation of religious and other forms of consecrated life. Sociological, psychological, and entrepreneurial analyses of religious life are necessarily self-limiting. They remain unable to reach up to the Trinity.

As important as institutes dedicated to works of the apostolate are, men and women hermits set the gold standard for consecrated life. They invite us, says John Paul, "never to lose sight of the supreme vocation, which is to be always with the Lord."[8] Thomas reflects this view when he writes that "solitude befits those already perfect."[9] While it is true that the hermit belongs to societies of hermits, the vocation to live alone with the Lord offers an outstanding example of the copenetration of *communio* and *missio*. Consider Philip Gröning's 2006 film, *Into the Great Silence*.[10] The Carthusian vocation, which essentially is eremitic, exemplifies the perichoretic ideal that stands at the apex of religious consecration: mission co-inhering in communion.[11] "Solitude befits those

7. Thomas Gilby, OP, trans., "*Writings on the First Book of the Sentences* II, 1, 4," in *St. Thomas Aquinas: Theological Texts* (Durham, NC: Labyrinth Press, 1982), 43–44.

8. *Vita consecrata*, §7.

9. *ST* II-II, q. 188, a. 8.

10. "Nestled deep in the postcard-perfect French Alps, the Grande Chartreuse is considered one of the world's most ascetic monasteries. In 1984, German filmmaker Philip Gröning wrote to the Carthusian Order for permission to make a documentary about them. They said they would get back to him. Sixteen years later, they were ready. Gröning, sans crew or artificial lighting, lived in the monks' quarters for six months—filming their daily prayers, tasks, rituals and rare outdoor excursions. This transcendent, closely observed film seeks to embody a monastery, rather than simply depict one—it has no score, no voiceover, and no archival footage. What remains is stunningly elemental: time, space, and light. One of the most mesmerizing and poetic chronicles of spirituality ever created, *Into Great Silence* dissolves the border between screen and audience with a total immersion into the hush of monastic life. More meditation than documentary, it's a rare, transformative theatrical experience for all." See http://www.zeitgeistfilms.com/film.php?directoryname=intogreatsilence (accessed August 12, 2008).

11. The view does not necessarily prejudice Thomas's position, which holds that the so-

already perfect," repeats Thomas. Whatever flows from consecrated life, whatever rightly may be called mission is to be interpreted within this Trinitarian model of mutual interpenetration. To put it otherwise, *communio* and *missio* go together in a way that is theologically controlled by the mystery of the Blessed Trinity. "Consecration inevitably implies mission. These are two facets of one reality."[12] *Vita consecrata* further develops this element of Trinitarian doctrine when it reminds us that "the consecrated life proclaims what the Father, through the Son and in the Spirit, brings about by his love, his goodness, and his beauty."[13] In order to assist common reflection on the theme of consecration as the foundation of mission, I enlist the help of Thomas to explain the significance for religious life of the Trinitarian triad of love, goodness, and beauty.

LOVE

When Thomas sets about to investigate the virtue of charity at the beginning of the *secunda-secundae* of the *Summa Theologiae*, he reminds his readers that charity looks to God as the Highest Good. "Now divine good, according as it is the object of man's beatitude, possesses a special aspect, and on this account the love of charity, which is the love of this divine good, is of a special kind."[14] In order to explain how charity works, Thomas, like St. John, turns to the notion of friendship. "Charity signifies not only the love of God, but also a certain friendship with him. This implies, besides love, a certain mutual return of love, together with mutual communion, as described in [Aristotle's] *Ethics*."[15] Thomas describes charity as a friendship not because of his esteem for Aristotle, but because Aristotle's explanation of friendship elucidates what the New Testament calls *koinonia*, or, in Latin, *communicatio*. For example, in the text of 1 Corinthians 1:9, we read: "God is faithful, and by him

called mixed life of contemplative and active religious holds the place of prominence in the Church because "it is better to illumine than merely to shine" (*ST* II-II, q. 188, a. 6). Thomas, who moreover does not comment on the difficulty of achieving this ideal of the Dominicans, makes his comparison on the basis of the end or objective that the religious institute achieves.

12. "Essential Elements," §23.

13. *Vita consecrata*, §20.

14. *ST* II-II, q. 23, a. 4.

15. *ST* II-II, q. 23, a. 1.

you were called to fellowship with the Son, Jesus Christ our Lord." The Thomist tradition adopts the view that the best human analogy for the fellowship or communion of charity is to be found in the human family. The reasons given by the sixteenth-century commentator Cardinal Cajetan for this choice are as follows: the fellowship of the family is rooted in nature; it is one of reverence and inequality; it is a proportionate relationship of justice and love; and it embodies a kind of excellence that arises from people loving each other.[16]

It is possible to adapt this analogy to suit the requirements of religious life. Of course, there is nothing natural about religious life. Indeed, if it were not for the communion of charity that the New Testament announces as a distinct and supernatural reality, there would be no reason why a group of people would constitute themselves as a communion of friendship based solely on achieving the perfection of charity. "Essential Elements" endorses this explanation of religious life: "Religious consecration establishes a particular communion between religious and God and, in Him, between the members of the same institute."[17] So religious life finds its expression in a communion that is rooted in supernature, but enjoys nonetheless the ontological density that belongs properly to the order of grace. We see this ontological density manifested, for instance, in the long-term traditions that adorn the Church, such as monasticism, the friars, and other institutes that may lay claim to the expectation of permanence in the Church. The Order of St. Dominic does not form a constitutive part of the Church, but it is hard (at least for me) to envisage the Church without the Dominicans. It may be easier for some Christians to see this assertion verified in the Franciscans. It is also easy to discover this ontological density in any authentic experience of religious life. As far as I am able to discern, it is a result of the encounter with this incarnate supernatural communion that first attracts new members to join religious life. In any case, it is not the spiffiness of philanthropic work that engages a designated group of professional people.

Religious life cannot proceed without the expression of reverence on

16. See the commentary on *ST* II-II, q. 23, a. 1, no. 1 of Thomas de Vio Cardinal Cajetan, which is printed in the Leonine edition of the *Summa*.

17. "Essential Elements," §18.

the part of the members of a religious institute. There is of course the reverence that exists between superiors and subjects, but there also is the reverence that should obtain among the members. As anyone who has lived in a properly ordered religious community recognizes, this reverence expresses itself differently according to the circumstances of a community's life, just as occurs in a natural family. Thus every *Rule* that stipulates for religious communities is bound to make provision for the care of the sick, for the formation of new recruits, for the discipline of wayward members, and the like. In other words, just as there exists an infinite inequality between the human creature and the God who calls us into fellowship with himself, so in religious life there exists necessarily an inequality among the members. Inequality does not result in subordination. Contrary to what is commonly held, it is possible to overcome inequality by means other than the exercise of brute power. Reverence in religious life develops to the extent that the members love one another, whereas when they do not, another figure of the Quattrocento emerges. He is the political theorist and realist Machiavelli.[18] It is my suspicion that many communities of religious life suffered the loss of their driving, charity-inspired dynamism when the dynamics of politics and power (for which the immigrant culture of the first half of the twentieth century afforded many, picturesque even, examples) subtly transformed the reverence of charity and covenant that had made religious communities so attractive to earlier generations.

The religious family like the natural family enacts justice differently from other cultural bodies. Because the family is considered to be the basic cell of society, one does not find within the family that alterity—the otherness—required for the exercise of justice. So the demands of justice are relativized, and the exercise of charity is given a freer rein than one might expect to discover within, for example, political societies. Take the case of forgiveness. Forgiveness occurs more readily, or at least it should,

18. Niccolò di Bernardo dei Machiavelli (May 3, 1469 to June 21, 1527) was an Italian diplomat, political philosopher, musician, poet, and playwright. He is a figure of the Italian Renaissance and a central figure of its political component, most widely known for his treatises on realist political theory (*The Prince*) on the one hand and republicanism (*Discourses on Livy*) on the other.

within families than it does in law courts. So also forgiveness should manifest itself more readily within religious communities than within other associations of like-minded persons.

Finally, the natural family affords the venue for people to love one another and to show the excellence that the human race is capable of achieving. Something similar occurs within the supernatural family that is religious life. Religious institutes should become places where it is evident that people love one another with excellence. In fact, it may be possible to argue that the decline in young people seeking admission to religious life exists in direct proportion to the decline in the manifestation of love among vowed religious. When one considers the contentiousness of the late '60s and the '70s, it is not difficult to imagine that there grew up a climate that was not conducive to caritative loving. Instead, religious combated one another along predictable ideological lines, with the proponents of exaggerated liberal positions oftentimes gaining the ascendance in the struggle. Ann Carey has documented one aspect of this history in her revealing *Sisters in Crisis: The Tragic Unraveling of Women's Religious Communities.*[19]

GOODNESS

In what does the goodness of friendship consist? We find an answer in another work that Thomas composed for use by Dominican missionaries, the *Summa contra Gentiles.* In Book Four, the Common Doctor sets downs some of the activities that are characteristic of friends. In other words, he describes the goodness that is shared among friends who are bound together within a *communicatio* of benevolent love—a love that wishes well to the other.[20] There are six characteristics that Thomas identifies as proper to friends. The first characteristic is openness, or the exchange of personal knowledge. Thomas reflects on the classical notion of the friend as the other half of one's soul, and suggests that when we reveal something to a friend it is as if the revealer has taken it out of

19. Ann Carey, *Sisters in Crisis: The Tragic Unraveling of Women's Religious Communities* (Huntington, IN: Our Sunday Visitor, 1997).

20. The following observations are drawn from *ScG* IV, ch. 21, 22.

his friend's own heart. From this mutual exchange follows the effective sharing of goods. Because the friend is looked upon as another self, the sharing of material goods serves to succor the friend. A further activity to consider is pardon among friends. Within the fellowship of divine charity one expects to find the pardon of every offense. Why? Friendship is opposed to every offense.

A fourth characteristic is contemplation of truth. Contemplation forms the foundational activity of friends. Even the ancient philosophers glimpsed the necessity of this activity for grounding friendship not so much in the friends themselves but in something other than the friends. As C. S. Lewis observes, he is a pathetic individual who wants only a friend.[21] Friendship must be about something. And for the highest friendship, the something required is the highest activity, which is contemplation. Interior joy follows upon contemplation. Friends delight in each other's presence and turn to each other in times of sorrow; one expects to discover harmony of wills among friends. Friends consent to the will of the other. It is characteristic of friends to get along, to find in each other not a source of division of wills but unity of wills. For Thomas and the Christian tradition, the fullest achievement of the friendship described in the above six points is to be found within the graced communion of the Church. For this reason, religious life may be thought of as embodying an intensification of ecclesial charity. Or, as "Essential Elements" notes, religious life "is itself a part of the Church as mystery and as social reality."[22]

It should not be difficult to adapt the description of what friends do with each other to the everyday life of religious communities. Members remain open to one another within the bounds of discretion in order to create the kind of psychological atmosphere that supports common life and fellowship. There is nothing less appealing than to try to share one's life with strangers. In order to ensure that he remains connected to the other members of the Charterhouse, even the Carthusian enjoys the fa-

21. C. S. Lewis, *The Four Loves* (London: Collins, 1965), 63: "That is why those pathetic people who simply 'want friends' can never make any. The very condition of having Friends is that we should want something else besides Friends."

22. "Essential Elements," §38.

mous three-hour walk on Sundays with fellow Carthusians. For religious, the effective sharing of goods is in fact institutionalized by the vow of poverty. When religious aim to replicate the sharing of goods that was practiced in the apostolic community, they introduce into the order of charity one of the requirements that even the ancient philosophers considered indispensable for friends. Friendship depends on a pooling of resources. Given the achievements of Christian monks throughout Western history, there is every reason to question whether the Weberian thesis that Calvinism jump-starts mainstream Western economies is verifiable. Pardon of every offense follows upon the religious community's commitment to pray together the "Our Father." Classical religious institutes that draw upon the monastic practice of the chapter of faults have made this feature of friendship a formalized part of their weekly routine. Members of the community accused themselves, and sometimes other members, of faults that disrupted the smooth running of the daily community life. For example, "I broke the simple silence five times and the solemn silence twice." At the end of this exercise, the superior would administer a symbolic penance and the members of the community would leave without the burden of hiding or rationalizing their own or others' faults. One effect of this practice is that the growth of widespread cynicism was checked.

The three remaining characteristics of friends should find unique and peculiar expression in religious life; for instance, contemplation. Inasmuch as individual, communal, and liturgical prayer form a necessary activity for each religious, contemplation becomes the occupation of all religious, and not only of those institutes that are dedicated fully to contemplation. When we speak about contemplation and friendship, we point to the fundamental necessity for each religious to look at the same truth and to behold it lovingly. Within this contemplative action, the religious embraces lovingly the unifying principle of friendship that establishes a community and enables the apostolate. As C. S. Lewis again has observed, travelers without a common destination will not be found walking along the same road.[23] When religious achieve this contempla-

23. Lewis, *Four Loves*: "Those who have nothing can share nothing; those who are going nowhere can have no fellow-travelers."

tive unity, they experience interior joy. As St. Thérèse of Lisieux reminds us, interior joy can coexist with sorrow, though never with sadness: *Dolor sed non tristitia.* This distinction was lost, however, on the secular readers of Blessed Mother Teresa of Calcutta's private correspondence with her spiritual fathers. "It also belongs to friendship," writes Thomas, "that a man consent to the things which his friend wills."[24] If harmony of wills does not exist within religious communities, then it is unlikely to be found anywhere. It is also unlikely that a religious community can survive without a harmony of wills. "Essential Elements" devotes five numbers to "communion in community." The *Rule of St. Augustine* has impressed on the Western Church the importance of living together with one will: "The chief motivation for your sharing life together is to live harmoniously in the house and to have one heart and one soul seeking God."[25] We find ourselves confronting another expression of the Trinitarian principle that *communio* and *missio* copenetrate each other. The reason is found in the overarching capacity of charity to unite *ad intra* and *ad extra* love.

BEAUTY

The third feature of the Trinitarian triad of love, goodness, and beauty follows from the second: "The good and the beautiful are the same in substance," says Thomas, "for they are established on a single real form; but they are different in meaning, for the good answers to appetite and acts like a final cause, while the beautiful answers to knowledge and acts like a formal cause. Things are called beautiful which give delight on being seen."[26] The category of the beautiful has entered into discussions of divinity especially through the theological aesthetics developed by Hans Urs von Balthasar. Popularized versions of his views may be found in books such as Richard Viladesau's *Theological Aesthetics: God in Imagina-*

24. *ScG* IV, ch. 22.

25. George Lawless, OSA, trans. *Augustine of Hippo and His Monastic Rule* (Oxford: Clarendon Press, 1987), §2.

26. *ST* I, q. 5, a. 4, ad 1 (Gilby translation: Thomas Gilby, OP, *God's Will and Providence,* vol. 5 (Ia. 19–26), *St. Thomas Aquinas, Summa Theologiae* [New York: McGraw-Hill, 1967]).

tion, Beauty, and Art.[27] By and large, proponents of theological aesthetics blur the formal distinction that Thomas makes between the good that elicits desire and the beautiful that informs knowledge. But there is no reason to abandon the knowledge character of beauty in order to adapt what Thomas sets down as the conditions for beauty to religious life.

If one takes seriously Thomas's distinction about the beautiful and knowledge, then one is led to reflect on what in the *Summa Theologiae* he identifies as the three conditions of beauty. Thomas puts it this way: "Three conditions of beauty—first, integrity or completeness, for broken things are ugly; second, due proportion and harmony; third, brightness and color."[28] It is possible to argue that John Paul issued "Essential Elements" in order to restore to religious life its own proper theological aesthetic. In other words, the pope wanted to make religious life beautiful again. We consider each condition for the beautiful in turn.

INTEGRITY OR COMPLETENESS

The very name of the document that we commemorated during 2008 points to this condition for the beautiful. The text lists the essential elements. "Broken things are ugly," says Thomas. It is easy to break up religious life. There are various conjectures to explain what happened to the great number of apostolic sisters in the United States who shouldered the burden of creating and sustaining the largest private school system, health-care system, and social work network since the Enlightenment. Today it is too late to worry about defining the causes. The unhappy effects are too far advanced. The Quinn Commission, in retrospect, was too optimistic or benign. The lesson that we can draw from the disappearance of the great mother houses once found in our country—to speak only about women religious for the moment—is the one that "Essential Elements" was written to illustrate. Beautiful religious life requires all of its parts. The document addresses directly the ques-

27. Richard Viladesau, *Theological Aesthetics: God in Imagination, Beauty, and Art* (New York: Oxford University Press, 1999).

28. *ST* I, q. 39, a. 8 (Gilby translation).

tion of integrity or completeness: "The nature, end, spirit and character of the institute, as established by the founder or foundress and approved by the Church, should be preserved by all, together with the institute's sound traditions."[29] Broken things are ugly. What lacks essential elements is broken. No one is drawn by the ugly. So "Essential Elements" warns: in order to preserve the identity of a religious institute, it is necessary to make following Christ "the supreme rule of life."[30]

DUE PROPORTION AND HARMONY

If there is a theme that runs through "Essential Elements," it is the theme of reconciling that which constitutes the classical with the reality of diversity, whether of gifts or of persons. Just as the broken is ugly, so is the distended. During the past forty years or so, many classical forms of religious consecration lost all sense of the proportionate and the harmonious. Consider the requirement of living together. It would be impossible to estimate the number of arrangements that have been established either to accommodate diverse commitments of apostolic activity or to facilitate the felt needs of personal preference. If we read "Essential Elements" as a prescription to avoid a diversification that results in a loss of identity, then it is possible to single out the several areas of religious life that have evaporated into what must honestly be called lay forms of living. I would place religious attire in this category.[31]

29. "Essential Elements," §14, citing *CIC*, §578.

30. Ibid., §13, citing *CIC*, §662.

31. Let me give an example of proportion and harmony adapted to the specific ends of contemplative life. I know a small community of Dominican nuns that is the first Dominican contemplative community since World War II to undertake a large-scale construction project. The new monastery stands on a hilltop in Linden, Virginia, surrounded by the Blue Ridge Mountains. The nuns of St. Dominic's Monastery are also among the few in the world to begin the day together at 3:30 a.m. with the recitation of the Night Office. Before these nuns left their temporary monastery in Washington, DC, they restored the monastic grille in the main parlor, and the nuns have returned to wearing the traditional habit of the contemplative nuns, the wimple and veil. This is one example of what is meant by maintaining due proportion and harmony within religious life. To borrow a phrase, the nuns are doing something beautiful for God.

BRIGHTNESS AND COLOR

Finally, there is the condition for beauty that is brightness and color. "Spiritual beauty," says Thomas, "which is the same as the honorable good, [consists] in fair dealing according to the candor of reason."[32] The world has lost the sense of spiritual beauty. There is no need to substantiate this assertion. It should be self-evident to anyone who opens his eyes. "Clearness and proportion are both rooted in mind," says Thomas, "whose function is to order and light up a symmetry."[33] Religious life proceeds as an exercise in sanctified reason. Although there is a sense in which one may experience religious life, the fact of the matter is that religious life is transmitted by learning. Misplaced efforts to manufacture experience result more often than not in producing the distractions that fog the light of intelligence, which is why Thomas goes on to affirm that "beauty, pure and essential, dwells in the contemplative life, wherefore it is said of the contemplation of wisdom: 'and I shall become a lover of her beauty' (Wis 8:2)." The Church in fact recognizes that in explaining the special value of the consecrated life, which enjoys "an objective superiority" among vocations in the Church, "men and women religious *completely devoted to contemplation* are in a special way an image of Christ praying on the mountain."[34]

There is another way that clearness and proportion are rooted in mind. Thomas points to the moral virtues. "Beauty is shed on the moral virtues in so far as they shine with the order of reason, especially on temperateness, which clears the lusts that fog the light of intelligence."[35] Moral virtue creates beauty; moral vice destroys it. "There cannot be a public witness to Christ poor, chaste and obedient without asceticism," says "Essential Elements."[36] The perfect continence in celibacy that the evangelical counsel of chastity requires serves both *communio* and *missio*. When unchastity takes over the fraternal life in communion, the

32. *ST* II-II, q. 114, a. 2 (Gilby translation).

33. *ST* II-II, q. 180, a. 2, ad 3 (Gilby translation).

34. *Vita consecrata*, §32, citing the Second Vatican Council, Dogmatic Constitution on the Church, *Lumen Gentium*, §46. Emphasis original.

35. *ST* II-II, q. 180, a. 2, ad 3 (Gilby translation).

36. "Essential Elements," §31.

results are obviously destructive. It bears saying that unchastity is not the sin reserved for the left wing and the unorthodox. Unchastity can also emerge within communities dedicated to reform and orthodoxy. It would require another essay to outline the threats that contemporary culture poses to the life of chastity, especially for young religious men and women. The threats come from the outside, so to speak, from the culture that is sex saturated, but they also come from within the person, especially from within those whose affective development has been short-circuited for one reason or another. When unchastity takes over *missio*, however, the results are equally disturbing. Leave aside the risks involved in allowing an unchaste religious access to other people who are wont to trust them as ministers of religion. Rather, consider the energy sapping caused in the person in whom unchastity has reached the status of a vicious personal habit, or what I prefer to call *habitus*. Put otherwise, what happens when unchastity so consumes a person that the religious finds himself or herself unable to concentrate or to engage in the contemplative act from which all *missio* or apostolic activity flows? When this circumstance is allowed to dominate, both the religious and the religious community lose the brightness and color that is the third characteristic of beauty. Instead, there emerges a "yellow fog that rubs its back upon the window-panes, / The yellow smoke that rubs its muzzle on the window-panes," to cite T. S. Eliot's "The Love Song of J. Alfred Prufrock."

This meditation on the Trinitarian features of religious *communio* and *missio* draws upon the insights of St. Thomas Aquinas on friendship, love, and beauty. The effort is meant to encourage institutes of consecrated life devoted to works of the apostolate to persevere in their fidelity to the directions set down by the Magisterium for the ongoing renewal and support of consecrated and especially active religious life. What Thomas helps to illustrate is a principle that "Essential Elements" endorses by referring to the conciliar document *Perfectae Caritatis*: "The entire religious life . . . should be imbued with an apostolic spirit, and all their apostolic activity with a religious spirit."[37]

37. Ibid., §12, citing *Perfectae caritatis*, §8.

CHAPTER 3

THE SACRAMENTAL MEDIATION OF DIVINE FRIENDSHIP AND COMMUNION

In this essay, Father Cessario develops the theme of friendship in light of the "theologal life" (CCC, §2607)—a life transformed by the theological virtues of faith, hope, and charity. While the previous two chapters consider theology and sanctity in relation to religious consecration, this chapter shows how all people—religious, sacerdotal, and lay—are called to live a fully "theological life." As Léon Bloy famously said to the young Jacques Maritain, "the only true tragedy in life is not to become a saint"—a true friend of God. A truly theological life—a life of theology and sanctity—is necessary for authentic human happiness.

Within the human person, authentic theology and sanctity are never cultivated one without the other. Moreover, the human person does not generate theology and sanctity within himself or by himself. As with all divine gifts, theology and sanctity are mediated realities. Of course, Christ is the one and supreme mediator. But "the One Mediator does not eliminate the need for many other mediations within the unique outpouring of divine grace that the hypostatic union

Originally published as "The Sacramental Mediation of Divine Friendship and Communion," *Faith and Reason* 27, no. 4 (2002): 7–41. Reprinted by permission.

effects in the world." Within the eternal plan of God's loving providence, Christ's mediation employs other, instrumental mediators. "The Incarnation is not magic, and the work of divine grace ... adopts a rhythm of continual transformation." This is why Jesus gave us the Church and the sacraments. "The mediation of divine truth stands at the heart of the Church's mission." Finally, Mary's unique maternal mediation emerges within this chapter. Each Christian believer discovers at some point in his or her life the truth that "all that the Church will become already exists in the Blessed Virgin Mary." Here Father Cessario reminds us that the theologal pattern of theology and sanctity is found (already and supremely) within she who is the "Cause of our Joy" (*Causa nostrae latitiae*).

"Man: The Image of God." Thus begins Part Three of the *Catechism of the Catholic Church*. We are reminded of the vocation of man created *ad imaginem Dei*. The promise of eternal life given to each of us at baptism initiates what the Church calls the "theologal life"—the way of faith, hope, and charity—a path that leads to beatific communion with the Blessed Trinity. When we ponder the extraordinary fulfillment that the gift of everlasting life offers to the human race, we can only be grieved to consider the vast number of our contemporaries who live without faith, hope, and charity. Many people remain without fruitful entry into the mediations that enable them to know why God made them, the love that he bears them, and the truth that sets them free. Even certain sons and daughters of the Church seem to have forgotten the universal importance and significance of the wise and well-known counsel offered by Léon Bloy to the young Jacques Maritain: the only true tragedy in life is not to become a saint.

Into a world that of itself can only approach, and this unsurely, the ultimate questions that treat man's final destiny, the Lord enters as the one who bears the gift of divine truth. The 1990 "Instruction on the Ecclesial Vocation of the Theologian" (*Donum veritatis*) summarizes the relationship of truth to the one order of sacramental mediation that finds its center in the Incarnate Son: "When God gives Himself to man as friend, man becomes free, in accordance with the Lord's word: 'No longer do I call you servants, for the servant does not know what his master is doing; but I have called you friends, for all that I have heard from my Father I have made known to you' (Jn 15:15). Man's deliverance from the alienation of sin and death comes about when Christ, the Truth, becomes the 'way' for him" (cf. Jn 14:6)."[1] This outpouring of divine grace, which St. Thomas Aquinas calls the "capital grace" of Christ, remains ordered to establishing the communion of friendship we call the Church.

If we look at things from the point of view of natures, every sacramental mediation that God offers to the world begins with the gift of his truth. Indeed, this truth appears preeminently in the Person of Jesus Christ, who himself embodies Divine Truth itself. The preaching of our blessed Savior therefore constitutes a privileged moment in the communication of this truth. The *munus petrinum*, which is the gift Christ gives directly to Peter, establishes the concrete link between Christ and the Apostle Peter and his Successors. From the moment that Christ confides to Peter the special grace that belongs to him alone in the Church, an order is established, one that is meant to continue until Christ comes again. The order is one of mediation. When asked whether Christ should have put his teaching into writing, Aquinas replied, predictably, in the negative.[2] Aquinas discovers one explanation why Christ left no writings pertains immediately to priests, consecrated persons, and those laity involved in evangelization. Christ, St. Thomas says, left no writings "so that his teaching might reach everyone in an orderly manner: namely, that he himself teach his disciples immediately, and that they subsequently teach others by speaking and writing. If, however, he himself had written, his teaching would have reached everyone immediately."[3] Evangelization

1. "Instruction on the Ecclesial Vocation of the Theologian," §1.

2. It is well known that Aquinas avoided doing theology in the hypothetical mood. He developed his theology from what was known through divine revelation, not from conjectures about what might have been possible. It never crossed the mind of the great theologians of the Church that Christ had failed to do what was in the best interests of his divine mission. This methodology leaves the Angelic Doctor free to discover "reasons" for why Christ did what the canonical Scriptures report he did.

3. *ST* III, q. 42, a. 4.

comes built in, as it were, with the divine plan. And because this divine plan has ordained that the teaching of Christ reach out mediately to the world, we should reflect on the implications of this divinely ordained mediation for the work of the Church.

The twenty-fifth chapter of Matthew's Gospel sets before us an enactment of the last judgment: "When the Son of Man comes in his glory" (Mt 25:31–46). If one were to enumerate the ways that form the basis for the divine judgment of the world (hungry, thirsty, stranger, naked, etc.), the list would include all the services that the human community provides for its members. For the developed world, these services have been variously taken up into the modern welfare state. Even recognizing a relative autonomy in the secular order, chapter 25 of the Gospel of Matthew makes it plain that the human community needs the theologal life. Indeed, our eternal happiness depends on it. In other words, the human project finds its true bearings in the Church. "I was hungry": agriculture, food and drug administrations, lunch programs and relief to the indigent, food processing, and so forth. "I was thirsty": ecological provisions for safe natural resources, alcoholic beverage bureaus, wine merchants and oenologists. "I was a stranger": immigration and naturalization departments, social welfare for displaced persons, refugees, and resident aliens; the hotel industry. "Naked and you clothed me": social welfare agencies, manufacturers and clothiers, the garment industry with its preference for low-cost labor. "I was ill": hospitals and clinics, drug manufacturers and pharmacists, doctors and nurses, the medical education establishment. "In prison and you came to visit me": criminal justice systems, lawyers and police forces, prison guards and rehabilitation workers. One could enlarge the list. How much do people need to know in order to fulfill these offices successfully? It would be an interesting exercise to ponder how much each of these endeavors requires a direction that only the Church can provide. The mediation of divine truth stands at the heart of the Church's mission. To cite but one text: the 1993 encyclical letter *Veritatis splendor*, §31, introduces a long meditation on the words of the Fourth Gospel—"You will know the truth, and the truth will make you free" (Jn 8:32)—and fixes our attention on "the fundamental dependence of freedom upon truth."[4] We are returned to the convertibility of the transcendentals, of the one, the true, and the good. Where there is truth, there is unity; where there is unity, there is the good. The theologal life comprises Christian faith and Christian love.

The publication of the "Instruction" *Dominus Iesus* in 2000 reminded the whole Church of the central confessions of the Christian religion: the Blessed Trinity and the Incarnation. It is a distinguishing characteristic of Catholic doctrine to recognize that the One Mediator does not eliminate the need for many other mediations within the unique outpouring of divine grace that the hypostatic union effects in the world. The picture that results is grand in scope; indeed, it is breathtaking. We behold one attempt to capture the momentousness of the mediations at work in the Church in the art and architecture of the Catholic Baroque period, with its many representations exhibited in the Eternal City and elsewhere in Europe. The mediations include the Sacred Humanity of Christ, which may be compared to what Aristotle said of the hand of a human person, namely, that it constitutes the instrument of instruments. Every other concrete medium through which divine grace is communicated to men depends on the humanity of the Son of God.[5] Obviously, the seven sacraments of the Church come first of all to mind. But the tradition obliges us to consider broadly the mediations that flow from the Incarnation.

It is sometimes difficult to impress on persons who are excessively conditioned by historical understanding that there exists anything in the world that possesses its identity without reference to historical accident or occurrence. Unfortunately, many Catholics consider the divinely authenticated mediations of the Church to be so many strategies that have been developed over the course of the ages for keeping alive the Christian message. In other words, we should not underestimate the difficulty that the people of our generation, especially in the West, experience

4. *Veritatis splendor*, §34.

5. The language of the creed expresses this mystery when it reminds us that for us "men" and for our salvation, the Eternal word "became man": "qui propter nos homines et propter nostram salutem . . . et *homo* factus est" (emphasis added).

when they come face to face with claims that are absolute. Take as two contemporary examples the dominical institution of the sacraments and the confiding to Peter of his special *munus*. The 1995 encyclical letter *Fides et ratio* has provided us all with the opportunity to consider the reasons for this retreat from the absolute, and also alludes to the difficulties that such an intellectual climate brings to the practice of the Christian religion. But the remedy at hand is not philosophical; rather, it is theological. The answer remains faith and the pondering that continues the assent of theological faith. The prayer that best sustains this theologal life is contemplative prayer. St. Teresa of Avila provides the *Catechism*'s definition: "Contemplative prayer [*oración mental*] in my opinion," she wrote, "is nothing else than a close sharing between friends; it means taking the time frequently to be alone with him who we know loves us."[6] We return to the theme of friendship and truth.

> When God gives Himself to man as friend, man becomes free, in accordance with the Lord's word: "No longer do I call you servants, for the servant does not know what his master is doing; but I have called you friends, for all that I have heard from my Father I have made known to you" (Jn 15:15). Man's deliverance from the alienation of sin and death comes about when Christ, the Truth, becomes the "way" for him (cf. Jn 14:6).[7]

Providence has ordained that the Latin verb *subsistere* enter into the vocabulary of the Church. We know the significance that it has for expounding the doctrine of the Incarnation. The Church believes that everything that his human nature requires for its personal realization, though without combining the divine *esse* with the created nature of Jesus Christ, depends, in a way that perhaps defies an exhaustive theological explanation, on the Eternal Word. Thus we confess that the human nature of Christ subsists in the Second Person of the Blessed Trinity. So also the Church of Christ subsists in the Church gathered around the Successor of Peter. "Be holy, for I, the Lord, your God, am holy" (Lev 19:1). In the Book of Leviticus, we find the divine subsistence associated with the commands that God enjoins upon Moses to speak to the chil-

6. See *The Book of Her Life*, 8, 5, as cited in *CCC*, §2709.
7. *Donum veritatis*, §1.

dren of Israel. Again and again, the universal call to holiness is punctuated by the announcement "I am the Lord." The mediation of divine truth that the Church enacts throughout the world points to God, whose Being not only causes but also sustains everything that exists. This explains why the worst evil that can befall any rational creature is error. Ignorance never helps the human person achieve the perfection of his nature. Error moves us away from being. What distinguishes education from indoctrination is the simple reality that truthful persons have experienced in their lives: the truth fits. Because it is the same God who established the heavens and the earth and who created man, divine truth communicates whatever is required for the free human being to achieve the perfection of his created being or nature. In the final analysis, the message God speaks in Leviticus holds good: "Be holy, for I, the Lord, your God, am holy" (Lev 19:1).

At the end of his encyclical *Fides et ratio,* the Holy Father reminds us that the philosopher's task leads him to the arms of the Blessed Virgin Mary: *Philosophari in Maria.* Why does a specifically human enterprise like philosophy find its perfection in a woman whose dignity no philosopher can fully uncover, but that only faith reveals? The answer of course is ultimately found in her Son, the Incarnate Wisdom of God. But in a special way the Virgin Mother of God helps us to embrace her Son's truth. It is significant that the doctrine of the Immaculate Conception, which has been devoutly held in one form or another from the earliest centuries of the Church—even Aquinas in his later years revealed a deep sympathy for the prerogative, as if he had come to realize that Mary's grace outstrips rational accounts of how she obtains it—only came into formal prominence at the end of the nineteenth century. Think of the shrine at Lourdes. I believe that this development of doctrinal explicitness has something to do with the overpowering difficulties that burden people in modern life. The challenges that sin creates for modern man, who, for whatever reason, is less likely to find a flight from the world attractive, indeed possible, and points to the need for a special divine assistance. When God through the Church reveals in an infallible way that the Mother of his Son has been preserved from all stain of sin, even from the first moment of her conception, he reveals a new dimension of her maternal mediation. She is the one in whom we can find refuge from all manner of sin and darkness.

THE MEDIATION OF THE HIERARCHICAL STRUCTURE OF THE CHURCH

"For just as from the heavens the rain and snow come down ... So shall my word be that goes forth from my mouth" (Is 55:10–11). Divine Truth is effective. God not only speaks the Highest Truth; he is the Highest Truth. As the scholastic theologians were accustomed to saying about the object of theological faith, God is First Truth in Being (*in essendo*) and First Truth in Speaking (*in loquendo*). It is of course God himself who communicates to the objects of divine faith their saving power and efficacy. (The objects are the propositions that communicate the reality of the divine.) The gift of truth communicated by Christ through the Apostle Peter to the Church not only provides instruction about God and the things that pertain to God, but also creates a world of divinely authenticated mediations that constitute the Church in her historical existence. It is a special sign of this divine strategy that the faithful throughout the world are accustomed on Sundays and feast days to join the Holy Father for the recitation of the Angelus. For from the moment that the Word becomes flesh in the womb of the Blessed Virgin Mary, there exists in the world a new creation whose "fullness of grace" is entrusted to the Catholic Church.[8] We return to the important connection between *subsistere* used of the Incarnation and *subsistere* used of the Church. The image of rain and snow watering the earth, making it fertile and fruitful, manifests a unified plan of divine action that is universal in its application. Nowhere in the world where people depend on vegetation for sustenance can one maintain a sufficient supply of plant life without the regular rhythms of waterfall that ensure the earth's fructification. "It shall not return to me void, but shall do my will, achieving the end for which I sent it" (Is 55:11).

8. See *Dominus Iesus*, §16.

Blessed Pio Nono marks an important moment in the designs of divine providence for this period of human history. Moved by the Holy Spirit, Blessed Pope Pius IX responded to the rapidly changing political circumstances of the modern period, and some forty years before the treacherous battles of the First World War would discredit the existing secular authorities on both sides of the conflict, he clarified the unique status of the Roman pontiff and his specific grace, the *munus petrinum*. In the modern period, Pio Nono made it possible for the faithful to recognize clearly the *munus petrinum* as a divine grace and not as a fixture of any political organization. And while the Holy See rightfully retains its political status among the nations, complete with the indispensable adornment of a diplomatic corps and formal exchanges with the nation-states, the fact remains that the administrative departments of the Holy See formally exist as mediations of divine grace. One may recall the "body and soul" metaphor that Pope Pius XI employed at the time of signing the 1929 Lateran Treaty: the Holy See's insertion into the political order is sufficient enough to ensure that the Church can breathe into the world of human affairs the life-giving grace of divine truth. Think how much Pope John Paul II did to give back to a weary world its "soul."

The Holy See offers a model for the work of the particular churches. Catholic believers must expend every effort to overcome the opposition that remains so manifest in the secular order between political exigencies and the demands of truth. Certain tensions are inevitable so long as the Church sojourns here below, and every power and principality have not yet been turned over to the Father of Lights. Still, the text of Isaiah about God's "word," quoted above, holds true: "It shall not return to me void, but shall do my will, achieving the end for which I sent it" (Is 55:11). One bishop recounts that shortly after he had appeared on the eleven o'clock evening news to comment on the cloning of the Scottish sheep Dolly, which had been announced earlier the same day, a Protestant pastor-friend called him and said, "You Catholics are lucky to have a Magisterium. I know nothing about cloning, and I suspect neither did you before tonight."

The Magisterium is not just an information service available to devout Catholics. The hierarchical structure of the Church serves above all to spread the grace of adoptive sonship throughout the world. The following story comes from a pastor of a large, typical Catholic community on the East Coast. A little girl "burst into tears, and startled her father. He stood, confused and somewhat embarrassed in the front pew of the church. What's wrong, he asked, as the rest of the congregation prayed the Lord's Prayer. 'I know this prayer, but I can't keep up. They're going too fast.'" We still learn from what comes out of the mouths of babes. Each day at Mass, the Liturgy places before us the prayer that Christ confided to his Church. It is the unique prayer of Christian revelation, and so no matter how many times we have recited the Lord's Prayer, we should never succumb to the temptation of quickly repeating only the words. This is the prayer of our inheritance. Only those persons whom God has renewed in his Son Jesus Christ possess a claim to sharing in beatific communion with Father, Son, and Holy Spirit. From the moment that Christ addresses God as Father, the main outlines of the salvation that he will win by his life-giving Passion and saving death appear. The salvation that God offers the world is marked by a deeply relational structure that images the inner life of God himself. The seventeenth-century English poet John Donne, though not a Catholic author, captures this mystery in his sonnet:

> Batter my heart, three person'd God; for, you
> As yet but knocke, breathe, shine, and seeke to mend;
> That I may rise, and stand, o'erthrow mee, and bend
> Your force, to breake, blowe, burn and make me new.
> ("Holy Sonnet X," *Poems*, 1633)

We know that the world remains like a usurped town that struggles to resist the captivating energies of the Trinitarian dynamism. At the same time, because grace perfects but never destroys nature, including political nature, this same world stands ready to be enthralled, indeed ravished, by God—Father, Son, and Holy Spirit.

More can be said about the hierarchical structure of the Church and the distinctive mediation of Trinitarian grace that it communicates, especially through the exercise of the episcopal *munera*: the *summa* of the sacred ministry. Because the bishops of the Church are "the principal stewards of the mysteries of God," the tasks of teaching the truth, sanctifying the people, and governing the Church of God belong to them in a preeminent way.[9] It is important to emphasize in our present circumstances that the great promises, captured summarily in *Gaudium et spes*, §22, reach the whole human race only through the mediation of the Church: "Reapse nonnisi in mysterio Verbi incarnati mysterium hominis clarescit." Where else than in the Church of Christ can the human person discover Christ, in whom man beholds who man is? Indeed, everything that the bishop does finds its meaning in this central text of the Second Vatican Council: "It is not therefore to be wondered at that it is in Christ that the truths stated here find their source and reach their fulfillment."[10] The reference points to the specific recommendations made in *Gaudium et spes*, but the same wonderment extends to everything that the Church teaches about the sanctification and reconciliation of the world. This conviction motivates the Church to reach outward to others.

The young French curé Eugene de Mazenod exemplified the permanent character of the Church's missionary mandate. The instruction of the founder of the Missionary Oblates of Mary Immaculate—go wherever the people are the poorest—still inspires and motivates the Church. The Church goes wherever the people are the poorest. In the nineteenth century, to be poor mainly meant being materially poor. Today we realize that the great expectations of modern learning that were only beginning to manifest themselves in the Europe of the 1830s possess less promise than had been envisaged by many enlightened persons of the nineteenth century. Some have argued that the today's culture of death comprises the last phase of the European Enlightenment. The sacramental mediation of the Church itself works to alleviate the poverty of the culture. It would be wrong, of course, to think of the Church's work in exclusively clerical terms. What matters most is that every member of the Church accomplish her work among all peoples. When priests and bishops fulfill their mandates in the Church, they are helping the People of God become all that God has ordained them to be.

9. See the Second Vatican Council's decree on bishops, *Christus Dominus*, §15.
10. *Gaudium et spes*, §22.

The ecumenical work of the Church may be seen in the light of the one sacramental mediation that flows from the Church of Christ. *Dominus Iesus* helped the Catholics of the world comprehend that ecumenical outreach is not the same as accommodation to the distortions that have entered, for a variety of reasons, into the Christian tradition. For causes that remain complex, the period after the Second Vatican Council has resulted in a transmutation of what the Council had taught about the Church's outreach to the ecclesial communions. In a country like the United States, this process of mutation has been abetted by the dominance of the institutions of a liberal, procedural democracy. As one American cardinal observed in the face of the immediate dissatisfaction expressed by many with the "Declaration," "It is not a question of style but of substance." Many Catholics had come to believe that ecumenism could only be advanced by promoting avenues of convergence among the various dialogue partners. We know now that ecumenical dialogue succeeds only to the extent that it remains rooted in the truth once and for all confided to Peter, "a perpetual and visible principle and foundation for the unity of faith and communion."[11]

Each new day brings time for renewal. Because Christ alone manifests man to himself, we know that this renewal can never be achieved without the grace of Christ. Christ reveals man to himself in the sense of not only speaking to us who we are but also making us to be what we must become. This grace, which observes the bipolarity of the Hebrew word of creation (*dabar*), remains the promise that Christ has given to the Church. He will never leave us. We must have confidence to return to Christ again and again because, in brief, there exists no alternative for the Christian but to turn to Jesus Christ. As St. Thérèse of Lisieux was fond of teaching her novices, no matter how grievous a sin she were to commit, she would always maintain confidence in the merciful love of God, and turn to Jesus. Every other solution to sin fails because it seeks its energy in something other than the mercy of God made manifest in Christ.

This brief advertence to the act of conversion suitably concludes our

11. *Lumen gentium*, §18.

consideration of the hierarchical structure of the Church and the way that it communicates divine grace to the world. The theologians of the conciliar period remind us that all that the Church will become already exists in the Blessed Virgin Mary. At the close of each day, the Christian people turn to the Mother of God as to their mother, and confide themselves to her maternal care. The *Salve Regina* represents not only a final salute to the Mother of God but also a plea for the clemency, the piety, and the sweetness that Mary brings in a uniquely personal way to the tired soul. We know that those who have forgotten about the place of the Mother of Christ in the Christian life are frequently those who have the most difficult time receiving the sacramental mediation of the Church as something willed by God for the salvation of the human race. Each Christian believer should turn with great devotion to Mary and place themselves in her company. There they will discover in ways that are new and refreshing the extraordinary importance of the Church's hierarchical structure and appreciate with a new seriousness the part that each one plays in keeping it alive in the world.

THE MEDIATION OF THE SACRAMENTS, ESPECIALLY OF THE BLESSED EUCHARIST

Among the specific mediations that Jesus Christ has instituted for the work of salvation stand the seven sacraments of the new dispensation. The Second Vatican Council has restored for us an appreciation of the larger context of Divine Liturgy in which each of the sacraments is set. We can draw benefit from the summary of the conciliar teaching that is found in the *Catechism of the Catholic Church*. Still, the tradition of the Church, especially as developed by the Fathers and also by the scholastic doctors, points us to consider each of the sacraments according to their individual sacramentality. It is helpful to recall the schema put forth by St. Thomas Aquinas, who organized the sacraments so as to make them correspond to the various moments and stages of human life. He thereby illustrated his prior theological conviction that grace perfects nature (*gratia perficit naturam*). The sacramental economy reminds us that the objectivity of the sacraments is something that requires careful oversight by the Church. The categories of licitness and validity, beyond their juridical significance, reveal that these sacred actions depend directly on Christ for their efficaciousness. They belong to no other person, individual or corporate: indeed, the sacraments are confided to the Church's care.[12]

The sacraments constitute privileged moments in the life of the Church. No day would be complete without a renewal of our own participation in the sacraments of new life. In what follows I can only highlight certain key aspects of the individual sacraments.

Baptism and Confirmation

The Church knows no other way in which the new life that Christ brings is communicated to the human person. Baptism evokes repentance from those who seek it not because of the threat of punishment but because of the promise of gifts that come to those who are renewed in the waters of the font. In these two enactments of divine judgment, we see the difference between the old law of fear and the new law of mercy and forgiveness clearly exposed before our eyes. Baptism brings new life. We therefore may ask ourselves why so many Catholics, at least in the industrialized countries, are given to forget the urgency of being released from the wickedness of the present age. The revised baptismal ritual places less emphasis on the fact that baptism releases a child from original sin and its punishment, and prefers rather to stress the newness of life in Christ Jesus that baptism bestows. This incorporation into the Body of Christ brings with it redemption. We have been bought back. The alternative to life in Christ remains life in oneself, and, given the weight of original sin in the world, the chances that a person can sustain a life of charity outside the sacramental structures of the Church are slim. "When we made our first profession of faith while receiving the holy Baptism that cleansed us, the forgiveness we received then was

12. For an illuminating comparison between the committal by God of both creed and sacraments to the care of the Apostles and their successors, see *ST* III, q. 64, a. 2, esp. ad 1.

so full and complete that there remained in us absolutely nothing left to efface, neither original sin nor offenses committed by our own will, nor was there left any penalty to suffer in order to expiate them."[13] Thus the *Roman Catechism* (as cited in the *Catechism of the Catholic Church*) tells us. This great grace, whether received as an infant or as an adult, requires careful shepherding.

Baptism forgives original sin, but it does not remove the concupiscence that original sin leaves in us. St. Thomas Aquinas recapitulates the rich teaching of the early Church Fathers about the wisdom that illuminates this disposition of divine providence. He points out that there are many reasons why the defects of the present life remain even in those who have been baptized. The most important reason, however, points to the need for each Christian to maintain a life fortified by what he calls "spiritual exercises." The struggle that the life of faith imposes on the one who takes up his cross is a cause for consolation, not despair. How many persons make a mistake about this crucial point of Christian life, and give up without recognizing that on the other side of the struggle stands Jesus? "Knowledge of God without that of our misery equals pride," wrote Pascal. "Knowledge of our misery without that of God equals despair. Knowledge of Jesus Christ strikes the balance, since in him we find both God and our misery."

Penance

The 1984 Post-Synodal Exhortation "On Reconciliation and Penance" merits more attention than it has received. In many places throughout the Christian world, its words of encouragement and sound doctrine continue to prompt in many frequent recourse to the sacrament of reconciliation. In the United States, while there are signs of renewal of sacramental practice, there are also indications that people confess their sins less frequently than their spiritual state may require. It should be observed as well that the decline in the number of available confessors also contributes to the decline in the celebration of the sacrament of penance. For many persons,

13. *CCC*, §979

the confession of venial sins can serve as an important source of grace for spiritual growth—for the "spiritual exercises" that Aquinas says we need to accomplish are part of the divine plan that leaves even the baptized with the *fomes peccati,* the broad concupiscence of sin.

Anointing of the Sick

Anointing the sick is among the most important sacramental mediations that can assist the Christian faithful to resist the culture of death. We can never meditate enough on the power of the risen Christ. He is the Lord of life and death. The healing that comes with the sacrament of the sick offers special consolation: we have it on the authority of the apostle James that the one who receives this anointing, "if he has committed sins, he will be forgiven" (Jas 5:15). Baptism, confirmation, the Eucharist, penance, and anointing of the sick are the sacraments that mark the beginning, the middle, and the end of the Christian life. Because of the unique intervention of the risen Christ and the power of the Holy Spirit, these sacramental mediations are more than symbolic expressions of religious convictions or public demonstrations of graces that have already been received without mediation. They are true sacraments of the new law, and they do something specific. They constitute efficacious instruments of the supreme grace confided to the Church. Without them, it is difficult to imagine the theologal life.

Sacramental mediations are open only to the eyes of faith. We know that the Eucharist is a mystery of faith because it is revealed only to "the eyes of faith," as St. Thomas Aquinas has impressed on the Christian imagination. Taste, touch, sight, hearing—none of the senses avails when it comes to recognizing under the appearances of bread and wine the body, blood, soul, and divinity of Christ, really, truly, and substantially present in this holy sacrament. Only the heart that assents to this mystery as expressed, preserved, reverenced, and cherished by the Church founded on the Apostles is able to open up to the reality of the Eucharistic Lord: *Mysterium Fidei.* The Holy Father has acknowledged that one text of the Second Vatican Council forms a leitmotiv of his postconciliar magisterium. He refers to the paragraphs of the "Pastoral Constitution on the Church in the World of Today" in *Gaudium et spes*, §22. The paragraphs bear the heading *De Christo novo homine*—"About Christ the New Man." We learn there that it is only in the mystery of the Incarnate Word that light is shed on the mystery of what it means to be human. The following constitutes a central portion of this conciliar document: "He who is 'the image of the invisible God' (Col 1:15) is the perfect man who has restored to the offspring of Adam the divine likeness which had been deformed since the first sin."[14] No wonder the Holy Father draws us back again and again to this foundational formulation of the Christian message. Into a world that has been deformed by human sinfulness, and deformed as a result of our own wrongdoing, not God's, comes God's gracious and paternal benevolence. One like ourselves but without sin who restores to the human creature not something alien to what it means to be human, but what is most connatural to being human, indeed, what from the beginning had been willed for the creature made in the divine image, namely, a life of friendship and intimacy with God, Father, Son, and Holy Spirit.

The Incarnation is not magic, and the work of divine grace throughout the long history—now two millennia—of the Christian Gospel adopts a rhythm of continual transformation. Herein lies one reason for suffering in the world. To create the new, the old must be broken. Yet even as it renews the face of the earth, the Eucharist consoles.

Gaudium et spes, §22, also refers to the sacrifice of Christ on the Cross: "Suffering for us, Christ not only set us an example to follow in his footsteps, but he also opened for us a way in which life and death are sanctified and given a fresh significance." One of the most familiar anthems known to the Christian people is the prayer composed for the Office of Corpus Christi: "O sacrum convivium in quo Christus sumitur recolitur memoria passionis eius, mens impletur gratia, et futurae gloriae nobis pignus datur." It sings of course of the Eucharist, Bread of Life that establishes the "new man," and a new world.[15] The Eucharist is a

14. Ibid.

15. What follows is inspired by the address of Bernard Cardinal Law, "Los Ojos de la Fe: Reflexión Theológica previa al Congreso Eucarístico," delivered in Havana on December 1,

sacred banquet, where the Bread of Life and of the Angels becomes food for a pilgrim people inclined to sin. A wonderful exchange occurs. As St. Augustine once and for all stamped on the Church's understanding, we do not consume this heavenly food, but rather this food consumes us in the fire of charity and unites us in the bond of unity. The anthem *O Sacrum convivium* recalls that the Eucharist is a living memorial of Christ's own Passion on Calvary. Every time that the priest eucharistizes the bread and wine, every time that he says, "This is my body, This is my blood," he reenacts in an unbloody manner the same sacrifice of the Calvary that *Gaudium et spes*, §22, tells us is the source of our new life in Christ. *O Sacrum convivium* announces that this new humanity, the human soul (i.e., the whole body-person, the whole man, the human creature), is filled with divine grace, the source of new life in us and of our union in friendship with God. Only the mystery of the Incarnate Word reveals—in the strong sense of manifests and effects—the mystery of man. If Godless and graceless strategies for perfecting the human race were able to answer the deepest aspirations of the human heart, then they surely would have succeeded better than they have over the course of the centuries. Strictly speaking, there is no human cure for atheism, but there are many indications that it remains an ideology without a future. The Eucharist points to the future, to a completion that is not limited by the constraints of fallen nature—where every tear will be wiped away—and that is promised as a time not of suffering but of glory: "There we hope to enjoy the vision of your glory." No longer a *Mysterium Fidei*, no longer an assent of the heart that the mind can barely glimpse, and now through a glass darkly, but a beholding.

The thought of the pledge of future glory, a future vision of glory that the Eucharist offers, transports us to an island that holds an important place in the spread of the Christian Gospel, a symbol of the islands of evangelization that exist throughout the world of today. I refer to the Island of Patmos in the Aegean Sea (southeast Greece), where we are told that St. John the Evangelist found himself in exile.

1998. The text is found in Romanus Cessario, OP, ed., *Boston's Cardinal: Bernard Law the Man and His Witness* (Lanham, MD: Lexington Books, 2002), 154–60.

> Then I saw a new heaven and a new earth; for the first heaven and the first earth had passed away, and the sea was no more. And I saw the holy city, new Jerusalem coming down out of heaven from God, prepared as a bride adorned for her husband; and I heard a great voice from the throne saying, "Behold, the dwelling of God with men. He will dwell with them, and they shall be his people, and God himself will be with them; he will wipe away every tear from their eyes, and death shall be no more, neither shall there be mourning nor crying nor pain any more, for the former things have passed away." (Rev 21:1–4).

This is the vision of the new world that the Eucharist creates in us, and in this present world signals the end term of the Church's sacramental mediation. God knew that once such a vision of blessedness was revealed to the human race in Christ, we would want to partake of the blessedness now, and not have to wait until after death. That is why Christ gave us himself in the Eucharist, for in this sacrament we taste the joy—Bread of Life!—that rejoices with the blessed in heaven, even as we journey along our way to join them.

THE THEOLOGAL LIFE: WHAT IS IT?

On November 22, 2000, John Paul II spoke these words during the general audience held in St. Peter's Square:

> Faith, hope and love are like three stars that rise in the sky of our spiritual life to guide us to God. They are the theological virtues *par excellence:* they put us in communion with God and lead us to him. They form a triptych, whose apex is found in love, the *agape* excellently praised by Paul in a hymn of the First Letter to the Corinthians. It is sealed by the following declaration: "So faith, hope, love abide, these three; but the greatest of these is love" (1 Cor 13:13).

The *Catechism of the Catholic Church* calls a life lived according to the theological virtues the theologal life.[16] The objective of the second part

16. The 1994 English version of the *Catechism of the Catholic Church* speaks about the "theologal path of our prayer" (§2607) and describes the first three petitions of the Our Father as "more theologal" (§2803).

of this essay is to examine the ways that this divinely bestowed theologal life flourishes in the communion of the Church. We have already examined the dynamics of the sacramental mediation that communicates the participated divine life to men and women. We now turn to examine how those who are members of the Church exhibit the graces that they have received.

First, however, we must establish the proper context for envisaging the concrete exercise of the theological virtues. Three theological coordinates govern a theological presentation of these divine virtues. The first is the threefold grace of Christ. Because "the one subject which operates in the two natures, human and divine, is the single Person of the Word," theologians have distinguished three graces that belong to Christ: the grace of the hypostatic union (the grace of the "single Person of the Word"), the grace resident in human nature (Christ's own sanctifying or habitual grace), and the grace that overflows into the members of Christ (the capital or ecclesial grace or the grace of headship).[17] Second, because "the human virtues are rooted in the theological virtues, which adapt man's faculties for participation in the divine nature," one must recall the form and dynamics of created grace: "for the theological virtues relate directly to God."[18] Some theologians have construed man's capacity for God in an inclusive way; in their account, grace and nature are so intertwined as to make it difficult to speak about the "dynamics" of an uplifted life of supernatural grace. The Thomist commentatorial tradition takes full account of the claim that the theological virtues "dispose Christians to live in a relationship with the Holy Trinity," and so are willing to talk about what is disposed.[19] This leads to the third coordinate. Recall what has been said above about the doctrine of the *imago Dei*, man made in the image of God.[20] The dynamism of the *imago* points toward God. Still, because man remains free under the movement of divine grace, it is possible to frustrate the inbuilt dynamic of the *imago*. Creation is not redemption. In a word, the *imago Dei* can

17. For one of the most recent employments of the Chalcedonian formulary, see *Dominus Iesus*, §10.

18. *CCC*, §1812.

19. Ibid.

20. See *CCC*, §1701–9, esp. §1708 and §1709.

be actualized or frustrated depending on how we fulfill God's will for us. Directly related to this fundamental Christian tenet is the claim "It must therefore be firmly believed as a truth of Catholic faith that the universal salvific will of the One and Triune God is offered and accomplished once for all in the mystery of the Incarnation, death, and resurrection of the Son of God."[21] The life of faith, hope, and charity establishes the believer in the communion of the Church. There he or she may dwell in one of three circles of ecclesial communion. We now turn to consider how these diverse vocations mediate the theologal life.

The Mediation of the Theologal Life by Priests

As we consider the mediation of the vocations that distinguish the Church, we recognize that there are three circles of ecclesial communion that exist within the one communion of the Church: the presbyterate of the priests, the fraternity of the consecrated, and the family of the laity. Because of their indispensable and irreplaceable ministry to the mediation of the theologal life, we consider first priests, especially diocesan priests. The priests of the late twentieth and early twenty-first century received great encouragement from Pope John Paul II through, for example, his Holy Thursday Letters, substantial reflections on fifty years of priesthood in 1996, and the 1992 Post-Synodal Apostolic Exhortation *Pastores dabo vobis.* The renewal of the priesthood that we hear about in many places in the world derives no doubt from this exquisite fulfillment of the Petrine Office. These documents help us to examine the way in which men exercise the sacred ministry confided to them at the time of their ordination. We need to reflect on the way in which priests live out the qualities of head and shepherd that distinguish the priest from other members of the Church.

It would be less than frank not to observe that in the United States the decline in the number of ordained ministers constitutes one of the most serious threats to the successful implementation of the New Evangelization. It is outside the scope of this essay to attempt a scien-

21. *Dominus Iesus,* §14.

tific analysis of the reasons for this circumstance. The adverse cultural factors that dominate in Western culture obviously have a great deal to do with the decline in vocations, not only to the priesthood, but also all forms of special consecration and dedication in the Church. There also exist intraecclesial factors that contribute to making the priesthood a less clear, and perhaps less desirable, vocation. I suggest that the major factor in this latter category remains the functionalization of the priesthood. To the extent that theologians continue to speak about ministry in the Church as if it were one homogeneous action performed by a class of generic ministers, the priestly office will be reduced to a "doing" without a "being."

A fairly thoroughgoing functionalism governs the thought of many Catholics. In some presentations, the priest emerges as one minister among many, and Catholics are left to conclude that the non-ordained or permanent deacon can substitute for the priest. It is reported, moreover, that some persons in the Church even favor the increased use of deacons and lay ministers to help meet the needs of Catholics in a time of fewer priests, and, what is more astonishing, that younger Catholics are least likely to say that they have noticed or have been affected by the decline in the number of priests. In many places, there exists a tremendous urgency to provide priests for the pastoral care of the faithful and to cultivate priestly vocations by promoting the specific ecclesial identity of the priest. At the same time, certain voices express the view that the decline in the number of priests is a cultural given, and that bishops should devise solutions that neither blatantly contravene canonical regulations nor depend upon the ministry of priests. Well did the 1997 Interdicasterial Instruction specifically warn against initiatives that "encourage a reduction in vocations to the (ministerial) priesthood and obscure the specific purpose of seminaries as places of formation for the ordained ministry."[22] Promotion of vocations to the priesthood must inform every baptized person's outlook on the Church.

The mediation of the priest is required in order for the Christian

22. "Instruction on Certain Questions Regarding the Collaboration of the Non-Ordained Faithful in the Sacred Ministry of Priest," §2.

people to learn the dynamics of the theologal life. Look back at the great movements within the Church that rescued whole segments of the population from the disastrous cultural alternatives to accepting the Gospel, whether in uncivilized lands, such as the Jesuit missionaries to the North American frontier in the seventeenth century, or in highly refined and advanced civilizations or societies, such as the spiritual renewal movements that started in Brittany and Normandy during the same period and extended into the eighteenth century. At the heart of such initiatives, one always discovers holy priests. To cite but one example, there is the French priest Louis Marie Grignon de Montfort, whose spiritual instruction about and ardent devotion to the Blessed Virgin Mary remains a constant source of inspiration for the Church. We need more priests moved with the fire and spirit of this missionary apostolic, as Pope Clement XI designated him in 1706. De Montfort's theology has become associated with a robust Marian piety, but scholarly studies have shown that the saint's intuition encompassed the whole relationship between the Creator and the creature—the plan of divine wisdom—and the special way in which the mediations that center on Christ and his Mother make it possible for the human creature to regain his proper status in the universe. In other words, de Montfort promoted the theologal life.

Special concern envelops the diocesan priest, who embodies in a *prima facie* way the ideal of priestly service inasmuch as he finds himself immediately dependent on the bishop of the particular church and collaborates with him in the priestly office. Among the responsibilities that the priest receives by delegation from the bishop is the authority to preach. Evangelization is a task that belongs to the whole Church, but preaching is reserved to those who participate in the "sacred power" of the priesthood, communicated through a valid episcopate with apostolic succession. Preaching is a sacred action. Because it communicates to the world truths on which the world has no claim, the preacher must rely on what has been handed over to him. How else, as the Apostle reminds us, can one preach unless he has been commissioned? "And how are they to hear without a preacher? And how can men preach unless they are sent?" (Rom 10:14–15). We return to the example of St. Louis Grignon de

Montfort: "The term 'apostolic' was a key word for Montfort. It properly described his 'missionary path.' Linked with the word 'missionary,' and having the etymological meaning of being 'sent,' it expressed something essential for St. Louie Marie."[23] We should also observe that "commission" meant a great deal to our saint. He walked from northwest France to Rome in order to receive from the Successor of Peter the designation and therefore the authority to undertake his missions.

What Louis Grignon de Montfort did at the beginning of the eighteenth century, a Spanish priest had done at the start of the thirteenth century. Dominic de Guzman also traveled to the Successor of Peter, and received a similar mandate from Pope Honorious III to participate in the tasks that belong by divine right to the bishops of the Church. It would be impossible to enumerate all of the other holy priests who have in one way or another taken up with seriousness the role of apostolic missionary. We learn from the spirit of St. Dominic that preaching issues forth best from a heart that is given over to praise and benediction: *laudare, benedicere, praedicare.* He reminds the priests of God's Church that if one is to communicate with enthusiasm and exactitude the truth of the Catholic religion, there exists no substitute for holiness of life. The spiritual adage *nemo potest dare quod non habet* captures the essence of this crucial truth. Priestly mediation is needed in the Church more than ever during a period when people have been distracted from the important truths that define their creaturehood and thus their relation to God. How much of what transpires in the culture of death, the consumer society, the new paganism of Western culture especially, shrouds a profound absence of what it means to be a creature? When we forget what it means to be a creature, then we ignore the urgency of the theologal life. Only the Christian priest who stands between God and men as a mediator can restore, I would argue, the orders of nature and grace. To accomplish this task, he must become a father, a head, a shepherd, but never remain just another religious functionary.[24]

23. Stefano de Fiores, *Jesus Living in Mary: Handbook of the Spirituality of St. Louie Marie de Montfort* (New York: Montfort, 1995), 24.

24. Note what is taught in *Lumen gentium,* §28: "It is in the Eucharistic cult or in the

The conciliar decree on priestly life and ministry stipulates that priests are obliged to "share the truth of the Gospel" and, further, that the virtue of the priest, pastoral charity, be exercised by "accepting and putting into effect in a spirit of faith whatever is enjoined or recommended by the Supreme Pontiff and their own bishops."[25] Number sixteen of the same document sets forth what the Second Vatican Council teaches about the value of clerical celibacy: fuller consecration to Christ to whom priests are especially conformed; greater freedom to pursue the ministry of the Church, specifically "to accept a wider fatherhood in Christ"; and the highest form of spousal love, which is that discovered in the communion of the Church with God. *Pastores dabo vobis* especially develops the theme of spousal love and links it to the identity and virtue of the priest, again, pastoral charity. The "Oath of Fidelity," which is considered an official document of faith, asks pastors (and all clerics) to unite themselves with bishops "as authentic doctors and teachers of the faith." It also enjoins the apostolic activity, especially preaching, that flows from the Church, not the individual, to be carried out "in the communion of the same Church."[26] Without this view of the ministry of the diocesan priest, it would be impossible to envisage a life of faith, which requires instruction, of hope, which requires encouragement, and of charity, which requires the exercise of headship. In other words, without the ministry of priests, it is impossible to sustain and develop the theologal life.

The Witness to the Theologal Life by Consecrated Persons

The fraternity of consecrated life offers a refreshing alternative to the isolation that envelops the modern individual, whose monad-like existence is oddly prefigured in the way that the eighteenth-century thinker Leibnitz imagined the concursus of human and divine freedom. The paradox of individualism is perhaps most realized in the culture that

Eucharistic assembly of the faithful (synaxis) that they [priests] exercise in a supreme degree their office."

25. *Presbyterorum ordinis*, §4 and §15.

26. See *CIC*, §833.

the United States has spawned since the end of the Second World War. The more that people strive to guarantee individual liberties, the more they find themselves isolated and alone, and thus inclined to substitute ersatz forms of being together for true community. Same-sex unions afford the most striking example, but there are others as well. Consecrated persons must remind a generation of lost individuals that truth and friendship are the only goods that perfect the human person. The *communio* of the Church offers the only authentic form of inclusiveness, to use the neologism that dominates so much of our public rhetoric. Within the *communio* of the Church, there exists a special form of communion whose intensity best represents the original coming together in the upper room, where the Apostles, united with Mary, the Mother of Jesus, received the parted tongues of fire that signaled a divine renewal of the whole face of the earth.

The witness of the evangelical counsels offers to the Church a constant reminder of the radical nature of Christian conversion. One can adapt to our present circumstances the way that the classical authors explained the perennial significance of the vows of religion. We can say that poverty opposes everything that is corrupt in the culture of consumption, chastity, everything that is disordered in the culture of permissiveness, and obedience, everything that is distorted in the assumption (which goes unchallenged in the politics of secular liberalism) that power is the only reality. It is a source of consolation for the Church that there are a large number of new initiatives throughout the world.[27] Many of these new initiatives, moreover, prove the thesis that Europe, especially France, is still a fecund source of renewal in the Church. A recent gift from France to the United States is Our Lady of Clear Creek, the new American daughter house of the French Abbey of Fontgombault—of the Solemnes Congregation. The new monastery is located outside Tulsa, Oklahoma.

Twentieth-century North American Catholicism, especially after the Second World War, when expansion to the suburbs proceeded at a rapid

27. For further information about the more prominent initiatives, see my interview on lay movements in the Catholic Church in *Catholic International* 11 (November 2000): 432–33.

pace, may have been the first time in the history of Christianity that members of the Church had to survive without some proximity to a monastery. For reasons that can be traced to historical occurrences in Europe (when hostilities against the Church prevailed) as well as to the need of the immigrant Catholic community, this circumstance was not so apparent in the nineteenth century: witness the Franciscan missions in California and especially the great Benedictine monasteries that grew up alongside the pioneer Church in the Midwest and Northwest. Today, however, only a very small percentage of American Catholics enjoy any experience of monastic life, and indeed of any formal representation of religious life such as was provided for them in the great urban centers of the Northeast by Redemptorists, Passionists, and Franciscans. Without a monastery—and now I use the term in the broad and analogical sense—we should ask ourselves to what extent the Church can protect herself against the adverse influences of a secular culture. How can the theologal life flourish without the witness of a true monastery?

The monk encourages people to trust in the paternal providence of God. Perhaps no more compelling analogy comes from the lips of our Blessed Savior than what He speaks in the Gospel of Matthew: "If you, with all your sins, know how to give your children what is good, how much more will your heavenly Father give good things to anyone who asks him!" (Mt 7:12). Confidence in the providence of God forms the foundation for everyday living out of Christian faith. In the period after the Council, some theologians began to interpret the value of evangelical obedience in terms of creating a disposition in the members of religious institutes for a more effective deployment of their corporate talents. These theorists missed the point of what religious profession or consecration accomplishes in the Church. The religious observes a life of obedience because obedience is foundational to the way of every Christian vocation. It is symptomatic, perhaps, of the kind of spiritual renewal needed in the Church today that the documents that come forth from the Roman Curia have found it opportune repeatedly to stress the "obedience of faith" (Rom 1:5), which is how the Apostle Paul defines his own ministry: "Jesus Christ our Lord, through whom we have received grace and apostleship to bring about the obedience of faith for the sake of his name among all the nations" (Rom 1:4–5).

The flourishing of consecrated life in the Church, as well as the various ways in which the classical forms of religious consecration have been adapted to suit the needs of the present time, reminds us of the importance of conversion of life. Without *conversio*, there is no theologal life. The Desert Fathers introduced the *conversio morum* into the vocabulary of their disciples. These stressed how much what is of the world needs to be left behind when one comes into the school of discipleship that the Lord has established for the members of his Church. We have subsequently developed our understanding of how the Church abides at the heart of the world, and how everything she does aims to draw all men into the center of the Church. At the same time, a misplaced emphasis on secularity has prompted a decreased appreciation for the values attached to retreat from the world. This phenomenon exemplifies one of the unforeseen but nonetheless undesirable effects of the emphasis that the Second Vatican Council—or, to be more precise, those who interpreted the Council's teaching, especially in the mass media—put on the notion of secularity. The decline in so many religious institutes of women in the United States surely finds part of its explanation in this mistaken interpretation of what the bishops of the Second Vatican Council had hoped to communicate about the "perfection of charity."

Consecrated chastity possesses its own objective in the communion of the Church. Religious—especially religious women, and among them, most especially, cloistered religious women—reveal the character of the Church as *Sponsa Verbi*. It may be difficult to formulate a mental picture of some religious—for example, the dogsled missionaries in the Arctic region of North America—as "Brides." And yet, by their wholehearted commitment to the work of evangelization, even these men of gnarled and leathery complexion demonstrate what it means for the Church to commit everything to prepare for the coming of the Lord. St. Paul, we know, appreciated virginity for the sake of the Kingdom because it allowed the Christian to do completely the one thing that is necessary: "I mean, brethren, the appointed time has grown very short"

(1 Cor 7:29). To this injunction, we should also add the accumulated wisdom of the Church, which St. Thomas Aquinas repeats: "sexual pleasure withdraws the soul from that perfect disposition of tending toward God."[28] In the Church, the witness of consecrated religious, especially the women who give themselves night and day to the worship of God, to prayer, and to cultivating the divine friendship, reminds each baptized person that he or she must remain clean of heart, with a mind fully centered on the Lord whose Church we inhabit in charity. The theologal life finds its eminent expression in consecrated, especially contemplative, life. In a word, there we find hearts transformed by the Lord. No wonder that the Holy Father places consecrated persons on Mount Tabor, the Mount of the Transfiguration.

Christ's Lay Faithful and the Work of Evangelization: The Spread of the Theologal Life

We have reflected on the "special activism" of priests and the unique vocation that consecrated persons embody in the task of the New Evangelization. We now turn to ponder the important and specific charge that the Second Vatican Council has given to Christ's lay faithful. While the distinction is a well-known one, it is also the case that some serious misunderstandings about the place of the laity in the Church exist, especially in the countries dominated by some recent German and Anglo-American theology. In certain places, the full recovery of the secular vocation of the laity has not been achieved, and a great deal depends on this happening. Many have observed the ways in which an elision is made between receiving certain tasks, such as teaching and liturgical duties, and becoming personally identified as a Catholic who performs such and such a task. The philosophical explanation lies, in my judgment, in the cultural proclivity to replace office (*munus*) and personal identity with a self-definition based on role and task. Because there exists no pre-Enlightenment culture in the United States, there is little to remind a citizen of this country of his "status," which is such an indispensable part of Christian revelation about who we are.

28. *ST* II-II, q. 186, a. 4.

Members of the Church must appropriate for themselves the teaching of the Council, and resist the Protestantization of the Church that four centuries after the Reformation of the sixteenth century once again threatens to undermine its sanctifying, teaching, and governing missions. The fruits of the Catholic Reform of the post-Tridentine period still remind us of the need to provide for the People of God clear and accurate guidance about how they sanctify the world. The list of tasks is too long to enumerate, and opportunities emerge as needs require. Still, it is imperative to impress on Christ's lay faithful their obligation to transform and sanctify the *saeculum*.

The People of God must live according to the spirit of the new dispensation. St. Matthew, whose account of the Sermon on the Mount has left its impression on the moral instruction given in the Church, exemplifies the apostle of interiority. External conformity only realizes half the grace of the Holy Spirit. Such observance never exhausts the theologal life. The full power of the new dispensation, of what Jesus introduces through the Paschal Mystery, informs every fiber of the human being. The "new man," of which Christian revelation speaks, is the person transformed from the inside out (see Eph 2:15). Without this kind of transformation, which may be summarized in the phrase "the moral conscience," there is little hope that the People of God will be able to do all that their distinctive vocation in the Church requires of them.

I found encouragement in the Jubilee Pentecost assembly held at St. Peter's. The lay ecclesial movements, which like all new stirrings of the Holy Spirit require time to find their precise point of insertion into the Church's hierarchical structure, offer to the People of God significant opportunities to live out their vocations. Recall that each of these movements provides a structured and organized program for spiritual formation. This program extends not only to initial formation, but also permanent formation. We are reminded of the earliest designation for the Christian life, namely, that it is a "Way." The pastors of the Church appreciate the spiritual formation that authentic lay movements give to the lay faithful. In my experience, the lay movements provide one of the best sources of authentic Catholic spirituality for Christians today. Sadly, some of what passes for spiritual theology or spirituality, at least in the United States, is not sufficiently informed by Catholic doctrine, and therefore becomes too much informed by secular if not pagan resources. The theologal life is defined by the theological virtues, not by ephemeral attempts to rejoice in the human spirit.

Interiority cannot be taught unless it is lived. Each person must show to the Church a living proof of the charity and unity that distinguish the Church of Christ. The theologal life flows from the Eucharist. As St. Paul reminded the Corinthians, "Because there is one bread, we who are many are one body, for we all partake of the one bread" (1 Cor 10:17). St. Augustine's exclamation in his commentary on John's Gospel becomes for the laity a warrant, a duty to be discharged, a sacred trust to be lived interiorly: "sacrament of piety, sign of unity, bond of charity!"[29] Because the Eucharist is the sacrament and source of ecclesial unity, the laity join consecrated persons gathered around the bishop and his priests in the one communion of the Church. From this experience of Christ's love, each member of the Body moves out to sanctify, diversely, the world.

Since the Second Vatican Council, we have become accustomed to ponder deeply on the relationship between *missio* and *communio*. Pope John Paul II's 1990 encyclical letter *Redemptoris missio* has helped the whole Church grasp and deal with the configuration of mission that confronts her in the third Christian millennium. Because the Church is missionary by her nature, I believe that it is fair to say that every member serves the Church's missionary mandate. The sacramental mediation of the Church achieves a certain transcendence when the Church reaches out as a sacrament of salvation to every human being on the planet. We comprehend the special circumstances that prompted the issuance of the "Declaration" *Dominus Iesus* in 2000. The truths of Catholic and divine faith that are recalled in that succinct catechism of essential Catholic doctrine possess a special meaning for the "missionary." No human person should be left to worship God in a way that does not allow for a full and active participation in the Eucharistic synaxis. The theologal life is sustained during this moment of participation in the Eucharist.[30]

29. *In Iohannis Evangelium*, 26:13.

30. The Second Vatican Council explicitly recognized the spiritual distress that results

Our meditation on the sacramental mediation of the Church in the context of the permanent validity of the Church's missionary mandate—of her *missio ad gentes*—leads us to reflect on inculturation. We know that the Church's missionary effort has been helped by a judicious use of findings from the anthropological disciplines. If I understand the history properly, when Émile Durkheim began his classical study of suicide victims, he already intuited that it would be important to examine the records of the civil authorities to determine the religion of those persons who had taken their own lives. This founder of modern statistical sociology supposed that the moral instruction given to Catholics would have had an influence on the statistical frequency of suicide victims. Durkheim's study, I understand, confirmed a higher statistical frequency of suicide among French Protestants. This anecdote suggests the importance of truth for life. In the culture wars, Christ conquers culture.

There is a similar lesson to be discovered from the more widely known and studied history of the Church's missionary efforts in China in the seventeenth and eighteenth centuries. Historians interpret the Rites Controversy differently, but the generally accepted view is that the episode was a damaging one. The distinguished Lutheran theologian George Lindbeck, who had been an ecumenical observer at the Second Vatican Council and is himself the son of Protestant missionaries to China, once recounted to me a different explanation of the Church's purposes. Whereas many thought the negative actions of the Holy See had impeded the growth of Christianity in China, it may be argued that the missionary strategy of the popes of the eighteenth century actually ensured that the authentic Gospel of Christ would flourish among people of every class and station. Well-educated and upper-class individuals may have been able to recognize Christianity in the proposed adaptations of Christian practices to accommodate the culture of the Chinese, but the rice farmer and the fisherman, the housewife and the spinster, may not have been so astute as to recognize Christian truth veiled in Chinese cultural practices. In other

---

from a paucity of priests in a given region when it urged bishops to "take special care of those regions of the world in which the word of God is yet to be proclaimed or in which, mainly because of lack of priests, the faithful are in grave danger of falling away from the moral standards of Christian life and of losing the faith itself" (*Christus Dominus*, §6).

words, the sophistication and ingenuity of the proposed adaptations may have made it difficult for ordinary people to recognize fully that the truths and the mysteries of the Christian religion in fact constitute something entirely "new" (see Eph 2:15). Ordinary people outside of the mandarin or ruling classes may have missed the specific distinctiveness of Christian life and worship—in other words, what makes things "new." In present-day terms, the People of God would not have recognized the "definitive and complete character of the revelation of Jesus Christ."[31] We return to the importance of the sacramental mediation of the Church, and of the definitive form that the theologal life takes within her communion. This form includes her liturgical rites. Inculturation should neither obscure the truth of the Gospel nor transmogrify the Catholic religion.

The layperson is called to the work of the evangelization. This witness requires a renewal of spirit. One must ask for the grace to enjoy a deeper love of the mysteries of the faith that we celebrate. Church members must do everything to ensure that the Church of faith and sacraments reaches the farthest corners of the globe, which can happen only to the extent that members live faithfully these gifts of grace. Missionary zeal always characterizes the saints. One thinks first of all of St. Francis Xavier and the flood of enthusiasm for evangelization that he unleashed, but also of St. Francis of Assisi and St. Dominic de Guzman, both of whom cherished and had desires that were never fully realized to carry out the *missio ad gentes*. The modern period affords examples of men, and especially of women, too numerous to mention, who have taken up this example. The missionary desires of a contemplative like Thérèse of Lisieux also serve to encourage and strengthen the Church. The bipolarity of monastics and missionaries, to borrow a designation from Hans Urs von Balthasar, will always serve as a mark of the true Church. Within these categories, laypersons will find their place during the new springtime of the Church.

Because Christ remains the unique savior of the world, no one can fulfill the two great commandments of love, love of God and love of neighbor, without experiencing within oneself the desire to make the Lord better known and loved everywhere. Recall Moses's words to the

31. *Dominus Iesus*, §5.

People of Israel: "You are to be a people peculiarly his own, as he promised you" (Dt 26:16–19). This promise is fulfilled in the Incarnation of the Son of God. The Church can never forget the ordering of the Joyful Mysteries of the Rosary: the Annunciation and the Visitation. The first thing that the embryonic Jesus does is travel, in the womb of his Mother, whose embrace of her cousin Elizabeth establishes Mary forever as the Cause of our Joy, *Causa nostrae latitiae*.

"In a word, you must be perfected as your heavenly Father is perfect" (Mt 5:48). We are reminded that the Christian Gospel is transformative. Well has Don Luigi Guisanni taught us that the Gospel introduces the believer into a "school of discipleship." For every member of the Church, growth in discipleship occurs according to the specific vocation that each one has received. We have examined the sacramental mediations that communicate the gift of divine grace to the human race. Only these mediations of the Church ensure that the human person attains beatifying friendship with God. At the same time, these gifts are received in freedom even as they transform our freedom, putting everything we do entirely at the disposal of the Lord. I have always taken consolation from a foundational principle of Christian discipleship, something that the theology of St. Thomas Aquinas teaches with special clarity, namely, that God loves us because he is good, not because we are. Since there exists no other motive for God to love anyone other than God's own goodness, we know that the priority of grace's transformative power belongs to God alone. Because of the way that the creature is dependent on God, to hold that our goodness belongs first of all to God in no way diminishes the dignity of human freedom. On the contrary, as the saints repeatedly remind us, the one who lives more fully in God becomes who he is, and achieves the freedom that ennobles. It is, as Aquinas again taught the Church, a freedom for excellence. The concrete name for this specifically Christian excellence is the theologal life.[32]

It is difficult to overestimate the importance of the sacred mysteries that God has ordained for the salvation of the world. Here I have

32. For more information about the theologal life, and the use of the term in contemporary theology, see my *Christian Faith and the Theological Life* (Washington, DC: Catholic University of America Press, 1996), 1–12.

reflected on the sacramental mediations from the perspective of the vocations that distinguish the Church. Nothing that happens for good in the Church affects only the one who accomplishes the good deed. The Mystical Body, as we know, is related in such a way that wherever charity increases in one, so charity increases in the other members—in ways known only to God, to be sure, but in real and measurable ways nonetheless. The renewal of all Christ's members in charity, their own rededication to prayer and spiritual discipline, their own recommitment to the work that is theirs, not only benefits the other members of the Church in the invisible workings of the Mystical Body, but also exists in the visible workings of the body that is the Church. Each Christian should expect to be renewed in the transformative power of divine grace and so experience a new urgency to extend and strengthen the sacramental mediations of the Church.

Among the lasting examples that Pope John Paul gave to the Church is the practice of appealing to the Virgin Mother of God. I suspect that it may become a rare instance of an infallible teaching that will remain unformulated, but continue as a custom that bishops and others will follow by some filial instinct, which will motivate them to observe and continue this noble and gracious practice. God knew what consolation it would bring to the brothers and sisters of the Lord to learn that the Mother of his Son is immaculately conceived, and so capable of exercising a sinless and perfect instrumentality in the Church. She who gave birth according to the flesh to the Eternal Son of God best understands what it means for the world to be saved by One like us in all things though free from sin. She who first held in her arms the one Mediator between heaven and earth best understands the sacramental mediations that flow from her son. She who lifted up the Lord of All for the adoration of kings who had come from the East best understands the evangelizing task that Christ has confided to the Church. In Mary, understanding breaks forth into love. In her, we find the theologal life in its fullness. So we bring this chapter to a close in the embrace of the woman whose maternal mediation remains, according to the teaching of Louis Grignon de Montfort, the sure promise of divine predestination for those who seek refuge in her.

CHAPTER 4

SONSHIP, SACRIFICE, AND SATISFACTION

The Divine Friendship in Aquinas and the Renewal of Christian Anthropology

This chapter shows how the salvific integration of divine friendship, adoptive sonship, mediation, sacrifice, and satisfaction occurs within and with regard to the *imago Dei*. The *imago Dei* is an essential element of Thomistic moral theology. The reason for its centrality is simple: the "*imago Dei* relates directly to our capacity to love God." Man's specific, rational nature is the essential foundation for the human reception of divine grace and the theologal transformation it enacts within his personhood. Theology and sanctity are only possible for human persons because they are created in the image and likeness of God. Thus the *imago Dei* is the key that explains both sin and redemption.

Considering the implications of alternative accounts of human nature, Father Cessario points to the inextricable link between theology and sanctity. Only St. Thomas's authentic teaching on the relationship between human nature and grace enables the theologian to account

Originally published as "Sonship, Sacrifice, and Satisfaction: The Divine Friendship in Aquinas and the Renewal of Christian Anthropology," *Letter and Spirit* 3 (2007): 71–93. Reprinted by permission.

for the "beloved awareness" that divine friendship produces within the adoptive son of God. The sacraments "supply the way that Christ makes make sons out of images." In short, the *imago Dei* "undergirds everything that is taught" in St. Thomas's sacramental theology. "We see, then, that the Church's sacraments and the practice of divine friendship go hand in hand."

One task of the theologian is to render an account of the *depositum fidei* contained in sacred Scripture and the Church's tradition. Because of his officially recognized ability to display the interconnectedness between elements of Catholic teaching that form part of this deposit of faith, St. Thomas Aquinas (1224/25–74) enjoys special standing among the Church's theologians.[1] This essay draws upon the writings of Aquinas to talk about the practice of the divine friendship that, as far as the Church knows, ennobles the human creature in this life as a gift given only to the baptized Christian believer.[2]

Jesus Christ himself announces the invitation to divine friendship: "I no longer call you slaves, because a slave does not know what his master is doing. I have called you friends, because I have told you everything I have heard from my Father" (Jn 15:15). In order to understand what it means that Christ no longer call us slaves but friends, we need to consider three theological points that receive extended treatment in the works of Aquinas—sonship, sacrifice, and satisfaction.

As Aristotle reminds us, friendship is an activity: only with a friend is one friendly.[3] St. Thomas demonstrates that the practice of divine friendship belongs properly to those who participate in the sonship of Jesus Christ. In illuminating the dynamics of this participation, Aquinas

1. See Pope John Paul II, "*Fides et ratio*, Encyclical Letter on Faith and Reason (September 14, 1998), 43, 44," *Origins* 28 (1998): 329–40.

2. Elements of this chapter were originally delivered as "The Image of God and the Sacraments of the Church: The Practice of Divine Friendship" at the Dominican House of Studies, Washington, DC, October 16, 2006, and as "The Sacraments of Healing and Satisfaction," at the Aquinas Center for Theological Renewal, Ave Maria University, Naples, Florida, February 3, 2007.

3. See Aristotle, *Nicomachean Ethics*, trans. Terence Irwin (Indianapolis: Hackett, 1985), 210: "For friendship is said to be reciprocated goodwill" (1155b 32, 33).

takes full account of what St. Paul reveals about the divine plan for our salvation. In sum, God "did not spare his Son, but handed him over for us all" (Rom 8:32). The Scriptures affirm that for Jesus to be "handed over" entailed sacrifice and the making of satisfaction. The Christian religion venerates a divine Redeemer who dies. Christ's divine status makes his death revelatory of the divine plan: "God sent his only Son into the world so that we might have life through him" (1 Jn 4:10). We discover the motive for Christ's death on the Cross—not in the historical circumstances of its accomplishment but in the sinful actions that, since the commission of the original sin, have marked the human race.

In Catholic culture and piety, the Blessed Virgin Mary is held to assist us to understand the place that sacrifice and satisfaction hold in Catholic doctrine about the atonement. On Calvary, Mary especially represents the "New Eve." From the Cross, Christ announces that his mother Mary has become the new mother of the living: "Woman, behold, your son" (Jn 19:26; Gen 3:20). In the person of St. John, Mary embraces a son in whom she receives each of us. She takes up actively her role as "Mother of the Church."

Mary's response in faith to the divine plan illuminates how Christian believers of all ages should regard the sacrificial and satisfactory character of the Christian life. While standing at the foot of the Cross, Mary, Our Lady of Compassion, exhibits the full dimensions of her maternal mediation that began at the annunciation. She teaches believers that profound joy can coexist even with exquisite sorrow. Mary's sorrow at seeing a bloodied and dying Jesus expresses the sorrow of God's elect. All those who find their salvation in the fulfillment of the divine plan identify with the Mother of God: "Be it done to me according to your word" (Lk 1:38).

Portrayals of Mary in a swoon appear late in the history of Christian art. The earliest representations of the crucifixion show Mary sorrowful of mien but recollected in spirit. She assents in faith to the working out of the divine plan. She accepts the sorrow that any mother would undergo upon seeing her son die, especially on a shameful cross. At the same time, the New Eve experiences the joy of embracing all those who have been bought back by the shedding of her Son's blood. Her spirit of acceptance is meant to inform the life of Christian belief practiced within the Catholic Church.

The Church is able to communicate the divine goodness to those who participate in her full communion. The Catholic theological tradition ascribes to Christ a threefold grace, including his capital grace, or that which establishes Christ as head of the Church. One expression of this outpouring of the divine goodness that flows from the capital grace of Christ is called *satisfaction*.

By his sacrifice on the Cross, Christ has accomplished satisfaction for the world's sins. Satisfaction, then, is related directly to restoring divine friendship to the sinful creature. Without Christ's sacrifice and satisfaction, the human race would have remained slaves of the Ultimate Divine. That is, all men and women would find themselves like those who do not know what the master is doing. Because of what happens on Calvary, however, human destiny is different. Jesus himself assures us of this comforting truth: "I have told you everything I have heard from my Father" (Jn 15:15). What do we learn? How we are to love unto eternal life. This text returns us to the theme of the *depositum fidei* and to the sacred tradition and sacred Scripture that it contains. Both Scripture and tradition make "present and fruitful in the Church the mystery of Christ, who promised to remain with his own 'always, to the close of the age' (Matt. 28:20)."[4]

THE IMAGE OF GOD AND CHRISTIAN ANTHROPOLOGY

In Aquinas's thought, the general themes of sonship, sacrifice, and satisfaction find their methodological and substantive underpinnings in the biblical and theological doctrine of man created in the image of God, *imago Dei*. In the early 1950s, a popular Dominican author expressed this startling view: "So vital is the doctrine that man is the image of God that we cannot understand the teachings of Christ apart from it."[5] This

4. *CCC*, §80.

5. See Elwood F. Smith, OP, and Louis A. Ryan, OP, *Preface to Happiness* (New York: Benziger Brothers, 1950), 4.

doctrine remains a foundational theme for Catholic theology, though, as the International Theological Commission has noted, few authors in the modern period appear to regard it as such.[6]

Dominican theologian J. Augustine Di Noia points out that the significance of the *imago* doctrine moves beyond the level of speculative anthropology to a consideration of its relation to moral theology.[7] *Imago Dei* relates directly to our capacity to love God. Our possession of the created *imago Dei* distinguishes us from other living beings and at the same time provides the basis upon which rests our adoptive sonship in Christ. The Christian participates in the divine sonship when he or she, through grace, becomes a living image of the Trinity. Therefore, in order to follow what Thomas has to say about sonship, sacrifice, and satisfaction, we first must consider how he sets forth the doctrine of the image of God. Aquinas is clear that in this image there is a dynamic movement toward fulfillment: "Man is said to be after God's image in virtue of his intelligent nature."[8]

Thomas supplies a fulsome treatment of the topic in his disputed question *De veritate* (On Truth) where, in thirteen articles devoted to *De mente* (On the Intellect), he provides an exegesis of the doctrine of the image as set forth by St. Augustine (†430) in the last books of his *De trinitate* (On the Trinity).[9] Because it employs the notion of relation, Au-

6. "Until the dawn of the modern period, the theology of the *imago Dei* retained its central position in theological anthropology. Throughout the history of Christian thought, such was the power and fascination of this theme that it could withstand those isolated critiques (as, for example, in iconoclasm) which charged that its anthropomorphism fostered idolatry. But, in the modern period, the theology of the *imago Dei* came under a more sustained and systematic critique." See International Theological Commission, "Communion and Stewardship: Human Persons Created in the Image of God," 18. Available at http://www.vatican.va/roman_curia/congregations/cfaith/cti_documents/rc_con_cfaith_doc_20040723_communion-stewardship_en.html.

7. J. Augustine Di Noia, OP, "*Imago Dei-Imago Christi*: The Theological Foundations of Christian Humanism," *Nova et Vetera* 2, no. 2 (2004): 267–78.

8. *ST* I, q. 93, a 4. This important article sets forth the first principle for subsequent developments in theories of universal human rights. See *Summa Theologiae*, 61 vols., Blackfriars ed. (New York: McGraw-Hill, 1964–80). There really is no adequate translation in English for *summa theologiae*. The closest would be the "sum of theology." For a general introduction to this classical theological source, see Jean-Pierre Torrell, OP, *Aquinas's Summa: Background, Structure, and Reception*, trans. Benedict M. Guevin, OSB (Washington, DC: Catholic University of America Press, 2005).

9. See *De veritate*, Question 10, "*De mente*." Text in Robert W. Mulligan, James V. McGlynn,

gustine's psychological model avoids the practical subordinationism that today shapes much popular preaching and instruction on the Trinity. Recall that relation is considered the weakest of the Aristotelian categories of accidental being: So the Church can use "substance" to designate the divine being in its unity and use "relation" to designate the fact that the distinction of persons lies in the relationship of each to the others.[10] Subordinationist accounts are pernicious not only for the understanding of God but also for the understanding of man. When the persons of the Trinity are not regarded as equal, as was the case in the Arianist heresy, it is the human creature that suffers. For, as Aquinas insists, man's imaging of God is related especially to the second person in God, the Logos-Son.[11] If that second person is believed to be a second and lower god, then the human creature is an image, not of God, but only of a higher form of creaturely existence.

Augustine, along with those who followed him in the patristic and medieval theological traditions, discussed the *imago* in light of Genesis 1:26: "Then God said, 'Let us make man in our image, after our likeness.'"[12] Patristic commentary on this verse alone makes up a voluminous collection of texts.[13] It is noteworthy that, whereas Augustine and several other patristic authors developed analogies for the image of God in man within their treatises on the Trinity, Thomas locates his discussion of the *imago Dei* in a treatise on man, specifically, in the first part of

---

and Robert W. Schmidt, trans., *Truth*, 3 vols., Library of Living Catholic Thought (Chicago: Regnery, 1952–54; reprint, Indianapolis: Hackett, 1994). Father William J. Hill was wont to alert his students that the use of St. Augustine's psychological model does not solve the mystery of the Trinity, although it does illuminate helpfully what remains a mystery. See William J. Hill, OP, *The Three-Personed God: The Trinity as a Mystery of Salvation* (Washington, DC: Catholic University of America, 1982), 215.

10. See *CCC*, §252.

11. See *ST* I, q. 35, a. 2, ad 3: "The image of one thing is present in one of two ways. The first, as in a being of the same specific nature, for example, the king's image in his son; the second, as in a being of a different nature, e.g., the king's image on a coin. The Son is the Image of the Father in the first manner; man is the image of God in the second."

12. Western Christianity based its reflections on the Latin translation of Genesis 1:26: "et ait faciamus hominem ad imaginem et similitudinem nostram et praesit piscibus maris et volatilibus caeli et bestiis universaeque terrae omnique reptili quod movetur in terra."

13. For example, see the still valuable and detailed work of John Sullivan, OP, *The Image of God: The Doctrine of St. Augustine and Its Influence* (Dubuque: Priory Press, 1963).

his *Summa Theologiae*.[14] He takes up the theme in considering "the end or term of man's production, insofar as he is said to have been made after God's image and likeness" (*factus ad imaginem et similitudinem Dei*).[15]

In addition to probing Augustine's psychological model for the *imago*, Aquinas also asks what the difference is between the two words used by Scripture, "image" and "likeness" (*ad imaginem et similitudinem*). He notes that the patristic period proffers at least two approaches to answering this question, and cites two familiar authorities: Augustine, who considered likeness as preliminary to image, and St. John Damascene († ca. 750), who thought that likeness signified the exactness or perfection of image.[16] Aquinas reconciles these apparently conflicting authorities by appealing to the Aristotelian doctrine of the transcendentals, which allows for properties of being, such as the true and the good, to be "both common to all things and applicable to any single thing."[17]

The twentieth-century Thomist Jacques Maritain captures the temper of Aquinas's mind: "To scatter and to confuse are both equally inimical to the nature of the mind. 'No one,' says [John] Tauler, 'understands true distinction better than they who have entered into unity.'"[18] Aquinas seeks to unite rather than to scatter image and likeness.

Aquinas knows that sometimes distinctions can scatter. In the second book of his *Sentences*, Peter Lombard insists on distinguishing image and likeness by strictly identifying one with intellect and the other with will. Lombard argues that because Scripture uses the two words, they are meant to be taken disjunctively. Aquinas replies by applying what might be described as a transcendental "method." He begins by pointing out that there is something of love in knowledge and something of knowledge in love: "love of the word (*dilectio verbi*), which is a

14. See Edmund Hill, OP, "St. Augustine on the Divine Image in Man," in *Man Made to God's Image*, vol. 13 (Ia. 90–102), *St. Thomas Aquinas, Summa Theologiae* (New York: McGraw-Hill, 1964), 209–12.

15. *ST* I, q. 93, prologue.

16. See *ST* I, q. 93, a. 9.

17. *ST* I, q. 93, a. 9: "Unum autem, cum sit de transcendentibus, et commune est omnibus et ad singula potest aptari, sicut et bonum et verum."

18. We recall Maritain's axiom "Distinguish to Unite"—"Distinguer pour unir, ou Les degrés du savoir"; Gerald B. Phelan, trans., "Preface to the Original French Edition," in *The Degrees of Knowledge* (New York: Charles Scribner's Sons, 1959), ix.

beloved awareness (*amata notitia*), belongs to the idea of 'image'; but love of virtue belongs to 'likeness,' just as virtue does."[19] He further suggests that the transcendental properties of being, the true and the good, make it difficult to impose a distinction that would render image one thing and likeness another. An *amata notitia* precedes virtue, which may be thought of as an instructed goodness (*docta bonitas*), even as the virtuous life perfects the *dilectio verbi,* which enjoys a special affinity to the second divine person, the Logos-Word. This reference is made without prejudice to Aquinas's position that the image of God in man remains that of the whole Trinity.[20] This text reveals that "image and likeness" both pertain to discerning the nature of authentic virtue, which Thomas insists remains the foundation of true friendship, both human and divine.[21]

NATURE AND THE SUPERNATURAL IN THE THOMISTIC REVIVAL AND BEYOND

The anthropology of the image, then, governs the moral theology of St. Thomas. And the teleology of the *Summa*'s second part finds its mooring in what theologians have called the obediential potency of human nature for completion in God—that which disposes the human creature to desire and seek the divine friendship. This question still vexes contemporary Catholic theology.

Since the mid-twentieth century, the whipping boy in many such arguments has been the theretofore revered sixteenth-century Thomist Cardinal Thomas de Vio Cajetan (1469–1534).[22] For nearly five centuries, most Catholic theologians considered his commentary on the *Summa* authoritative. But in the twentieth century, his theological trustworthiness came under assault, as he was charged with distorting Aquinas's

19. *ST* I, q. 93, a. 9, ad 4: "Ad quartum dicendum quod dilectio verbi, quod est amata notitia, pertinet ad rationem imaginis; sed dilectio virtutis pertinet ad similitudinem, sicut et virtus."

20. See *ST* I, q. 93, a. 5: "God's image is in man with reference to both the divine nature and the Trinity of persons."

21. See *ST*, II-II, q. 106, a. 1, ad 3: *cum vera amicitia supra virtutem fundetur.*

22. See my "Cardinal Cajetan and His Critics: Review of *Culture and the Thomist Tradition: After Vatican II* by Tracey Rowland," *Nova et Vetera* 3, no. 1 (2005): 109–18.

meaning. For instance, lay philosopher Étienne Gilson called into question Cajetan's essentialism, while the Jesuit and later Cardinal Henri de Lubac criticized Cajetan's conception of human nature's openness to divine grace. The Dominican intellectual historian Marie-Dominique Chenu, who earlier in his career had inveighed against the Baroque systematization of Thomas's thought, encouraged these critical voices. Chenu himself was persuaded that much of the Thomism developed during the late Renaissance and Baroque periods reflected the outlook of the secular rationalist Christian Wolff (1679–1754) more than it did an authentic development of the Thomas's thought.[23]

Ralph McInerny has rebutted these modern critiques of Cajetan and Renaissance and Baroque Thomism.[24] He does so on the basis of the common principles of Catholic theology. McInerny, the philosopher, clears the way for the theologian. He shows that it makes a great deal of difference how one conceives of the sinful creature's disposition both to want and to receive the gratuitous gift of the divine friendship. To put the question in terms redolent of John 15:15: it is important to distinguish the ways that a person may be said to want to know what the master is doing. That returns us again to the question of the *imago Dei*. If we know nothing of human nature, we can say neither what it is, nor whether it is, nor whether it has been assumed by Christ's Incarnation. We also do not know what claim human nature has on God.

De Lubac expresses well the Catholic doctrine that is jeopardized when lack of proper nuance introduces confusion about what it means to claim that man is created in the *imago Dei*: "In my view, which is that of every Catholic, any idea of a claim of created nature in relation to the supernatural should be absolutely excluded."[25] De Lubac is treating the papally condemned view of Flemish theologian Michael Baius (1513–89), who argued that in the state of original justice innocence and its

23. See my review: "*Aquinas and His Role in Theology* by Marie-Dominique Chenu, OP," *Theological Studies* 64 (2003): 440–41.

24. Ralph McInerny, *Praeambula Fidei: Thomism and the God of the Philosophers* (Washington, DC: Catholic University of America Press, 2006), 125. See my review in *First Things* (May 2007): 48–51.

25. *Augustinisme et Théologie Moderne* (Paris: Aubier, 1965); English translation: *Augustinianism and Modern Theology* (New York: Herder, 1969).

promised eternal reward were not supernatural gifts of God to man, but the necessary complement of human nature itself.[26] Oddly, Baius's view resembles the practical presumption that today informs the outlooks—if not the developed theories—of many good-willed Christians. In his avowal of this view, de Lubac recognizes that it is important to ensure that the order of nature remains distinct from and enjoys no claim upon the supernatural.[27]

Later, certain continental and American theologians would radicalize de Lubac's ideas about the human creature's natural desire for God. But they failed to understand the degree to which de Lubac himself constrained the radicality of his own thesis by this prior affirmation that created nature can make no claims on the supernatural. It would be beneficial for theologians of every stripe to take another look at Pope St. Pius V's initial condemnations of Baius, whose teachings are often considered a likely forerunner to Jansenism. Recall that the Louvain-based Baius repudiated the received scholastic thought of his day and claimed to have discovered a pristine account of grace and nature in the writings of the Church Fathers, especially St. Augustine. Baius, then, would have been thought of as a conservative reformer.

The point is to observe that the interpretation of how the *imago Dei* works within the dynamics of Christian living and salvation occasioned friendly, and sometimes not-so-friendly, disputes among Catholic theologians even during the heyday of the Thomistic revival encouraged by

26. For example, an error of Baius cited by Pope Pius V, *Ex omnibus afflictionibus* (October 1, 1567): "Vita aeterna homini integro et angelo promissa fuit intuitu bonum operum, et bona opera ex lege naturae ad illam consequendam per se sufficiunt." A. Schönmetzer and Heinrich Joseph Dominik Denzinger, *Enchiridion symbolorum, definitionum et declarationum de rebus fidei et morum* (Freiburg: Herder, 1963), 1904; English translation: *The Sources of Catholic Dogma* (Fitzwilliam, NH: Loreto, 1992).

27. De Lubac's avowal of Baius's view is all the more arresting because he did not concur with Aquinas's teaching (in *De malo*, q. 1, a. 5, ad 15) that deprivation of the beatific vision in a hypothetical state of pure nature would not be a punishment. Hence even an author who is associated with denial of the claim that human nature could in a different order of providence be ordered to a lesser felicity apart from what grace creates also affirms that the order of nature is distinct from and enjoys no claim upon the supernatural. The International Theological Commission, in "The Hope of Salvation for Infants Who Die without Being Baptized" (2007), adverts to these discussions within the context of discussing the hope for salvation that one may have for unbaptized infants. See http://www.vatican.va/roman_curia/congregations/cfaith/cti_documents/rc_con_cfaith_doc_20070419_un-baptised-infants_en.html.

Pope Leo XIII in the late nineteenth and early twentieth century. In my view, while theologians may think that they have moved beyond the difficulties, they have not. Moreover, there can be no sidestepping of the question of the status of man created *ad imaginem Dei*. In short, there has not yet been any resolution of the questions about man's natural desire for God that were debated through the mid-twentieth century.

One of the best contemporary examples of sound Thomist teaching on the *imago Dei* and its reaching out for God, however, is Lawrence Feingold's *The Natural Desire to See God According to St. Thomas Aquinas and His Interpreters*.[28] The conclusion of Feingold's lengthy study is titled "Summary of the Arguments Showing That There Is No Innate Appetite for the Vision of God, but Only an Elicited and Imperfect Natural Desire." This should be required reading for anyone wishing to affirm that a natural desire for intrinsically supernatural beatitude is innate in man.[29] Indeed, Feingold clarifies from within the Thomist tradition how the *imago Dei* provides the anthropological basis for achieving the status of friendship with God through sharing in Christ's natural sonship.[30]

CREATION, GRACE, AND GLORY IN THE CHRISTIAN LIFE

To understand how we share in Christ's natural sonship requires that we do some thinking about the nature and efficacy of the sacraments of the Church. Aquinas takes up theological topics associated with the Incarnation and the sacraments in the third part of the *Summa*. In this part, he makes only two direct references to the *imago Dei*—both appear in discussions of man's capacity for beatific fulfillment.[31] This perhaps

28. Lawrence Feingold, *The Natural Desire to See God According to St. Thomas Aquinas and His Interpreters* (Ave Maria, FL: Sapientia Press, 2010). For further discussion of the contemporary issues that the natural desire in man for God raises, see the "Book Symposium" on Feingold's work in *Nova et Vetera* 5, no. 1 (2007).

29. For further discussion, see my "Duplex Ordo Cognitionis," in *Reason and the Reasons of Faith*, ed. Paul J. Griffiths and Reinhard Hütter (New York: T&T Clark, 2005), 327–38.

30. See my *A Short History of Thomism* (Washington, DC: Catholic University of America Press, 2005).

31. One reference occurs when Aquinas discusses whether the Holy Spirit should be called the Father of Christ in respect of his humanity, and the other when Aquinas explains

explains why one rarely sees the theme of the *imago Dei* discussed in connection with the sacraments of the Church—even though Aquinas compares the sacraments to the humanity of Christ as separate to conjoined instruments of his divinity.[32] At the same time, the doctrine of the *imago Dei* undergirds everything that is taught (and indeed what would have been taught) in this third part of the *Summa*.[33] In order to see why, however, we must return to the discussion of the *imago* in the first part of the *Summa*.

Aquinas there concludes that some realization of the *imago Dei* occurs in all men, even in sinners.[34] Thomas formulates the following distinctions as to how the image is realized. The first mode of realization is man's natural aptitude for understanding and loving God. The second mode appears in those who actually or habitually, though while on earth imperfectly, know and love God. The third mode is in those who know and love God perfectly. This last group is composed of the saints in heaven who have attained the image according to the likeness of glory, that is, those in whom the practice of divine friendship has achieved beatific consummation. So the first image is found in all men, the second only in the justified, and the third only in the blessed.

This tripartite division of the *imago Dei* is not peculiar to Aquinas. Christian tradition returns frequently to the image of creation, the image of grace, and the image of glory, although some recent spiritual and theological authors eschew this tripartite understanding of man's relationship to God.

The International Theological Commission acknowledges Aquinas's tripartite distinction and contrasts his teaching on the *imago Dei* with that of St. Bonaventure and of the fourteenth-century Dominican Meister Eckhart (ca. 1260 to ca. 1328).[35] The commission also observes that

---

that Christ enjoys possession of the beatific vision while still a wayfarer on earth. These texts are found in *ST* III, q. 32, a. 3, and *ST* III, q. 9, a. 2, respectively.

32. But see my *The Godly Image: Christ and Salvation in Catholic Thought from Anselm to Aquinas*, Studies in Historical Theology 6 (Petersham, MA: St. Bede's, 1990).

33. Aquinas did not finish his masterwork. For an account of the composition of the *Summa Theologiae*, see Jean-Pierre Torrell, OP, *Saint Thomas Aquinas*, vol. 1: *The Person and His Work*, rev. ed. (Washington, DC: Catholic University of America Press, 2005).

34. *ST* I, q. 93, a. 4.

35. See International Theological Commission, "Communion and Stewardship": "In

the sixteenth-century reformers rejected the notion that this image was ontological, reducing it instead to the category of a relation, something extrinsic to man. Catholic theology, on the other hand, aims mightily to follow Thomas's lead—envisioning that image gives way to sonship, that the *imago Dei* of creation gives way to the adoptive sonship of grace. Nothing qualifies with greater profundity the human person than the gift of sanctifying grace. And the Church always explains sanctification in terms of transformation.

Di Noia identifies this dominant theme of Thomas's theology in the teachings of the Second Vatican Council, Pope John Paul II, and Pope Benedict XVI. The Council and postconciliar Popes, he says, also express the vision that "the human person is created in the image of God (*imago Dei*) in order to grow into the image of Christ (*imago Christi*)."[36] Because the human person is created after the image of God, and inasmuch as this imaging enjoys a special relationship to the second divine person, who is the divine Logos of creation, there exists an affinity between the image of creation and the sonship of grace—*imago creationis* (*naturae*), and *imago recreationis* (*gratiae*).

Thomas distinguishes the causal communication of divine goodness that sustains all that is created from the grace of adoptive sonship made complete by glory. One commentator explains Thomas's distinction this way:

> The mystery of Christ is that hidden for all ages until revealed in him. It is the mystery of the sonship and of the Father whose Son he is. That revelation means that the divine relation to creation is paternal in having reference to the natural filiation of Jesus Christ and to all who are conjoined to him. That is to say that all creation is ordered to the per-

---

Thomas Aquinas, the *imago Dei* possesses an historical character, since it passes through three stages: the *imago creationis* (*naturae*), the *imago recreationis* (*gratiae*), and the *similitudinis* (*gloriae*) (*STh* I, q. 93 a. 4). For Aquinas, the *imago Dei* is the basis for participation in the divine life. The image of God is realized principally in an act of contemplation in the intellect (*STh* I, q. 93, a. 4 and 7). This conception can be distinguished from that of Bonaventure, for whom the image is realized chiefly through the will in the religious act of man (*Sent.* II, d. 16 a. 2 q. 3). Within a similar mystical vision, but with a greater boldness, Meister Eckhart tends to spiritualize the *imago Dei* by placing it at the summit of the soul and detaching it from the body (*Quint.* I, 5, 5–7; V, 6.9s)."

36. Di Noia, "*Imago Dei-Imago Christi*," 269.

> sonal fatherhood: of the Father to Jesus Christ and of the Father to the sons by adoption; "All things are yours for you are Christ's and Christ is God's" (1 Cor 3:22–23).[37]

It follows that before and outside of the revelation communicated by Christ, there is never any question of speaking about God as Father, except metaphorically. Nor can we speak of the Christian believer as an adopted son, except as a way of expressing the relation of creation that sustains in existence the intelligent creature, that is, the image of creation. This becomes important when we seek to understand the necessity of the sacramental life of the Church. We must remember that the infusion of divine grace that makes us sons in the Son results from a causal exercise of the divine goodness that is distinct from what produces the intelligent creature *ad imaginem Dei.*

Christ stands at the center of the mystery of adoptive sonship. Thomas observes with great care the distinction between natural and adoptive sonship. Christ perfectly embodies the divine sonship: "Christ, however, remains Son of God according to a perfect definition of filiation"—"Christus autem est Filius Dei secundum perfectam rationem filiationis."[38] Christ, again, is "the Son of God by nature, [and who] under no aspect may be said to be an adoptive son."[39]

Adoptive sonship, on the other hand, remains the preferred way to speak about the divine image of God actualized in those who have been born into the new life of water and the Holy Spirit in baptism. The graced image appears in the form of what the New Testament calls adoptive sonship (Rom 8:23; Gal 4:5). The proximate source of this grace in the Church remains Christ, Son by nature, not adoption. But "the whole Trinity adopts men as sons of God."[40]

Aquinas invents nothing. His language of sonship comes from Scripture, and he seeks the connections between the truths revealed there. Thus the Dominican theologian Colman O'Neill can explain: "The member of Christ is an adopted son of God because he is to share in Christ's

37. See T. C. O'Brien, *Father, Son, and Holy Ghost,* vol. 7 (Ia. 33–43), *St. Thomas Aquinas, Summa Theologiae* (New York: McGraw-Hill, 1976), 247.

38. *ST* III, q. 32, a. 4.

39. *ST* III, q. 23, a. 4.

40. *ST* III, q. 23, a. 2.

inheritance."[41] The doctrine of the image as realized in sonship illustrates the dynamic interpretation of the *imago* that permeates Aquinas's thought. The movement of the *imago Dei* remains Godward, teleological, perfective, bound for glory. We recognize, then, a familiar sequence for modern theology: anthropology, Christology, and eschatology.[42]

O'Neill argues that three theological topics are required to illuminate the meaning of adoptive sonship—*imago Dei*, likeness to God, and participation in the divine goodness. As we have seen, Thomas locates the reason for man's privileges and responsibilities in the divine imaging that occurs in the intellect and in freedom. The human creature can know and love, and this native "capacity for the supreme good" can be fulfilled by a revelation of God's inward life that summons man to a participation in the divine knowledge and love.[43]

The adopted son knows what the master is doing. To the adopted son, Christ reveals all that he has heard from the Father. This revelation creates a special kind of friendship between man and God. Sonship of this kind, on Thomas's account, consists of the reproduction of the life of the Blessed Trinity in man through his activity of supernatural knowledge and love. For the Catholic theologian, the emphasis in sonship remains theological—knowing and loving God in faith, hope, and charity—not principally humanistic. This is why, in order to stress the ontological difference that precedes the practice of the theological virtues, the *Catechism* speaks of a "theologal" life.[44]

In considering adoptive sonship, likeness to God is always to be understood analogically. The adopted son does not share a specific nature with God. So adoptive sonship resembles the image of a ruler on a coin.

41. Colman E. O'Neill, OP, "Adoptive Sonship," in *The One Mediator*, vol. 50 (3a.16–26), *St. Thomas Aquinas, Summa Theologiae* (New York: McGraw-Hill, 1965), 250. Pages 250–57 summarize the content of this dense essay.

42. See Di Noia, "*Imago Dei-Imago Christi*," 267–68: "Over thirty years ago, in one of the first theological commentaries on *Gaudium et Spes* . . . Cardinal Joseph Ratzinger argued that it is essential to take into account the intrinsic linking of anthropology with Christology (and thus with eschatology) which unfolds across the entire text and which in his view constitutes its crucial insight."

43. See *ST* I, q. 93, a. 2, ad 3.

44. See *CCC*, §2686. For further discussion, see my *Christian Faith and the Theological Life* (Washington, DC: Catholic University of America Press, 1996), esp. 1ff.

Finally, the adoptive son's participation in the divine goodness achieves its highest degree only in those to whom God himself chooses and positively transmits it to through predestination.[45] There is no room in the Thomist vision of sonship for naturalism or Pelagian strategies.

O'Neill sums up: "If the adopted son of God is to be equated with man as the image of God by grace, then it must be said that sonship consists in the reproduction of the life of the Blessed Trinity in man through his activity of supernatural knowledge and love."[46] This knowledge and love of the persons of the Trinity occur only within the context of the theological and infused moral virtues, which, under the impulse of the gifts of the Holy Spirit, can produce a "semi-experimental" awareness of the divine persons.

Aquinas develops the doctrine of the image so as to bring us to realize that our awareness of the Trinity develops through the image that we bear in ourselves. Friendship produces a beloved awareness of the Beloved, an *amata notitia*. The teaching on adoptive sonship is as startling in its conclusion as it is overarching in its complete command and delicate treatment of several key elements of Catholic doctrine related to sacramental life in Christ.

THE DIVINE LOVE AND THE "EFFICACY" OF THE SACRAMENTS

The life of adoptive sonship finds its external expression and source in the sacramental structures of the Church. A heavy emphasis on sacramental symbolism has dominated much theology since the Second Vatican Council's *Sacrosanctum Concilium*.[47] This has sometimes obscured the plain truth of Catholic sacramental theology that each of the sacraments does something.[48] They are signs to be sure, but signs that cause.

45. See *ST* I, q. 23, a. 1.

46. O'Neill, *One Mediator*, 253.

47. Second Vatican Council, "*Sacrosanctum Concilium*, Dogmatic Constitution on Divine Revelation (December 4, 1963)," in *The Documents of Vatican II*, ed. Walter M. Abbott (Piscataway, NJ: New Century, 1966).

48. See my "The Sacraments of the Church," in *Vatican II Renewal within Tradition*, ed. Matthew L. Lamb and Matthew Levering (Oxford: Oxford University Press, 2008), 129–46.

Pope Benedict XVI expresses this truth with clarity: "Since the Eucharist makes present Christ's redeeming sacrifice, we must start by acknowledging that 'there is a causal influence of the Eucharist at the Church's very origins.'"[49]

No account of a sacramental theology is complete without addressing the question of sacramental causality—how the sacraments bring forth their effects.[50] Dominican theologian Benedict Ashley reminds us of the importance of Thomas's concept of efficient causality in explaining the hierarchic reality of the sensible universe.[51] In short, nothing comes into being without some exercise of efficient causality. This assertion is made within a classical philosophical context and applies to the order of being. But the same principle applies as well to the order of supernature. It is difficult to conceive that the order of nature would exhibit a richness that does not exist in the order of supernature. Efficient causality offers to explain what brings something into existence.

Today, however, this is difficult for people to recognize because, since the Renaissance, discussions about efficient causality have become almost exclusively the concern of the observational sciences. Modern philosophy remains strong on developing accounts of formal and final causality. But the moderns retreat from expounding efficient causality, preferring to consign that to scientific theorists. As a consequence, Catholic theology no longer possesses philosophical concepts to describe "hierarchic reality" and the unity and plurality of creation. This turn of events further leaves Catholic theology without a useful tool for explaining the double agency at work in the sacraments.

In the Christian understanding of the sacraments there is an ordered

49. Pope Benedict XVI, *Sacramentum Caritatis*, Post-Synodal Apostolic Exhortation, February 22, 2007 (Washington, DC: US Catholic Conference, 2007), 14, quoting John Paul II, *Ecclesia de Eucharistia*, Encyclical Letter on the Eucharist in Its Relation to the Church, April 17, 2003 (Washington, DC: US Catholic Conference, 2003), 21.

50. Belgian Cardinal Godfried Danneels has observed that in the Scientific Revolution, which suggests that the theses dealing with sacramental causality require reworking, "Classical theologians have worked out a wide array of theories in response to this question [how do the sacraments bring forth their effects], but most of them are extremely difficult to uphold today." See "Current Challenges for Sacramental Theology," *Antiphon* 5 (2000): 44–45, at 45.

51. Benedict M. Ashley, OP, *The Way toward Wisdom: An Interdisciplinary and Intercultural Introduction to Metaphysics* (Notre Dame, IN: University of Notre Dame, 2006).

series of causes that are necessary to explain the effect that the Christian Church holds out as either the result or the promise of sacramental administration. Only God sanctifies. Still, each of the sacraments does something. Take the example of holy orders. Catholic theology must account for why a man is not deputed, licensed, authorized, designated, or simply chosen for ministry, but rather is radically transformed in order to exercise the sacred power of the priesthood. The Church speaks about an "ontological bond" with Christ.[52] The explanation will entail some account of efficient or agent causality that can illuminate the truth that only God makes a man a priest and at the same time that this change never occurs outside of the sacramental act duly performed.

What is true for one sacrament holds true for the practice of divine friendship. Catholic theology today faces a serious challenge when asked to give an account of the transformation worked by grace. One needs to provide some explanation for how man created in the image of God becomes an adoptive son, when this sonship consists precisely of the actual or habitual knowing and loving of the triune God. What transforms the human person? How does one account for the newness of life that the New Testament makes part of its central proclamation?

The ordinary ways in which adoptive sonship is bestowed and sustained are discovered in the divine agency mediated through the sacraments, especially the sacraments of initiation and of healing. Thus we recall the well-known teaching that baptism remains the only way known to the Church by which the gift of justification is bestowed.[53]

The Eucharist stands at the center of the Church's life. The Church comes forth from the Eucharistic sacrifice. There exists a reciprocal relationship between the Eucharist and growth in the practice of divine friendship. Theologians speak about the grace of the Eucharist as charity and unity. Beatific fellowship or communion finds its anticipation here below in the Eucharist. It is necessary, however, to understand this sacramental consecration of the Christian life, of the theological life of

52. See Pope John Paul II, "*Pastores Dabo Vobis*, Post-Synodal Apostolic Exhortation (March 25, 1992)," in *The Post-Synodal Apostolic Exhortations of John Paul II*, ed. J. Michael Miller, CSB (Huntington, IN: Our Sunday Visitor, 1998), 11, 13, 72.

53. *CCC*, §1257.

faith and hope, and of charity, with reference to the sacrificial character of the Eucharist.[54]

Pope Benedict, referring to 1 John 4:19, uses the language of causality to explain how divine love comes to exist in the world: "The causal influence of the Eucharist at the Church's origins definitively discloses both the chronological and ontological priority of the fact that it was Christ who loved us 'first.'"[55] Where does Christ first show on earth his maximal love? The tradition expressed by Aquinas replies: on Calvary. Discussing the efficacy of Christ's passion and death, Thomas says, "Christ, suffering in a loving and obedient spirit, offered more to God than was demanded in recompense for all the sins of mankind, because first, the love which led him to suffer was a great love [*propter magnitudinem charitatis*]."[56]

THE ADVENT OF MERCY

To inquire about the purpose of the sacraments is to inquire about the divine goodness and mercy. Recall St. John's words: "he first loved us" (1 Jn 4:19). Aquinas speaks about the sacraments as instruments of the divine saving mercy—*qui sunt instrumenta divinae misericordiae salvantis*.[57] This is a cardinal feature of his sacramental theology. The sacraments communicate God's saving mercy within the structure of a twofold movement of image restoration and image perfection. The basis for communicating these perfections is the divine goodness. God is merciful inasmuch as his goodness casts out from us every defect.[58]

54. John Paul II, *Ecclesia de Eucharistia*, 12: "The Church constantly draws her life from the redeeming sacrifice; she approaches it not only through faith-filled remembrance, but also through a real contact, since this sacrifice is made present ever anew, sacramentally perpetuated, in every community which offers it at the hands of the consecrated minister."

55. Benedict XVI, *Sacramentum Caritatis*, 14.

56. *ST* III, q. 48, a. 2.

57. "In hoc autem pro tota natura meruit, in quo debitum naturae, scilicet mortis, quae pro peccato ei debebatur, exsolvit ipse peccatum non habens; ut sic non pro se mortem solvere teneretur, sed pro natura solveret; unde satisfaciendo pro tota natura, sufficienter meruit peccatorum remissionem aliis qui peccata habebant. Tertio modo dicitur agens instrumentale; et hoc modo sacramenta delent peccata, quia sunt instrumenta divinae misericordiae salvantis." See Aquinas, *Scriptum super libros sententiarum magistri Petri Lombardi Episcopi Parisiensis* (Paris: Sumptibus P. Lethielleux, 1929), bk. 3, d. 19, q. 1, a. 1.

58. See *ST* I, q. 21, a. 3.

The expression *adventus misericordiae*, or "the coming of [the divine] mercy," evokes a theme in Thomist theology that today remains misunderstood.[59] How does the divine mercy take hold of one who receives worthily the sacraments of Christ? Pope Benedict XVI takes up this question in discussing "the connection between the eucharistic form of life and moral transformation."[60] Moral transformation remains a serious question for Catholic theology to the extent that many contemporary efforts to resolve moral problems remain disconnected from the Eucharist and from Christ. The Catholic tradition, however, regards both the sacramental life and the moral life as a single expression of the divine goodness active in the world.[61] Christian satisfaction forms part of the Church's sacramental life. It derives its efficacy from the sacramentalization of contrition that we call the sacrament of penance or reconciliation. We move, then, to discuss the place that medicinal satisfaction holds in the life of Christian sacraments and conversion.

The French Benedictine theologian Ghislain Lafont, among others, suggested that Aquinas had placed too much emphasis on the medicinal effects of the sacraments.[62] Lafont's work brings us back to the theological airs of the late 1950s. In fact, he represents a class of mainly European theologians who easily assumed that the sixteenth-century reformers' critiques of satisfactory expiation were valid reactions to Aquinas's teaching on satisfaction. These theologians went on to argue that Aquinas's treatment of the sacraments places too much emphasis on the need for satisfaction for sin. In support of their contention, they highlighted the medicinal metaphors used by Aquinas.

We may wonder whether these theological criticisms, which so reflected a certain temper of the times, did not contribute to what we now recognize as a general breakdown and retreat from the discipline of the

59. See *ST* III, q.1, a. 6, ad 3: "Unde patet quod non debuit adventum misericordiae differre usque in finem mundi." Here Aquinas treats the fittingness of the timing of the incarnation.

60. Benedict XVI, *Sacramentum Caritatis*, 82.

61. The very structure of the *Catechism of the Catholic Church* makes this point explicitly. Part Two treats the sacraments. Part Three treats the moral life, life in Christ.

62. In his 1961 *Structure et méthode de la Somme théologique de saint Thomas d'Aquin* (Paris: Le Cerf, 1996).

sacraments of healing—penance and holy anointing—in the postconciliar period.[63] But when full account is taken of the careful way that St. Thomas treats the coming of the divine mercy, the *adventus misericordiae*, we can see how seriously these critics misunderstood Thomas.

It is true that Thomas speaks frequently about healing the wounds of sin (*vulnus peccati*). But the overall context of his *Summa Theologiae* makes clear that his treatment of healing is influenced more by his understanding of the divine goodness than by therapeutic metaphors.[64] Thomas presents satisfaction as a sweet grace to embrace, not a bitter medicine to avoid. And his account should be the basis for a reformulation of sacramental theology, one that explains forcefully how and why the sacraments are "instruments of mercy."

THE SEVENTH SEAL AND THE THEOLOGY OF SATISFACTION

Fortunately, French theology has not been monolithic. One should observe the influence that French-speaking theologians from the Suisse Romande and Provence have played and continue to play in the reshaping of contemporary Catholic theology. This influence can be seen especially in the reformulation of Catholic beliefs in satisfaction, which, like Aquinas's teaching on sin, has been subject to caricature in the modern period.[65]

63. The generation (and spirit, *l'esprit parisien*) that Lafont represents may be excused for thinking that one ought to explain the dynamics of Christian salvation by softening the emphasis on the medicinal effects of the sacraments, and in general on the role that personal reformation of life plays in the Christian dispensation. Many European theologians of that period, including the *nouveaux théologiens*, seem to have flourished as the Marshall Plan (1947–51) restored economic prosperity in Catholic Europe. These circumstances, along with more scholarly explanations such as the findings of historical-critical biblical studies, made it seem out-of-date to talk much about sin and original sin. At the same time, the Parisian critiques of sacramental causality and of nature and grace dynamics coincided with radical changes in the way Catholics observed the duties of their religion, especially in the area of the sacraments of healing. The effects remain. It does not require the services of a sociologist to observe that the two sacraments of healing—penance and holy anointing—exemplify the sacraments least administered to the Christian people, even though contemporary Catholics, it may be supposed, require these "instruments of divine saving mercy" as much as did Catholics of earlier ages.

64. See *ST* I-II, q. 87, a. 7, ad 3.

65. In the United States, much of this influence may be found in the work done by the

One good illustration of the misconstrual of the role that medicinal practices hold in Christian life dominates Ingmar Bergman's (1918–

Aquinas Center for Theological Renewal located at Ave Maria University in Ave Maria, Florida. Matthew Levering deserves great commendation for the efforts that he has expended to translate the works of authors such as Gilles Emery, OP, and to publish articles from French authors in the journal *Nova et Vetera*.

In some oblique way, I can associate myself with this respected strain of theological reflection that traces its modern origin to 1859, when Père Lacordaire bought back a portion of old Saint-Maximin, the Var property that preserved the relics of St. Mary Magdalene and that had been securely in Dominican hands since the fourteenth century, in order to base a *studium*, or study house, of the Dominican Order. The *couvent* had been seized in 1791 by the Revolution—the Dominicans taking flight. Lacordaire was not able to buy back all of the old property, and a good part of the *couvent* remained and remains still the property of the *mairie* of St. Maximin. It is said that the basilica was spared because Napoleon's brother Lucien ordered "La Marseillaise" to be played on the eighteenth-century classical organ housed in the church. (The 1773 organ was built by J. E. Isnard at the basilica of Ste. Marie Madeleine in St. Maximin-en-Var in south France.) After 1859, Saint-Maximin remained an important intellectual center of Thomist theology for almost a century, until 1957, when the Provençal Dominicans transferred the location of their study house to Toulouse. One illustrious carrier of the southern French tradition was Father Jean-Hervé Nicolas, OP, who was one of my directors at Fribourg in the 1970s. In 1976, I arrived in Fribourg to begin my doctoral studies under the tutelage of the Irish Dominican Eugene Colman O'Neill. The results were published first in 1981, and a second edition, with a different title, in 1990. See my *Christian Satisfaction in Aquinas* (Washington, DC: University Press of America, 1982), and *Godly Image*. The revised edition is still available at Fordham University Press.

In the 1970s, with the ecumenical impetus launched by the Second Vatican Council in full and optimistic swing, Father O'Neill had become actively involved in ecumenical exchanges, especially with reformed theologians in Switzerland. O'Neill had read his Calvin: "We are indignant," John Calvin replied to the reforming Cardinal Jacobo Sadoleto (1477–1547), "that in the room of the sacred Supper has been substituted a sacrifice, by which the death of Christ is emptied of its virtues." "Reply by John Calvin to Cardinal Sadoleto's Letter (Basel, September 1, 1539)," in *A Reformation Debate*, ed. John C. Olin (New York: Fordham University Press, 2000), 68. In Catholic Fribourg during the 1970s, Catholic worship—*la sainte messe* and *Heilige Messen* (the Holy Mass)—was celebrated more frequently than these Lord's Supper celebrations. Still, O'Neill had come to the realization that Catholics eventually would need to dialog with reformed and other Christian believers about the nature of the Eucharistic sacrifice. His conviction was based on what Pope Benedict XVI has expressed so succinctly in *Sacramentum Caritatis*: "We hold that eucharistic communion and ecclesial communion are so linked as to make it generally impossible for non-Catholic Christians to receive the former without enjoying the latter." To embrace ecclesial communion with the Catholic Church requires embracing what she holds about the Eucharist. We witness another example of the interconnectedness of the *depositum fidei*.

Here O'Neill was persuaded that before discussions about the nature of Eucharistic sacrifice and therefore communion could begin, the nettlesome question of satisfaction must once more be taken up by both parties to the ecumenical dialogue. It had been exhausted in the period of the Catholic reform. O'Neill was convinced that what Aquinas had taught about satisfaction did not conform to the modern caricatures of medieval theologies, which had continued to inhabit Protestant and some Catholic thought throughout the Eisenhower years (1953–61).

2007) captivating 1957 film, *The Seventh Seal.* By aiming to exhibit medieval practices, Bergman purported to portray what he thought constituted Catholic teaching on satisfaction. In his contemporary apocalypse, Bergman depicts survivors of Death whipping themselves so that God will spare them, hoping to atone for their sins through self-flagellation. The son of a Swedish Lutheran pastor, Bergman in fact visualized what was generally held to be the Catholic—that is, the medieval—outlook on medicinal Christianity. The film appeared during the waning years of post-Tridentine polemics about Christian satisfaction. The cinematic effects were mesmerizing. Through the well-crafted lens of Ingmar Bergman, the image of Christians observing the rubrics of satisfaction approached the sadistic.

Yet it was another Swede who more directly shaped (or misshaped) twentieth-century theological reflection about Christian satisfaction in Aquinas: Lutheran Bishop Gustaf Aulén (1879–1978). His 1931 book *Christus Victor* provided a historical account of what he considered the misadventures of St. Anselm's medieval treatise, *Cur Deus Homo?* (Why Did God Become Man?) and the supposed perpetuation of Anselm's errors by Aquinas.[66] *Christus Victor* was translated into English in the same year that Bergman's film was released.

Against these strongly negative and distorted views perpetuated by the filmmaker and theologians both Protestant and Catholic alike, we must return to a correct understanding of Aquinas and satisfaction.[67] The way that St. Thomas treats Christian satisfaction affects profoundly his account of the sacramental dispensation. He discussed the healing that Christ brings under three headings: the anthropology of healing, the cause of healing, and the objective of healing. These headings correspond to three of the four causes that Aristotle considers necessary to explain what something is: material (man), efficient (God), and final (Beatitude).

The fourth cause, the formal cause of the sacraments, is located in

66. Gustav Aulen, *Christus Victor: An Historical Study of the Three Main Types of the Idea of Atonement*, trans. A. G. Herber (New York: Macmillan, 1977).

67. See my "Aquinas on Christian Salvation," in *Aquinas on Doctrine: A Critical Introduction*, ed. Thomas Weinandy, OFM, Cap., Daniel Keating, and John Yocum (London: T&T Clark International, 2004), 117–37.

the divine mercy that the Incarnation introduces into the world—the *adventus misericordiae.* The sacraments follow the Incarnation of the Eternal Son and prolong and continue the *adventus misericordiae* that his Incarnation represents.

Again, Aquinas insightfully distinguishes principal and instrumental efficient causes and, among the instrumental causes, those conjoined from those separated. He thus shows that there exists one causal flow of divine goodness that moves from the Trinity to Christ to the sacraments to the adopted son. We see, then, that the Church's sacraments and the practice of divine friendship go hand in hand. We recall a familiar text from Aquinas concerning the effects of Christ's passion:

> When we say that Christ's passion reconciled us to God, we do not mean that God has begun anew to love us, for it is written in Jeremiah 31:2, "with age-old love I have loved you." Thanks to Christ's passion the cause for hatred has been removed, both because sin has been wiped away and because compensation has been made in the form of a more agreeable offering.[68]

By his sacrificial death on the Cross, Christ introduces into the world a mercy that otherwise would not exist. This fulfillment of the *adventus misericordiae* changes the human creature. Our defects are removed. We no longer find ourselves without a place to turn in the face of our sins. We no longer have reason to doubt that God loves us. In other words, we are able to think credibly of ourselves as friends of God.

THE SACRAMENTS AND THE "NEW MAN"

Only God makes us his friends. But if one were to inquire about the reasons for the eclipse of discussion about how God makes us his friends—the aforementioned sacramental causality—the inquiry would point back to erroneous views in some contemporary presentations of Christian anthropology.

O'Neill, whose important work was discussed above, said that ignorance of the modes in which the *imago Dei* can exist explains why

68. *ST* III, q. 49, a. 4, ad 2.

so many theologians of our period have thought an adequate account of the sacraments can be rendered by appeal only to the categories of formal and final causality.[69] The sacraments, however, as we have seen, are about more than symbols and promises of heaven. They also figure in the working out of predestination. O'Neill put it this way: "Through Christ and his grace the goal [of life] becomes immediate knowledge and love of God, the Blessed Trinity, as he is in himself. Such a goal, which is beyond man's natural resources, can be won only by those whom God himself chooses and positively transmits to it through predestination."[70]

Predestination represents a form of divine agency. Efficient causality transposed into the proper theological and biblical categories—for example, the biblical category of the vine and the branches—provides an adequate philosophical basis to account theologically for this transmission.[71] We discover how God communicates to his creatures the benefits that only he can bestow on—and, to be more precise, create in—man. Thomists adopted a view of sacramental causality that they described as "physical." They did this in order to emphasize that the new man of Ephesians 4:24—"And put on the new man, who according to God is created in justice and holiness of truth"—and the new nature of Colossians 3:10—"And have put on the new nature, which is being renewed in knowledge after the image of its creator"—are more than mere metaphors for expressing mental relations or religious sentiment.

In sum, as we have said before, the sacraments do something. We are now in a position to state more precisely what it is that they do. The sacraments enact the work of image restoration and image perfection. They supply the way that Christ makes sons out of images. Image restoration, as the phrase suggests, brings about healing, whereas image perfection creates and serves communion. Beatific fellowship or communion finds

69. O'Neill did not view sacramental theology as a subspecialty within the theological sciences. He rather interpreted the sacraments within the overall context of the *depositum fidei*. See his *Meeting Christ in the Sacraments*, rev. ed., ed. Romanus Cessario, OP (New York: Alba House, 1991), and his *Sacramental Realism* (Chicago: Midwest Theological Forum, 1998). The latter forms a long essay on sacramental causality.

70. O'Neill, *One Mediator*, 253.

71. See John 15:5: "I am the vine: you the branches. He that abideth in me, and I in him, the same beareth much fruit: for without me you can do nothing."

its anticipation here below in the Eucharist. The Eucharist introduces the themes of charity and communion, which epitomize the work of image perfection. Healing and satisfaction are ordered, on the other hand, to image restoration. Both image restoration and image perfection represent expressions of the communication of divine goodness that the Incarnation of the Son of God makes possible for the human race.

DIVINE HEALING: THE COMMUNICATION OF PERFECTION

Why does the Christian require sacraments of healing? The divine love that communicates itself through the sacraments must first of all remove the obstacles to itself before raising men to a participation in itself. We find ourselves back to considering the effects of Christ's passion: "Thanks to Christ's passion the cause for hatred has been removed, both because sin has been wiped away and because compensation has been made in the form of a more agreeable offering."[72] *Adventus misericordiae*!

To wipe away sin entails satisfaction. It is a work that the Christian cannot omit. Why? Because only the saints love one another in a bond of authentic friendship. Sinners do not. Commenting on that passage in the *Summa* in which Thomas inquires whether sinners love themselves,[73] the sometimes-maligned Cajetan tells us why:

> Guard in your heart the conclusions of this article: (1) that evil is the kind of thing that makes it impossible for sinners to love themselves; (2) that there are five signs of authentic self-love which can only be found in the good: to want to live a spiritual life in accord with right reason; to want to develop within this life the good of virtue; to want to act so as to realize this; to be free of anxiety, and to want to get along peacefully with others. Examine your conscience on these points if you want to know whether you are good or not, whether you truly love yourself, whether you truly are a friend to yourself. And do this frequently, at least once a day![74]

72. *ST* III, q. 49, a. 4, ad 2.

73. *ST* II-II, q. 25, a. 7.

74. Thomas de Vio Cardinal Cajetan, *In secunda-secundae*, q. 25, a. 4. Text in Tommaso de Vio Cajetan, *Summa totius theologiae D. Thomae Aquinatis cum commentariis* (Rome: Apud Iulium Accoltum, 1570).

These considerations are hardly what one would describe as prescriptions drawn up by a man who is fixated on essentialism. They rather express the view of a man who understood the predicament of the human condition without Christ. Cajetan's reflection on love within the *communio* of the Church would not have made the final cut of Bergman's *The Seventh Seal*. The true Cajetan simply does not correspond to the caricatures that certain northern Europeans have made of him and of the Thomism he represents.

The practice of the divine friendship follows upon Aquinas's teaching on the tripartite modes of the *imago Dei* and his strong teaching on sacramental causality. What else can explain how fallen human beings can rise up to become authentic lovers of God and neighbor?

But in order to reestablish Aquinas's teaching, Thomists must criticize what I call "inclusivist theologies"—theologies that take umbrage at nature and grace distinctions. Promoters of this outlook, whether stridently orthodox or shadowy heterodox, take too much for granted when it comes to explaining the dynamics of conversion. Leaving aside the orthodox inclusivists, who in any event are usually loyal to what the Church prescribes for the moral life, we find ourselves left with the widespread presumption promoted by the shadowy heterodox. When one reflects on the list of things that those who profess themselves to be Catholics hold to be compatible with Christian truth and virtue, the results are sadly disappointing. It would serve them well to make every dissenting moral theologian read Cajetan's commentary on whether sinners love themselves.

We are made for happiness with God. But our capacity to achieve the realization of this beatitude, whether inchoatively on earth or consummatively in heaven, depends on the absolute priority of the divine initiative. God loves us because *he* is good, not because *we* are. As Thomas says: "Purely and simply, other considerations apart, it is of his goodness that God communicates perfections."[75]

The divine prevenient grace that governs all that transpires in the world for the good moves the human creature to the Church of Christ and to baptism, which, as I have noted, remains the only way that the

75. *ST* I, q. 23, a. 3.

Church knows to introduce a human creature into the fellowship of divine friendship.[76] Baptism, as Aquinas says, is the door to the other sacraments.[77] Sacramental mediation marks every step of the Christian life and of the spiritual life. Baptism requires no satisfaction of the one who receives it. The power of Christ takes hold of the whole person, "just as if he himself had sufficiently made satisfaction for all his sins."[78]

The rest of the sacramental economy involves satisfaction. Thomas stopped writing his *Summa* as he was discussing the place that satisfaction holds in the sacrament of penance. The few passages in the *Summa* that mention holy anointing (*extrema unctio*)[79] suggest that this sacrament of healing completes penance in a way that is parallel to the way that confirmation completes baptism. In each of the sacraments, we discover a special *adventus misericordiae*. Each of the sacraments brings effectively a remedy against some effect of sin. The sacraments of healing accomplish this objective poignantly:

> Penance against actual sins committed after Baptism; Extreme Unction against those elements of sin which remain, those namely which, whether through negligence or ignorance, are not sufficiently removed by Penance.[80]

To be specific, this effect occurs through the satisfactory works that penance sacramentalizes, which brings us back to confessional lines and Catholic deathbeds.[81] The urgency is great. Young men should willingly sacrifice their lives to become ministers—and only priests can serve as the ministers of these sacraments of healing—of these saving instruments of Christ's mercy. Aquinas compares extreme unction to diet and exercise in the human life. This specific *adventus misericordiae* removes what remains of sin in us and renders us *paratam ... ad finalem gloriae*—"ready ... for final glory." This means ready for the fullness of the *imago*

76. The 2000 declaration *Dominus Iesus* reaffirms the advantages that one finds only within the circle of full communion with the See of Peter. See Congregation for the Doctrine of the Faith, *Dominus Iesus*, Declaration On the Unicity and Salvific Universality of Jesus Christ and the Church, August 6, 2000 (Vatican City: Libreria Editrice Vaticana, 2000).

77. *ST* III, q. 68, a. 6. See also *ST* III, q. 66, a. 2.

78. See *ST* III, q. 69, a. 2.

79. For example, see *ST* III, q. 65, a. 1.

80. Ibid.

81. See note 63 above.

Dei, ready to possess a filial fear that expresses itself as reverence.[82] The Church allows the priest to anoint a Catholic so long as there is some expectation that the breath of life remains, a period that is not determined by the declaration of physical death. At the very end, the dying man—no matter how holy a life he may have led—still needs the *adventus misericordiae* that Christ imparts through the sacraments of the Church: penance, holy anointing, Eucharist. To get ready for final glory, even the saint needs spiritual medicine to cast out every defect.

FREED FROM SIN BY WAY OF SACRIFICE

"It is finished" (Jn 19:30), Jesus completes his redemptive work on Calvary. Mary, according to the tradition, holds on her lap the lifeless body of her Son. The *Pietà*! She remains the sorrowful Mother, though she never succumbs to being a sad Mother. There is a difference between experiencing sorrow and being sad. Sadness arises when one is overcome by evil. While caressing Jesus's dead body, Mary contemplates the supreme goodness that the Incarnation reveals. At the same time, she ponders the plain fact that God "did not spare his Son, but handed him over for us all" (Rom 8:32). Mary touches the pierced side of her Son, the fountain of sacramental life. Her sorrowing affords Mary time to meditate on the benefits that we receive from Christ's death: "In all these things we conquer overwhelmingly through him who loved us" (Rom 8:37).

Mary comprehends the divine plan better than any other member of the Church. For this reason, she is able to participate fully in her Son's redemptive work. She merits the unique title of *Co-Redemptrix*. Though she is conceived without original sin and so escapes the burden of making up for sin, Mary is the first to experience vicariously in the dead body of her Son the price paid for our sins. The sacraments of healing and the sacramentalized practices of penitence allow Catholics to enter deeply into the mystery of conversion that Christ's death on the Cross makes possible. Without his divine power, nothing in us would change. Let St. Thomas have the last word:

82. See *ST* II-II, q. 19, a. 11.

When Christ's passion is viewed in relation to his divinity, it can be seen to act in an efficient way; in relation to the will which is rooted in Christ's soul, by way of merit; in relation to the very flesh of Christ, by way of satisfaction, since we are freed from the guilt of punishment; by way of redemption, inasmuch as we are thereby freed from the slavery of sin; and finally, by way of sacrifice, thanks to which we are reconciled to God.[83]

83. *ST* III, q. 48, a. 6.

CHAPTER 5

CIRCA RES . . . ALIQUID FIT

Aquinas on New Law Sacrifice

Here Father Cessario develops the theme of sacrifice introduced in chapter 4. St. Thomas explains that "the Eucharist is at once a sacrifice and a sacrament: it has the nature of a sacrifice in that it is offered, and of a sacrament in that it is received" (*ST* III, q. 79, a. 5). Father Cessario observes that the majority of twentieth-century Catholic theologians largely ignored the sacrificial nature of the Mass. John Paul II's 2003 papal encyclical *Ecclesia de Eucharistia*, however, reminded all of the Christian faithful about this essential truth of the Christian faith. Within St. Thomas's teaching on the Holy Sacrifice of the Mass, we discover that "the Mass is an icon of Calvary." Thus the saving graces of the Most Blessed Sacrament "exist in cruciform composition." "The satisfaction of Christ and of his members provides a template through which the theologian is able to explain a central act of the Christian religion, namely, the death of Christ on the Cross."

The "sacrificial meaning" of the Mass is important because it enables the theologian to explain how there is "in the Eucharist the power to create authentic love"—a love that even moves those conformed to Christ's sacrificial image to sacrifice themselves out of love for their

Originally published as "*Circa res . . . aliquid fit*: Aquinas on New Law Sacrifice," *Nova et Vetera* 4, no. 2 (2006): 295–312. Reprinted by permission.

Savior. Father Cessario illustrates the salvific implications of Christ's sacrificial love through the life of one of St. Thomas's favorite saints: St. Agnes. Participation in Christ's sacrificial love is open to all. In a word, those in whom theology and sanctity find full theologal union withhold nothing from their Beloved.

In his treatise "On Virgins," St. Ambrose praises a Roman teenager named Agnes: "Today is the birthday of a virgin; let us imitate her purity. It is the birthday of a martyr; let us offer ourselves in sacrifice."[1] The Roman Church observes the feast of St. Agnes on January 21. The Roman Canon includes her name in the list of saints found in the prayer *Nobis quoque peccatoribus,* which is said by the priest after the consecration of the Mass. Her witness to Christ is recalled following the proclamation of the "Mystery of Faith": "We proclaim your death, Lord Jesus."[2]

I cite this patristic text for two reasons. First, it introduces the theme of the present chapter, Aquinas on new law sacrifice. It does so by identifying the connection between martyrdom and sacrifice: *circa res . . . aliquid fit.* In the example of a martyr, of course, the "something" that is done to the *res*—in this case, a living person—is the delivery of a deadly blow. Second, St. Thomas Aquinas cherished a special devotion to this Roman virgin and martyr, whom both St. Ambrose and St. Augustine eulogized as a great witness to the power of the new law of grace. Twice in his writings, Aquinas himself mentions St. Agnes in order to show how the virtues of temperance and fortitude are found united exemplarily in the virgin martyrs.[3] Those familiar with the work of Aquinas recognize that he does not customarily offer personal examples of the theoretical lessons that he develops. We may reasonably infer, then, that his direct references to St. Agnes afford rare glimpses into the personal piety of Friar Tommaso D'Aquino.

One of Aquinas's early biographers tells us that he also kept relics of St. Agnes on his person: "reliquias dicte sancte, quas ad pectus suspen-

1. St. Ambrose, "On Virgins," bk. 1, cap. 2.5 [PL 16 1845]: 189.

2. See the 2003 encyclical letter of Pope John Paul II, *Ecclesia de Eucharistia,* no. 11.

3. We find at least two mentions of St. Agnes as an example of purity to the point of martyrdom: *IV Sent.,* d. 49, q. 5, qc. 3, ad 9, and *Quodl.* III, q. 6, a. 3 [17], ad 3.

sas ex deuotione portabat." In other words, Aquinas piously wore the relics of St. Agnes at his breast. On one occasion we know that St. Thomas used these relics to obtain the intercession of the young saint in order to cure his sick socius or priest-companion, Friar Reginald of Piperno. When St. Agnes's mediation was discovered to have been successful, and Reginald's health had improved, Aquinas spontaneously promised to sponsor a special meal for his students on every twenty-first of January.[4] This cure took place in 1272, and thus it happened, as a contemporary chronicler observes, that Aquinas was able to fulfill his votive promise only once—namely, in the winter of 1273.[5]

By January of 1274, Aquinas himself had been taken ill, though he was still preparing to journey on the road toward France whence Blessed Pope Gregory X had summoned him to attend the Second Council of Lyons (1274). While en route to Lyons on the Rhône, Aquinas, in the early hours of March 7, 1274, died at the Cistercian monastery of Fossanova, whose white monks guarded his body for nearly a century thereafter. His present place on the liturgical calendar, January 28, commemorates the day in 1369 when his relics were transferred solemnly from that venerable monastery, located off the old Via Appia south of Rome, to the church of the Jacobins in Toulouse, where they have been preserved since. (With the exception of about two centuries when Aquinas's mortal remains were kept out of harm's way in the neighboring basilica of St.-Sernin, which, though the largest Romanesque church in the West, serves as a parish church in Toulouse.) This temporary transfer happened toward the end of the eighteenth century, when the French Revolution threatened to expel the Dominicans from one of their most spectacular Gothic installments in Europe, *l'église des Jacobins*. In any case, divine providence so arranged that the bones of Aquinas would return to the city where, as Father Weisheipl observes, the Dominicans had begun their existence: Toulouse on the river Garonne.[6] There is something fit-

4. See Jean-Pierre Torrell, OP, *Saint Thomas Aquinas*, vol. 1, *The Person and His Work*, rev. ed., trans. Robert Royal (Washington, DC: Catholic University of America Press, 2005), 271.

5. See Tolomeo of Lucca, *Ptolomaei Lucensis Historia ecclesiastica nova*, lib. XXIII, 10.

6. James A. Weisheipl, OP, *Friar Thomas D'Aquino* (Washington, DC: Catholic University of America Press, 1983), 331.

ting in this providential turn of events, *conveniens* as Aquinas himself would say.

NEW LAW SACRIFICE

Our theme is Aquinas on new law sacrifice. The new law refers to the grace that the Incarnation of the Son of God introduces into the world. This grace distinguishes new law sacrifice from the divinely ordained sacrifices of the old law. St. Thomas explains this distinction by appeal to the reality of a sacrament: "The sacrifice of the New Law [*sacrificium novae legis*], the Eucharist, contains Christ himself, the author of our sanctification, for 'he sanctified the people by his own blood' (Heb 12:12). Hence this sacrifice is also a sacrament. The sacraments of the Old Law, however, did not contain Christ, but prefigured him, and so they are not called sacraments."[7] We may further conclude that new law sacrifice is to be distinguished from sacrifices that pertain to the natural law, which every human creature is required to offer to God.[8] One fact is clear. Aquinas helps us to recognize that when Christians speak about new law sacrifice, they mean only one thing: the passion and death of Christ "sacramentally perpetuated" in the Eucharist.[9]

There is something fitting about returning in 2006 to the theme of the Eucharist as sacrifice. For example, consider the October 2004 apostolic letter *Mane Nobiscum Domine,* which announced the Year of the Eucharist. This period of grace and indulgence began during October of that year and came to an end at the Ordinary Assembly of the Synod of Bishops held in Rome in October 2005.[10] Pope John Paul II himself urged us to ponder during that year the unique sacrificial character of the Eucharist. I would suggest that the Pope directed us to undertake a reconsideration, even a rehabilitation, of the theological notion of sacrifice. His successor, Pope Benedict XVI, aimed to complete this project as the *instrumentum laboris* for the fall synod suggests.

7. *ST* I-II, q. 101, a. 4.

8. *ST* II-II, q. 85, a. 1.

9. See *Ecclesia de Eucharistia,* §12.

10. For details, see the "Decree of the Apostolic Penitentiary on the Gift of an Indulgence during the 'Year of the Eucharist'" [in Italian and Latin], *L'Osservatore Romano,* January 15, 2005.

What prompted this papal directive? In the abovementioned apostolic letter, Pope John Paul II suggested, at least implicitly, that a certain amnesia has enveloped many theologians of the postconciliar period.[11] What have they forgotten? That the sacrifice of the new law, the *sacrificium novae legis*, finds its proper expression in the Eucharist, "which makes present what occurred in the past."[12] Pope John Paul II suggested that too exclusive an emphasis has been put on the Eucharist as shared meal: "It must not be forgotten," he wrote, "that the Eucharistic meal also has a profoundly and primarily *sacrificial* meaning."[13] This papal admonition follows the publication of two important magisterial documents, the 2003 encyclical letter *Ecclesia de Eucharistia* and its companion, the 2004 dicasterial document *Redemptionis sacramentum*, which provides detailed instruction about the reverence that is owed to the Blessed Eucharist, especially during the actual celebration of the Holy Sacrifice of the Mass. *Ecclesia de Eucharistia* is built around the infallible Catholic truth that "the sacrifice of Christ and the sacrifice of the Eucharist are *one single sacrifice*."[14]

The encyclical recalls the ancient Catholic dogma that the "sacrificial meaning" of the Eucharist remains indissociable from the promise of "universal charity" that this sacrament of Christ's love embodies.[15] Many persons who have been catechized during the last forty years will find this strong papal assertion about the "sacrificial meaning" of the Eucharistic banquet surprising. They may also wonder why they came away from their lessons in Christian doctrine with the notion that the Eucharist is a shared meal and were not taught about sacrificial meaning one way or another. They may even ask themselves whether to think of the

11. There are some indications that the notion of sacrifice has begun to interest theologians, however. For example, see the essays collected by E. Mazza, ed., *L'idea di sacrificio: Un approccio di teologia liturgica* (Bologna: EDB, 2002).

12. *Mane Nobiscum Domine*, §15.

13. Ibid.

14. *Ecclesia de Eucharistia*, §12, citing *CCC*, §1367.

15. *Ecclesia de Eucharistia*, §12: "This aspect of the universal charity of the Eucharistic Sacrifice is based on the words of the Savior himself ... Jesus did not simply state that what he was giving them to eat and drink was his body and his blood; he also expressed *its sacrificial meaning* and made sacramentally present his sacrifice which would soon be offered on the Cross for the salvation of all."

sacrament only in terms of a shared meal is adequate to dispose the communicant to recognize in the Eucharist the power to create authentic love. In order to put this surprise or disappointment into some perspective, we need to step back from our present moment, and take a look at some aspects of Catholic liturgical life during the past four decades.[16]

It is generally agreed among Catholic theologians that the Second Vatican Council (1962–65) failed to address at length three areas of theological investigation. To acknowledge this omission is not to signal a defect. No ecumenical council addresses every aspect of Catholic doctrine. The reception given to the Second Vatican Council, however, favored the impression among many persons that 1965 marked a fresh start for the Catholic Church and her teachings. Moreover, events that transpired in the secular culture of the period encouraged the spread of this false impression. By the mid-1960s, cultural changes were expected routinely. In any case, the view developed among some Catholics that the documents of Vatican II were meant to serve as the founding articles of a new period in the history of the Church. No previous ecumenical council had generated this sense of discontinuity with what had gone on before, with what had been taught before, in short, with the tradition.

Something else occurred after the Second Vatican Council that was unprecedented. A new class of "theologians" came into prominence. These "popularizers," as Father Matthew Lamb has characterized them, were mainly responsible for ensuring that the spin about this "new period" reached a wide audience.[17] Many Catholics, including certain bishops who themselves were present at the Council, were persuaded by this new brand of theologians to view the mid-1960s as the dawn of a new day. Many of the popularizers, however, were not trained theologians who had become well versed in the sacred Scriptures and in sacred tradition;

16. For further reflection on this movement, see Leslie Woodcock Tentler, *Catholic and Contraception: An American History* (Ithaca, NY: Cornell University Press, 2004), esp. 233–34.

17. Father Matthew Lamb mentions popularizing at the end of a response to Margaret Farley in the *Fellowship of Catholic Scholars Quarterly* 21 (1998): 2–5: "Any effort to spin Papal and Vatican concern for Catholic theological orthodoxy as 'stifling scholarship' is just plain false. The dissent is not based upon serious theological scholarship but on superficial popularized distortions. Orthodox Catholic faith enlightens human intelligence. Dissent weakens both faith and intelligence."

they were rather journalists, essayists, and other frequent contributors to the mass media who claimed the mantle of the professional theologian.[18] Before the Council, the Church had recognized certain "approved authors" whose views could be absorbed without risk of falling away from Catholic doctrine. These *auctores probati* only became such after death, moreover. Somehow, in the fall of 1965—a period when rather commonly authority, especially that exercised by either civil or religious officials, lost standing—anyone who could write a newspaper column gained putative approbation. And as we know, these freelance theologians considered themselves competent to pronounce on everything from the hierarchical structure of the Church to the moral structure of human sexuality. It is easy now to see why the first significant expression of Catholic life in this new climate was the rejection of the 1968 encyclical letter *Humanae vitae.*

It is not the case that every Catholic in the United States adopted the outlook of the popularizers. Still less is it true that every Catholic joined the ranks of the dissenters. At the same time, the Second Vatican Council left work to be done. The fathers did not address, except to call for a genuine renewal, fundamental issues in moral theology; they did not take up a project left undone at the First Vatican Council—namely, developing the *praeambula fidei,* or apologetics—and they chose to address liturgical reform without at the same time considering the long elenchus of accepted theses that made up classical sacramental theology. Even the casual observer of things Catholic recognizes that today a certain chaos surrounds Catholic moral teaching, Catholic sacramental life, and, what is perhaps less apparent, Catholic apologetics, the artful science that provides arguments designed to persuade those outside full communion with the Church to embrace Her truths.

These lacunae have begun to be filled during the postconciliar mag-

18. In a private communication to the author, Father Lamb recalls the history as follows: "The mass media began the process during the second session of Vatican II when they imposed a framework of conservative versus liberal on all the proceedings. Those theologians and *periti* who went along with this found they were media stars, quoted often. After the Council bishops and religious superiors turned to them, rather than approved theologians, for how to implement the Council. So the liberal progressives were all over the place, and continued the Xavier Rynne tradition by writing columns, etc. The truth came with *Humanae Vitae* in 1968 and then we had the mass media supporting widespread dissent."

isterium of Pope John Paul II. First, in 1993, the encyclical letter *Veritatis splendor* provided an authentic statement of the Church's teaching "regarding certain fundamental questions of the Church's moral teaching." Second, in 1998, the encyclical *Fides et ratio* provided a reaffirmation of what the Church recognizes as the powers of natural reason to discover the existence of God, citing the First Vatican Council's dogmatic constitution *Dei Filius* IV: "'There are two orders of knowledge, distinct not only in their point of departure, but also in their object.'"[19] In 2003, we received the encyclical on the Eucharist, "On the Eucharist in Its Relationship to the Church," as the English title runs, whose content illuminates in some measure the other sacraments as well. Further magisterial clarifications in these and other areas of Catholic doctrine may be required in the future. Again, this contingency does not signal defect. It rather shows how the Church carries on in the person of the Successor of Peter the teaching mission that Christ has confided to her.

It would not be frivolous to opine that each of the aforementioned papal documents challenges not a few of the prevailing theological outlooks that have gained acceptance among professional theologians, especially those who enjoy standing in the learned academies of theology. Many moral theologians still avoid *Veritatis splendor*. Other theologians cavil with words in *Fides et ratio*. And though it is still too early to evaluate the reception that *Ecclesia de Eucharistia* will receive, it is likely that an assortment of avant-gardist theologians, both liturgical and sacramental, will be surprised to discover that in the early numbers of his encyclical on the Eucharist, the Holy Father returns priests and laity to doctrinal determinations that were formulated in the sixteenth century: "How can we not admire," he says, "the doctrinal expositions of the Decrees on the Most Holy Eucharist and on the Holy Sacrifice of the Mass promulgated by the Council of Trent?"[20] Forty years later, this newest (and, as it turns out, the last) encyclical of Pope John Paul II gives mo-

19. See the 1998 encyclical letter of Pope John Paul II, *Fides et ratio*, §53. See also the prologue: "Faith and reason are like two wings on which the human spirit rises to the contemplation of truth; and God has placed in the human heart a desire to know the truth—in a word, to know himself—so that, by knowing and loving God, men and women may also come to the fullness of truth about themselves."

20. *Ecclesia de Eucharistia*, §9.

ment for pause to those who have been persuaded that it was a complete fresh start after 1965.

The reference to the doctrinal discussions about the "Holy Sacrifice of the Mass" and the sacraments that were carried on at the Council of Trent points us back to the figure of Thomas Aquinas. It is well known that his doctrine, especially as set forth in the *Summa Theologiae*, guided the work of the drafting committees that served the bishops at Trent. In the 1920s, Dom Anscar Vonier wrote in his book *A Key to the Doctrine of the Eucharist*, which is now enjoying a renaissance in Catholic circles, "The remarkable feature . . . of that most scholarly and exact presentment of the Catholic doctrine of the Eucharistic sacrifice by the Fathers of Trent is this, that it gives an exact reproduction of the doctrine of St. Thomas, whose line of thought and whose very expressions are easily recognized in the more classical treatment of the subject by the great council."[21] What Abbot Vonier does not mention is that the theological consultants responsible for these decrees of the Council of Trent were drawn mainly from the ranks of Spanish Dominicans, whose native land it was thought had not been compromised by the introduction of Lutheran theology.[22]

Whatever Martin Luther held about the Eucharist, and we may assume that his views were closer to being Catholic than those of many present-day Lutherans, the reformer of Wittenberg inveighed against the notion that the Eucharist is a sacrifice. His important 1523 pamphlet *Forma Missae et Communionis* explained the new Protestant rite of the Lord's Supper. To this day, Protestants refer to the Eucharist as "the Lord's Supper." Since the sixteenth century, Eucharistic sacrifice has occasioned theological debate between Catholics and Protestant theologians, especially Lutherans. The history of this argument falls outside the scope of today's topic, as does speculation on the interesting question of how much *periti* at the Second Vatican Council allowed burgeoning ecumenical considerations to influence their proposals.[23] I would

21. Anscar Vonier, *A Key to the Doctrine of the Eucharist* (Eugene, OR: Wipf and Stock, 1946, 2002), 145–46.

22. See Angelo Walz, *I Domenicani al Concilio di Trento* (Rome: Herder, 1961).

23. It was sometimes argued that the Catholic position on sacrifice had become distended as a result of several centuries of sometimes-heated rhetorical polemic.

like to mention, in any case, that my own doctoral work was done under the direction of the Irish Dominican Father Colman O'Neill, who taught sacramental theology at the University of Fribourg in Switzerland. Because he was convinced that it would be impossible to explain the sacrificial character of the Mass in ecumenical circles without first discovering the original presentation of satisfaction that St. Thomas gave to the "theory" that he had inherited from St. Anselm, Father O'Neill encouraged research on the notion of satisfaction in Aquinas.[24] It is well known that the *Cur Deus Homo?* nowadays is a difficult text for most Catholic and Protestant theologians. One thing is sure: Aquinas does not repeat the commercial and juridical metaphors that seem to color Anselm's account of satisfaction.

However much the acrimonious debates that alienated Protestants from Catholic during the four-hundred-year period before 1965 may have shaped theological attitudes at the Second Vatican Council, one circumstance now appears evident. The well-known liturgical renewal that issued from this Council seems to have unwittingly contributed to the eclipse of attention paid to the Eucharistic sacrifice. On December 4, 2003, we observed the fortieth anniversary of the Second Vatican Council's constitution on the sacred liturgy, *Sacrosanctum Concilium*. It may be startling for some to learn that this conciliar document on the Church's liturgy mentions the Eucharistic sacrifice itself only four times.[25] *Ecclesia de Eucharistia* cites this conciliar constitution once, namely, number 47, which sets forth the Catholic doctrine that "our Savior instituted the Eucharistic sacrifice of his body and blood, in order to perpetuate the sacrifice of the Cross throughout time, until he should return."[26] That the liturgical renewal failed to encourage reflection about the Eucharist as sacrifice and that its proponents took up themes other than that of sacrifice may require no more elaborate explanation than the sudden shift in quantitative emphasis on sacrifice that many persons observed in a document that was the first pronouncement from the Fathers of the

24. The book is still available under the title *The Godly Image: Christ and Salvation in Catholic Thought from Anselm to Aquinas* (Petersham, MA: St. Bede's, 1990).

25. *Sacrosanctum Concilium,* ʃ10, §12, §47, and §55.

26. See *Ecclesia de Eucharistia,* §11n9.

Second Vatican Council. The distinguished then-Lutheran scholar Jaroslav Pelikan wrote in 1966 that "this Constitution on the Sacred Liturgy . . . does not merely tinker with the formalities of liturgical worship, but seeks to form and to reform the very life of the Church."[27] He may have been right.

The first chapter of the 2004 encyclical in its opening paragraph sets the notion of Eucharistic sacrifice within the biblical context of the Passion of Christ: "'The Lord Jesus on the night he was betrayed' (1 Cor 11:23) instituted the Eucharistic Sacrifice of his body and his blood. The words of the apostle bring us back to the dramatic setting in which the Eucharist was born. The Eucharist is indelibly marked by the event of the Lord's passion and death, of which it is not only a reminder but a sacramental representation. It is the sacrifice of the Cross perpetuated down the ages."[28] This affirmation reflects what Aquinas himself set down when he discusses the ritual for the Eucharist in *Summa Theologiae* III, question 83, article 2: "in celebratione huius mysterii attenditur repraesentatio dominicae passionis." In the celebration of this mystery (of the Mass), attention is paid to the representation of the Lord's Passion. In another place, Aquinas uses the provocative phrase "celebratio huius sacramenti est imago repraesentativa passionis Christi."[29] The celebration of this sacrament is a representational image or icon of the passion of Christ.

The remainder of the first chapter of the encyclical contains in summary form a basic catechesis on Eucharistic theology. The Holy Father explains how the sacrifice of the Mass fulfills God's saving purpose in the world; specifically, what happens at Mass relates to the establishment of communion in Christ among the Catholics: "The Eucharistic Sacrifice is intrinsically directed to the inward union of the faithful with Christ through communion; we receive the very One who offered himself for us."[30] It remains a fair generalization to remark that this intrinsic re-

27. Jaroslav Pelikan, "A Response," in *The Documents of Vatican II in a New and Definitive Translation*, ed. Walter M. Abbott, SJ (New York: Herder & Herder, 1966), 179.

28. *Ecclesia de Eucharistia*, §11.

29. *ST* III, q. 83, a. 1, ad 2. For a brief but incisive commentary, see Inos Biffi, "Eucharist as the Perfect Sign of Christ's Passion," *L'Osservatore Romano*, March 30, 2005, 10.

30. *Ecclesia de Eucharistia*, §6.

lationship between sacrifice and communion has not informed many theological or catechetical or even preaching exercises over the past forty years. On the contrary, the impression has been given oftentimes that communion among persons results from the collective goodwill of those who choose to join a community whose focal point happens to be God. Even the Lutheran theologian Robert W. Jenson laments a "transformation of the Eucharist into a religious social event, celebrating believers' own commitments and feelings for each other."[31] Within this sort of perspective, it would be easy to forget about the sacrifice of Christ, the thought of which may even, from this perspective, be judged to throw up an obstacle to fostering bourgeois sensibilities. One may recall some of the histrionic reactions to the realism of Mel Gibson's film *The Passion of the Christ*.[32]

It, of course, would be wrong to conclude that the eclipse of sacrifice in Eucharistic theology followed logically from the Second Vatican Council's pronouncements on the liturgy. *Sacrosanctum concilium* was meant to renew the liturgy. While journalists and other popularizers imposed their own spin on things, some professional theologians took the occasion of liturgical renewal to instigate doctrinal revisions. Although gathering the testimony required to justify the claim that theologians conspired to sabotage Catholic doctrine on the Eucharist would require extended research, it is possible to point out at least one influential book that illustrates the directions that were being set by English-speaking liturgical theologians during the period after 1963. In 1987, a priest who has taught liturgy and sacraments at the Catholic University of America, David. N. Power, OMI, published a slim volume titled *The Sacrifice We Offer: The Tridentine Dogma and Its Reinterpretation*. Toward the end of this study, which is based on doctoral research done by the author at a much earlier date, Father Power affirms: "The most serious conclusions that follow from this interpretation [of what Trent said about the

31. Robert W. Jenson, "The Church and the Sacraments," in *The Cambridge Companion to Christian Doctrine*, ed. Colin E. Gunton (Cambridge: Cambridge University Press, 1997), 222.

32. For further information, see my "Mel Gibson's Movie & Thomas Aquinas's Modes: How the Passion of Christ Works," *Saint Austin Review* 4 (2004): 27–32.

Mass] are the need for the Catholic Church to reconsider the role of the priest and the language of sacrifice on the one hand, and the possibility of doing this in a differentiated historical continuity with Trent on the other."[33] Power's conclusion in fact reveals a program that had been pursued since the 1970s at least and that would be promoted aggressively after 1987: redefine the role of the priest and reinterpret the language of sacrifice.[34] Confusion about these two issues continues to hamper both the pastoral care given in parishes and priestly formation offered in seminaries.

One area of Church life that illustrates this claim is catechetical instruction given to children and young adults. Archbishop Daniel Buechlein, who was appointed in 1994 as chair of the Bishops' Ad Hoc Committee for the Use of the Catechism, reports that "the fullness of doctrine" has suffered much since the Second Vatican Council. In a report commissioned by this same committee, it was observed that deficiencies in catechetical material can be cataloged under ten headings. One of these headings cites "a pattern of inadequate presentation of the sacraments."[35] "Particularly," the archbishop declares, "the sacraments of the Eucharist and Holy Orders evidence deficiency."[36] Whatever may someday be determined as the cause of the departure from the fullness of doctrine, the practical results are clear. Many Catholics have forgotten what the Church teaches about the Holy Sacrifice of the Mass. *Ecclesia de Eucharistia* signals a reversal in this downward and disturbing trend. The Pope now wants us to ponder deeply the sacrificial character of the Eucharist. To do this we, like the theologians at Trent, can depend on the help of the saint who found in St. Agnes a model of sacrificial love.

33. David N. Power, *The Sacrifice We Offer: The Tridentine Dogma and Its Reinterpretation* (New York: Crossroad, 1987), 161.

34. Edward Schillebeeckx, OP, *The Eucharist*, trans. N. D. Smith (New York: Sheed & Ward, 1968), had been published in Europe only the year before. This small volume takes up a reconsideration of the Tridentine decrees on the Eucharist.

35. Archbishop Daniel Buechlein, "The *Catechism of the Catholic Church* Ten Years Later: The Challenge of Inculturation," address given at Saint John's Seminary, Brighton, MA, April 2002.

36. Ibid.

AQUINAS ON THE EUCHARISTIC: SACRAMENT AND SACRIFICE

The "infallibility with which the divine Redeemer willed his Church to be endowed in defining a doctrine of faith and morals" never fails.[37] *Ecclesia de Eucharistia* provides the warrant for a reconsideration of Eucharistic sacrifice, which, as we have seen, remains a central element of Catholic doctrine. Because the Holy Father has chosen to remind the Church about the Eucharistic sacrifice, Catholics are encouraged to take up again the question of what distinguishes a sacrifice made to God from other kinds of offerings that are not sacrificial. The title of this chapter is taken from a text of St. Thomas: *circa res . . . aliquid fit.* It is found in the *secunda secundae* of the *Summa Theologiae,* where Aquinas discusses the external acts of the virtue of religion, one of which is sacrifice. In order to examine what Aquinas teaches about sacrifice as an act of the virtue of religion, however, we need to gain some perspective on the theological compositions of the Common Doctor that treat of the Eucharist.

The treatise on the Eucharist comprises eleven questions in the *tertia pars* of the *Summa Theologiae*. The exposition on the Eucharist is the last sacrament that Aquinas was able to develop completely. The experience that brought his writing of the *Summa* to a halt occurred while he was working on questions related to the sacrament of penance. It was in fact shortly after having completed his work on the Eucharist that something out of the ordinary happened to St. Thomas while he was saying Mass in the Chapel of St. Nicholas at the Dominican church in Naples. "I cannot do any more," said Aquinas to his astonished companion Reginald. The date was around December 6, 1273. We know then that Aquinas's theology of the Eucharist as found in the *tertia pars* of the *Summa* represents a work of both spiritual and scholarly maturity.

The bishop-theologian William Barden (1908–2004), who taught the treatise on the Eucharist for many years before becoming Archbishop of Ispahan in Iran, observed that "a piety which would express

37. Second Vatican Council, *Constitution on the Church, Lumen gentium,* §25.

the theological interest of St. Thomas might find its centre rather in the tabernacle and in the monstrance than on the stone of sacrifice."[38] This description is true inasmuch as the bulk of Aquinas's work on the Eucharist aims to clarify issues relating to the Real Presence and transubstantiation. In these discussions, moreover, Aquinas remains without equal. At the same time, Archbishop Barden acknowledges that all the elements for a fruitful study of what happens at the Mass will be found in his discussion of the effects of the Eucharist (particularly in q. 79) and of the ritual that surrounds its celebration (q. 83).

"The Eucharist is at once a sacrifice and a sacrament: it has the nature of a sacrifice in that it is offered, and of a sacrament in that it is received."[39] Aquinas makes this distinction in the context of replying to the question: "Is the entire punishment for sin pardoned through this sacrament?" Like everything associated with evil, the punishment for sin resides in the privation of the good that the sinner lacks, which explains why Aquinas begins his direct reply to the question by reminding his readers that the Eucharist, "considered as a sacrifice, has the power of rendering satisfaction."[40] The Latin expression is *vim satisfactivam.* In Christian theology, satisfaction is a way of talking about how the punishment for sin is acquitted, to use a juridical metaphor to express a grace that is ontological, transformational. It would be wrong to think that the identification of sacrifice as satisfaction reduces Eucharistic sacrifice to an outmoded theological oddity. Christian satisfaction is not a theological throwaway. Within Aquinas's scheme of things, in fact, the satisfaction of Christ and of his members provides a template through which the theologian is able to explain a central act of the Christian religion, namely, the death of Christ on the Cross. Aquinas pays full heed to the assertion that St. Paul makes in the Letter to the Romans: "While we were yet helpless, at the right time Christ died for the ungodly" (Rom 5:6).

In his theology of the Passion, satisfaction supplies one of the five

38. Abp. William Barden, OP, *The Eucharistic Presence,* vol. 58 (3a.73–78), *St. Thomas Aquinas, Summa Theologiae* (New York: McGraw-Hill, 1965), xxii.

39. *ST* III, q. 79, a. 5.

40. Ibid.

modes that Aquinas considers sufficient to account for everything that the Passion and death of Christ accomplish for the human race. The reason why the notion of penal satisfaction—which always involves the embrace of something that is painful, something that runs against the grain—figures in any complete account of Christ's Passion hinges on the nature of Christ's redemptive mission. It is impossible to explain within the context of divine revelation why Christ had to suffer apart from the fact that the first man, Adam, sinned and so introduced into the world a reign of sin from which the human race alone was unable to extricate itself. Again, the Letter to the Romans: "If, because of one man's trespass, death reigned through that one man, much more will those who receive the abundance of grace and the free gift of righteousness reign in life through the one man Jesus Christ" (Rom 5:17). St. Anselm summarized this teaching when he affirmed of the satisfaction of Christ that only God could do it and that only a man ought to do it. The mystery, as Anselm explains it, revolves then around this pairing of *qui potuit* and *qui debuit*. There is much that exists within the divine plan for salvation that flows from the satisfaction that Christ makes during the course of his dolorous Passion: in particular, the seven sacraments of the new law, each of which remits the punishment due to sin. Suffice it for now to observe that satisfaction comes into play whenever the effects of sin require Christian healing.

Aquinas mentions the Eucharist as a sacrifice in the course of answering the question of whether the entire punishment for sin is pardoned through the Eucharist. He makes this identification in order to show that the perfective graces of the Eucharist, which are unity and charity, proceed to the extent that we are released from disordered attachment to sin (which is itself a punishment of sin). Punishment for sin is another one of those categories that has not received much attention during the past forty years. We are led to consider another reason that explains why the sacrificial aspect of the Eucharist was neglected. That we forget, however, does not mean that God forgets. Every Eucharistic community is obliged to ask itself to what extent the frequency of communicating and the numbers of communicants translates into a community that is identified as a place where the truth about the human and divine good flourishes in the lives of each member.

Aquinas's discussion of the ritual that celebrates the Eucharist more clearly connects the sacrifice of the Eucharist with the Sacrifice of Golgotha. In *Summa Theologiae* III, question 83, article 1, Aquinas asks whether Christ is sacrificed in this sacrament. Two lines of consideration are offered, one that justifies calling the Mass a sacrifice, and the other the communication of the benefits of the Passion. The key affirmation is found when Aquinas asserts that "the celebration of this sacrament is a definite image representing Christ's Passion, which is his true sacrifice."[41] As one commentator observes, "*Imago* should be charged with its full sense, that which proceeds or issues forth according to a likeness and specific meaning."[42] We could say that the Mass is an icon of Calvary. Then we can recall what Aquinas teaches in an earlier question of the *tertia pars* when he explains that reverence is given to a representation of Christ as to Christ himself, not as an artifact but only as an image—*solum inquantum est imago.*[43]

The Eucharistic sacrifice insofar as it is a representational image of Christ's Passion is a true exemplar cause (*exemplar effectivum*) of the graces God bestows in this sacrament.[44] We could say that the graces of the Eucharist exist in cruciform composition. *Ecclesia de Eucharistia* references an important teaching of the Council of Trent, one that addresses the objection lodged by the reformers that a strong representational account of the sacrifice of the Mass leads people to imagine that the once and for all—*semel, hapax*—sacrifice of Calvary stands in need of multiple repetitions or reiterations in order to accomplish the work of redemption. The mystery runs deeper than this mechanical view of things. "It is one and the same victim here offering himself by the ministry of his priests, who

41. *ST* III, q. 83, a. 1: "Celebratio autem huius sacramenti . . . imago quaedam est repraesentativa passionis Christi quae est vera eius immmolatio."

42. Thomas Gilby, OP, *Holy Communion*, vol. 59 (3a. 79–83), *St. Thomas Aquinas, Summa Theologiae* (New York: McGraw-Hill, 1975), 134–35, note c.

43. See *ST* III, q. 25, a. 3.

44. See *ST* III, q. 83, a. 1, ad 1: *Hoc autem sacrificium exemplum est illius.* Father Gilby renders this text as "Christ offered once, and that was the exemplar of our offering" (*Holy Communion*, 137).

then offered himself on the Cross; it is only the manner of offering that is different."[45] What is different between the representational image of the sacrifice of Calvary and the death that Christ actually underwent on the Cross? In a word, the sacrifice that is offered daily in the Mass is sacramental, whereas the sacrifice of Christ on the Cross, his offering to God in obedience and love, is expressed in the physical event of crucifixion.

The way that divine providence allowed Christ to die brings us back to the title of this essay: *Circa res . . . aliquid fit.*[46] I have mentioned that even a connoisseur of Aquinas's Eucharistic theology such as Archbishop Barden felt compelled to admit that the *Summa* devotes more time to explaining the metaphysics of Real Presence than it does to the way that the sacrifice of the Mass makes present the sacrifice of the Cross. One explanation for Aquinas's ordering of his materials is the fact that sound theologians, like Aquinas, address more freely those topics that are challenged than those that remain uncontested. For instance, Aquinas does not theorize a great deal about community, but he surely appreciated the dimensions of community life, given the way that it was lived in the thirteenth century, more than do the theoreticians of community who seldom leave their individual studies.

There is another way to view Aquinas's treatment of new law sacrifice. We discover what Aquinas thinks by looking at what he says about sacrifice in general. This discussion is not in the Christological and sacramental questions found in the *tertia pars,* but in the *secunda pars* where Aquinas treats the moral life. In particular, sacrifice belongs to the virtue of religion, which itself is placed under the cardinal virtue of justice as one of its potential parts.[47] A potential part means that while the allied virtue corresponds to the main virtue, it exercises the power or *potentia* of the virtue within a limited sphere of activity. In the case of religion, the just man renders what is owed to God. Because it is impossible to render to God all that is owed him, religion is a potential part of

45. *Ecclesia de Eucharistia,* §12 at note 16, Ecumenical Council of Trent, session XXII, *Doctrina de ss. Missae Sacrificio,* ch. 2 (*DS,* no. 1743).

46. *ST* II-II, q. 85, a. 3, ad 3.

47. See *ST* II-II, q. 80: "There are certain virtues which render another his due, but not to its full extent . . . Religion is a potential part of justice."

the cardinal virtue of justice.[48] The virtue of religion expresses itself in internal acts, devotion and prayer, and also through the external acts, such as adoration, sacrifice, and vows. Sacrifice falls within the category of those acts whereby men give things to God: sacrifice, oblation, first fruits of the harvest, and tithes. It is easy to see that Aquinas is organizing large amounts of biblical material, especially religious duties prescribed by the Law of Moses.

In question 85, article 3, Aquinas records the argument that states, "anything offered to God seems to be a sacrifice. Yet many things are offered to God, such as devotion, prayers, tithes, first fruits, oblations, and holocausts. Therefore, sacrifice does not seem to be a distinct act of a definite virtue."[49] In the body of the article, Aquinas explains that, generally speaking, a sacrifice is any good action offered to God, especially in order to cling to God in spiritual union.[50] In the reply to objection 3, however, Aquinas introduces a more proper notion of sacrifice: "A sacrifice in the proper sense of the word means that something is done to the thing offered to God, for example, when animals were killed and burned and when bread is blessed, broken, and eaten."[51] This text affords a glimpse of the theological coherence that informs the *Summa Theologiae*. Deep within the *secunda pars,* which treats the moral life, Aquinas is obviously thinking about the Eucharist: bread blessed, broken, and eaten.

To ponder in faith the sacrifice of Calvary requires understanding what makes a sacrifice. *Ecclesia de Eucharistia* develops this point: "The sacrificial nature of the Eucharistic mystery cannot therefore be understood as something separate, independent of the Cross or only indirectly referring to the sacrifice of Calvary."[52] Catholic faith recognizes that on Calvary something was done to the one who was crucified. Christ's self-offering on the Cross is "a sacrifice that the Father accepted, giving, in

48. Ibid.

49. *ST* II-II, q. 85, a. 3, obj. 3.

50. See *ST* II-II, q. 85, a. 3, obj. 1 and ad 1: "the act of any virtue assumes the character of sacrifice if it is performed in order to cling to God in spiritual union."

51. *ST* II-II, q. 85, a. 3, ad 3.

52. *Ecclesia de Eucharistia,* §12.

return for this total self-giving by his Son, who 'became obedient unto death' (Phil 2:8), his own paternal gift, that is to say the grant of new immortal life in the resurrection."[53]

I began this essay by drawing your attention to the example of St. Agnes. The mystery of the Eucharistic sacrifice achieves its highest expression among the saints in the life of the martyrs. The witness of a teenage girl is meant to encourage all Christians to know that participation in Christ's sacrifice is open to them. One reason the Church reserves priestly ordination to men is because the priest immolates at the altar.[54] Each Mass enacts a true sacrifice. The Catholic holds "that Christ's Eucharistic Body under the appearance of bread, and Christ's Eucharistic Blood under the appearance of wine, represent Christ's natural Body and Christ's natural Blood as they were on Calvary. This is the true and final expression of sacramental representation; and such representation suffices by itself to constitute the sacrifice, because the representation is of that period of Christ's wonderful existence when he was nothing but sacrifice, as his Blood was separated from his Body."[55] *Circa res . . . aliquid fit.*

I would like to close by suggesting how young men may serve the mystery of the Eucharist. The proposal is self-evident. Some young men must sacrifice certain of their potentialities so that this precious gift of Christ to his Church will continue to sanctify the world. There is special reason to appreciate the example of the virgin martyr Agnes. Purity of life prepares for sacrifice. This axiom applies especially to the priest. A young man makes every effort to lead a chaste life so that he will be fully disposed spiritually to handle the bread and wine of the Eucharist. And young women should help them in imitation of St. Agnes. Both men and women believe that in the double consecration the sacrificing priest plays his role in representing the sacrifice of Christ on Calvary. God has provided no other solution to take away the sins of the world and to establish the reign of universal charity. These supernatural gifts

53. *Ecclesia de Eucharistia,* §13, citing Pope John Paul II, Encyclical Letter *Redemptor Hominis* (1979), §20: *Acta Apostolicae Sedis* 71 (1979): 310.

54. Father Benedict Ashley discusses this argument in his *Justice in the Church: Gender and Participation* (Washington, DC: Catholic University Press of America Press, 1996), 82–84.

55. Vonier, *Key to the Doctrine,* 118–19.

Christ won for us by his obedience and love expressed externally during his crucifixion by Roman soldiers some two thousand years ago. From his pierced side flow blood and water, which the Church proclaims to be the fountain of sacramental life in the Church. This is the message that Pope John Paul II wants us to ponder as we read his encyclical *Ecclesia de Eucharistia*. It is also a message that comes to us from St. Thomas Aquinas through the mediatorship of the Catholic Church, which continues to recognize his perennial contributions to Catholic thought.

CHAPTER 6

THE LIGHT OF TABOR

Christian Personalism and Adoptive Sonship

Father Cessario in this chapter integrates the themes introduced in the previous five within a consideration of their relevance for happy living. The transformation of creatures made in the image of God into adoptive sons encompasses the whole of the Christian life. This essay examines how God accomplishes this transformation in members of the human race he has predestined for glory.

As we have already seen, St. Thomas teaches that "men become adopted sons of God by a certain conformity to the image of the natural Son of God"—Jesus (*ST* III, q. 45, a. 4). This conformity to the image of the Eternal Son finds a twofold expression in the human person: (1) through the grace of "imperfect" conformity proper to wayfarers here on earth and (2) through the glorious, perfect conformity realized in the saints of heaven. Thus St. Thomas teaches that there is a "twofold state of sonship," with the imperfect filial conformity ultimately ordered toward the perfect conformity proper to beatific communion. Father Cessario explains that this "dynamic" movement from imperfect to perfect conformity to the image of Christ is what the Church calls the "Christian moral life." This filial conformity to Christ

Originally published as "The Light of Tabor: Christian Personalism and Adoptive Sonship," *Nova et Vetera* 2, no. 2 (2004): 237–48. Reprinted by permission.

is what his Passion on Calvary enabled and what his sacraments effect in the lives of Christians. In short, the person and work of Christ enable the adoptive sons of God both to know and to love the perfective truth of the moral life.

Commentators have observed the significance of the date on which the Holy Father chose to sign the encyclical.[1] The August Feast of the Transfiguration illuminates the themes contained in *Veritatis splendor*, especially the divine reality in man that Catholic moral theology guided by the Magisterium seeks to explicate and promote. It is axiomatic that all the mysteries of Christ's life, death, and resurrection sanctify those who are members of his Body. "Every act and suffering of Christ," Aquinas assures us, "acts instrumentally in virtue of his divinity for man's salvation."[2] The mystery of Christ's Transfiguration points in a special way to the theme that occupies many theologians of the period: preethical anthropology and its relationship to a Christian anthropology of sonship. The Transfiguration assures us that a rational nature can participate through grace and charity in the divine glory and majesty.[3] We are left to consider the following question: How does God accomplish this transformation in members of the human race he has predestined for glory?[4]

THE CHRISTIAN ANTHROPOLOGY OF ADOPTIVE SONSHIP

We find in the *Summa Theologiae* of St. Thomas Aquinas (1224/25–74) certain considerations essential to a proper theological understanding

1. See, e.g., J. A. Di Noia, OP, "Veritatis Splendor: Moral Life as Transfigured Life," in *Veritatis Splendor and the Renewal of Moral Theology*, ed. J. A. Di Noia, OP, and Romanus Cessario, OP (Chicago, IL: Midwest Theological Forum, 1999), 1–10. This volume was published to commemorate the encyclical's fifth anniversary in 1998.

2. *ST* III, q. 48, a. 6: "omnes actiones et passiones Christi instrumentaliter operantur in virtute divinitatis ad salutem humanum." Cited in Jean-Pierre Torrell, OP, *Saint Thomas Aquinas*, vol. 2, *Spiritual Master*, trans. Robert Royal (Washington, DC: Catholic University of America Press, 2003), 135.

3. See *ST* III, q. 23, a. 3.

4. Aquinas holds that the splendor that Christ assumed at his Transfiguration was that of a glorified body "as to essence, but not as to mode of being" (*ST* III, q. 45, a. 2).

of a Christian anthropology of sonship. One line of inquiry is found in Aquinas's discussion of the mystery of Christ's life that governs the central message of *Veritatis splendor*. When he treats the Transfiguration in *tertia pars* question 45, Aquinas includes in article 4 what at first glance appears to be a throwaway question: "Whether the testimony of the Father's voice, saying, *This is my beloved Son*, was fittingly heard."[5] In fact, this article contains an important distinction. Aquinas's express inquiry is about the "convenience"—the fittingness or suitableness—of the text that is recorded variously in each of the Synoptic accounts (Mt 17:5; Mk 9:7; Lk 9:35): "This is my beloved Son, with whom I am well pleased; listen to him" (Mt 17:5).[6] The authority of the canonical Gospels supplies an *in contrarium*. Because Aquinas accepts the sacred texts themselves as sufficient warrant for the fittingness of the testimony, the article contains no *sed contra*. God spoke these words, so there is no reason for theological discussion about their coherence with the economy of salvation. Still, the testimony of the Father's voice at the Transfiguration points to the question of sonship, both of Christ's own and, according to the principle of instrumentality, of that possible for the rational creature.

The reply to question 45, article 4, sets forth, as I have indicated, a first and crucial distinction for a Christian anthropology of sonship: "Men become adopted sons of God by a certain conformity of image to the natural Son of God. Now this is accomplished in two ways. First of all, by the grace of the wayfarer, which is an imperfect conformity; secondly, by glory, which is a perfect conformity."[7] Aquinas includes in this article the text of 1 John 3:2: "Beloved, we are God's children [in the Vulgate Latin, 'filii Dei'] now; it does not yet appear what we shall be, but we know that when he appears we shall be like ['similes'] him, for we shall see him as he is." A first thing to consider, therefore, about a Christian

5. *ST* III, q. 45, a. 4: "utrum convenienter auditum fuerit testimonium paternae vocis in transfiguratione."

6. Scripture references are taken from the Revised Standard Version, Catholic edition (1965).

7. *ST* III, q. 45, a. 4: "Dicendum quod adoptio filiorum Dei est per quamdam conformitatem imaginis ad Filium Dei naturalem. Quod quidem fit dupliciter: primo quidem fit per gratiam viae, quae est conformitas imperfecta; secundo, per gloriam patriae, quae erit conformitas perfecta." Translations, sometimes slightly modified, are taken from *Summa Theologiae*, 61 vols., Blackfriars ed. (New York: McGraw-Hill, 1964–80).

anthropology of sonship is that it exists for now in a twofold state or degree of likeness or similitude, one here below that is imperfect, another above on high that is perfect. A second thing to consider is that this likeness or similitude is impressed on the human being after the fashion of an inhering form, which according to the adage *forma dat esse* becomes the principle of the Christian's image activity. The final perfection of this activity is called beatific vision.

To distinguish a twofold state of sonship gives theologians a way to talk about the eschatological expectations that Christians cherish in accord with what St. Paul writes in Romans 8:17: "and if children [*filii*], then heirs, heirs of God and fellow heirs with Christ." It also affords a way to understand growth in holiness; for, as *Veritatis splendor* observes, there is a close connection "between eternal life and obedience to God's commandments."[8] The dynamic relationship between what here below remains imperfect and what at the same time tends toward being perfect is lived out by each believer in what the encyclical calls the "Christian moral life."[9] "Dynamic" is not, in this context, a superfluous modifier. The term serves to signify any movement that proceeds both from the inner dimension of the reality itself and according to some kind of necessity, as an acorn contains imperfectly the perfect oak tree that (barring external impediments) will develop from it.

The necessity that attaches to natural dynamic movements is not absolute. Aquinas usefully points out in his commentary on Aristotle's *Physics* that movement in nature proceeds according to a necessity that is suppositional, *ex suppositione finis*.[10] At the beginning of the *tertia pars*, without diminishing the excellence of the grace of union, he also applies this mode of necessity—that is, when something is required for a better and more expeditious attainment of an end—to the Incarnation itself.[11] Some acorns will be eaten by squirrels, just as some wayfarers, though

8. See *Veritatis splendor*, §12.

9. For example, "The Spirit of Jesus, received by the humble and docile heart of the believer, brings about the flourishing of Christian moral life and the witness of holiness amid the great variety of vocations, gifts, responsibilities, conditions and life situations" (§108).

10. *Physics* II, c. 9 (200a14). For further discussion, see William A. Wallace, OP, *The Modeling of Nature* (Washington, DC: Catholic University of America, 1996), 20ff.

11. See *ST* III, q. 1, a. 2.

they may receive initially the grace of adoptive sonship, will sin and fall away. In the orders of nature and grace, *ex suppositione finis* works to illustrate how the God-given dynamism that belongs to a particular created form interacts with other natural or voluntary agents in the course of moving toward the perfective end proper to the form.[12] Our transformation into sons proceeds in accord with this kind of necessity.

THE IMAGE OF THE SON

Aquinas builds his anthropology of sonship around the notion of the image: "per quamdam conformitatem imaginis ad Filium Dei naturalem." Equally important is that Aquinas does not hold that adoptive sonship is to be thought of as a participation in the natural sonship that is Christ's. Just as the human image is related to the Trinity as its model, adoptive sonship is contracted in respect to the whole Trinity. Although some New Testament texts, such as Galatians 4:4—"God sent forth his Son ... so that we might receive adoption as sons"—may appropriate adoption to the natural Son within the Trinity, the bestowal of the grace of adoption, including the eschatological promises that this grace brings, results from the work of the whole Trinity.[13] In accordance with a way of speaking about God, which is in fact what appropriation is, adoption is attributed "to the Father as its author, to the Son as its model, to the Spirit as the Person who imparts to us the likeness of this model."[14] As part of the divine economy, adoptive sonship itself is the common work of the three divine persons.

In order to grasp what Aquinas means when he says that "adoptive sonship ... is similar to natural sonship," it is necessary to return to his discussion of the Blessed Trinity and in particular to recall his absolute consideration of each divine person found in *prima pars* questions

12. The difference between providence and predestination is understood.

13. See *CCC*, §258: "The whole divine economy is the common work of the three divine persons."

14. *ST* III, q. 23, a. 2, ad 3. See Colman E. O'Neill, OP, *The One Mediator*, vol. 50 (3a.16–26), *St. Thomas Aquinas, Summa Theologiae* (New York: McGraw-Hill, 1965), Appendix 6, esp. 254–56.

33–38.[15] After a single question devoted to the First Person, Aquinas turns "to study the Person of the Son. The names given him are three," says Aquinas, "'Son,' 'Word' and 'Image.' We know," he continues, "the meaning of the term 'Son' from that of the 'Father'; there remain to be examined, then, the names 'Word' and 'Image.'"[16] The examination continues in questions 34 and 35 of the *prima pars* where we learn that the Christian tradition agrees that the names "Word" and "Image" are both personal names in God and names proper (*proprium*) to the Second Person of the Blessed Trinity. It is not possible to develop a theologically accurate Christian anthropology of sonship without including proper reference to the other personal names of the Son, Word, and Image. This is the case because of the nature of the Trinitarian processions. The Christian tradition, following the lead of St. Augustine, holds that the Second Person is considered first as Word and only then, in terms of intellectual procession, as Son.[17] As Aquinas expresses it, "the procession of the Word corresponds to the action of the intellect [*actionem intelligibilem*]."[18]

Two considerations follow. First, about the Word. As the biblical accounts of creation suggest, the divine Word bears a special relationship to creatures. In his commentary on John's Gospel, Aquinas observes that *Logos* was not, as it could have been, translated as *ratio* because the Prologue expresses the effective power of the Word, "all things were made through him" (Jn 1:3), whereas *ratio* expresses only the cognitive character of the concept or mental word.[19] The name Word connotes, then, a reference to creatures inasmuch as, though God's knowledge of himself is cognitive, his knowledge of everything that is outside of himself is both cognitive and causative (*factiva*). Logos nonetheless connotes pattern or

15. *ST* III, q. 23, a. 3.

16. Prologue at *ST* I, q. 34: "Deinde considerandum est de persona Filii. Attribuuntur autem tria nomina Filio, scilicet Filius, Verbum et Imago. Sed ratio Filii ex ratione Patris consideratur; unde restat considerandum de Verbo et Imagine."

17. See *ST* I, q. 27, a. 2: "Unde processio verbi in divinis dicitur generatio et ipsum verbum procedens dicitur Filius."

18. *ST* I, q. 27, a. 3: "Processio autem verbi attenditur secundum actionem intelligibilem."

19. *Lectura super Ioannem* 1, lect. 1. For further information, see T. C. O'Brien, *Father, Son, and Holy Ghost*, vol. 7 (Ia. 33–43), *St. Thomas Aquinas, Summa Theologiae* (New York: McGraw-Hill, 1976), 38nC.

model, an *actionem intelligibilem*.[20] Interestingly, when *Lumen Gentium* comments on the text of Colossians 1:15, "He is the image of the invisible God, the first-born of all creation; for in him all things were created," the conciliar text carefully expresses itself: "[Christus] est *imago Dei* invisibilis, in eoque *condita sunt* universa."[21] In Christ, all things receive their foundation. In this foundation, living things find their ends: "creatures are said to do God's word inasmuch as they carry out some effect toward which they are directed through the begotten Word of divine wisdom."[22]

The causal relationship that exists between God and creatures remains a central element of Aquinas's Christian anthropology. When it is said that all things are created in the Word, this means that everything that God creates enjoys the special causal relation of creation. Anti-Arian caution excludes this relation being affirmed with reference to the Second Person, who is Son "origine non adoptione; veritate non nuncupatione; nativitate non creatione."[23] Human beings, on the other hand, bear a likeness to the intelligible Word of divine wisdom because they have been created in him. Preethical anthropology concerns what is proper to this kind of creature, who because he is endowed with mind and will is also said to bear the natural image of the Trinity.[24] The encyclical refers to "man's proper and primordial nature, the 'nature of the human person' (*Gaudium et spes*, §51), which is the person himself in the unity of soul and body, in the unity of his spiritual and biological inclinations and of all the other specific characteristics necessary for the pursuit of his end."[25]

Second, about the Image. The Son is properly said to be the image of God because he is the Word of God: "the Son proceeds in the manner of a word, whose meaning it is to be alike in kind [*similitudo speciei*] to the source from which it proceeds."[26] Adopted sons in the Son do not pos-

20. See note 18 above and *ST* I, q. 27, a. 3.

21. *Lumen gentium*, §7.

22. *ST* I, q. 34, a. 1, ad 4: "creaturae dicuntur facere verbum Dei inquantum exsequuntur effectum aliquem, ad quem ordinantur ex verbo concepto divinae sapientiae."

23. Hilary of Poitiers, *De Trinitate*, bk. 3, 11 (PL 10:82).

24. See *ST* I, q. 45, a. 7, where Aquinas takes up the distinction between the image and the trace (*vestigium*) of the Trinity in creation.

25. *Veritatis splendor*, §50.

26. *ST* I, q. 35, a. 2.

sess this *similitudo speciei*, however, and so we find ourselves compelled to recognize some form of analogical agreement. In order to ensure that the work of adoptive sonship, of making us like the natural Son, is seen as a work of the whole Trinity, recourse to analogy of proper proportionality is required: The natural Son is to the Father as the adoptive son is to the whole Trinity. God's adoptive sons are, in the fullest sense of the word, his creation, and thus they cry out, "Abba! Father!" (Rom 8:15).

Now we can interpret what Aquinas means when he says that "men become adopted sons of God by a certain conformity of image to the natural Son of God."[27] Because image also requires analogical predication when said of the Son and of the human creature, it is necessary to identify what is similar and different in the analogy: "The image of one thing is present in another in one of two ways. The first, as in a being of the same specific nature, e.g., the king's image in his son; the second, as in a being of a different nature, e.g., the king's image on a coin. The Son is the Image of the Father in the first manner; man is the image of God in the second."[28] When it is said that man is created after the image of God, this means that there exists within a specifically different nature from that of God an analogical likeness to God that is able to undergo transfiguration.[29] The existence of a natural likeness that is apt for receiving a new form that grace or glory confers remains a central notion of St. Thomas's theological anthropology and, I would argue, the supposition of the encyclical *Veritatis splendor*.

To minimize the distinction between what is created by God through the Word and what is brought forth through the redemptive action of the Incarnate Son in the Church risks confusing the orders of nature and grace, with the result that it would be difficult to treat rightly a Christian anthropology of sonship. To cite one example from the encyclical, it is

27. See note 7 above.

28. *ST* I, q. 35, a. 2, ad 3: "imago alicujus dupliciter in aliquo invenitur: uno modo in re ejusdem naturae secundum speciem, ut imago regis invenitur in filio suo; alio modo in re alterius naturae, sicut imago regis invenitur in denario. Primo autem modo Filius est Imago Patris; secundo autem modo dicitur homo imago Dei."

29. See also *ST* I, q. 33, a. 3: "The quality of being God's son is present in a creature not in the full sense, but on the basis of a limited likeness, and one that becomes fuller the nearer it approaches the absolute expression of this sonship."

sufficient to recall what it says about a sometimes fashionable exaggerated personalism: "This heightened sense of the dignity of the human person and of his or her uniqueness, and of the respect due to the journey of conscience, certainly represents one of the positive achievements of modern culture. This perception, authentic as it is, has been expressed in a number of more or less adequate ways, some of which however diverge from the truth about man as a creature and the image of God, and thus need to be corrected and purified in the light of faith."[30]

To take full account of "the truth about man as a creature and the image of God," it is necessary to insist upon a threefold distinction that governs the relationship between preethical anthropology and a Christian anthropology of sonship. (1) God may be called "Father" with respect to intelligent creatures on account of the likeness of the natural image, but not with the priority of a personal name, and therefore by way of metaphor not by proper analogy. In order for the analogical deployment of Father to be valid, there must be a relation of one person to another. This personal analogy applies, as has been observed already, (2) to adoptive sons on earth who enjoy likeness to the divine by grace and (3) to full-blown saints in heaven who enjoy the likeness of glory, in accord with what St. Paul says in Romans 8:17, "and fellow heirs with Christ, provided we suffer with him in order that we may also be glorified with him."[31] One may speak of the dynamism of discipleship. In fact, adoptive sonship includes a missionary aspect, as the Holy Father so clearly indicated in his Apostolic Letter *Novo Millennio Ineunte*: "Did we not celebrate the Jubilee Year in order to refresh our contact with this living source of our hope? Now, the Christ whom we have contemplated and loved bids us to set out once more on our journey: 'Go therefore and make disciples of all nations, baptizing them in the name of the Father, and of the Son and of the Holy Spirit' (Mt 28:19). The missionary mandate accompanies us into the Third Millennium and urges us to share the enthusiasm of the very first Christians: we can count on the power

30. *Veritatis splendor*, §31.

31. The material is set forth in *ST* I, q. 33, a. 3: "Utrum hoc nomen Pater dicatur in divinis per prius secundum quod personaliter sumitur."

of the same Spirit who was poured out at Pentecost and who impels us still today to start out anew, sustained by the hope 'which does not disappoint' (Rom 5:5)."[32] Only God can effectuate this movement.

THE CHRISTIAN MORAL LIFE

What is apparent to those persons who, over the past decade, have welcomed the encyclical? The limitations of space allow me to comment only on certain themes that had been suggested by those who organized the Roman symposium at which this essay was first read.[33] First are questions of the present moment. Three areas of concern that have emerged in the past several years include: stem cell research, which makes it difficult to work in the area of bioethics; the state approval of same-sex unions, which makes it more difficult both to instruct about chastity and to promote the full truth about marriage; and lack of agreement on just war criteria, which relates to the general theme of political prudence. When one addresses these questions, following the method of *Veritatis splendor* makes it possible to avoid giving the impression that the Church promotes sectarian or private moral views. What is at stake is man's participation in the divine goodness: "Each creature is stretched out toward the attainment of its own perfection, which is a likeness of the divine perfection and goodness."[34] As the important teaching found in chapter 1 of the encyclical reminds us, "Only God can answer the question about what is good, because he is the Good itself."[35] The themes of adoptive sonship and the image of God find their completion in beatitude, or in the beatific vision. But these themes also are to be understood within the context of the fundamental participation in the divine goodness that informs everything that exists. The basic teleological dynamism of creation emerges against the background of the

32. *Novo Millennio Ineunte*, §58.

33. The symposium, composed of international scholars, was held during the month of September 2003.

34. *ST* I, q. 44, a. 4: "Et unaquaeque creatura intendit consequi suam perfectionem, quae est similitudo perfectionis et bonitatis divinae."

35. *Veritatis splendor*, §9.

divine will from which all striving after perfection springs.[36] The challenge for the Christian evangelist and theologian is to persuade people to consider this truth of creation when they engage in ethical issues.

Second is the question of conscience. The formation of the moral conscience requires adherence to the truth about the good. As the encyclical points out, "in the practical judgment of conscience, which imposes on the person the obligation to perform a given act, the link between freedom and truth is made manifest. Precisely for this reason conscience expresses itself in acts of 'judgment' that reflect the truth about the good, and not in arbitrary 'decisions.'"[37] It is impossible for anyone to make a judgment of conscience that conforms to the truth about the good without possessing the virtue of prudence. In my view, there is more reason today than there has been in the past to employ the distinction between infused and acquired prudence. This distinction helps one to explain the Gospel and its requirements to people who possess some appreciation of what moral goodness imposes on every human being.

Prudence perfects the practical intellect. A moral anthropology that purports to serve *Veritatis splendor* must take account of all the capacities in the human creature that require development and perfection. Sin in the broad sense occurs when these capacities do not produce an action that achieves the perfective ends that together realize the good of man. To cite Aquinas, a person sins when he performs an action deprived of its proper ordering to the end, *actus debito ordine privatus.* Both moral conscience and sin are properly explained within the larger context of the goods that perfect man as an individual (particularly the virtues of personal discipline, temperance, and courage) and as a social being (the virtue of justice and its parts). None of these virtues can operate outside of the directive function that is unique to prudence and that ensures the harmony of right reason and right appetite. Every sin therefore involves some departure from prudence.

It seems to me that most of the commentary, at least in English, that the encyclical has received centers on the rich instruction, found in sec-

36. See O'Neill, *One Mediator,* 252.

37. *Veritatis splendor,* §61.

tion 4 of chapter 2, on the nature of the moral act. Competent moral theologians have sought to expound especially on the meaning of the phrase "in the perspective of the acting person" as it applies to the specification of the moral act.[38] It would not be useful to rehearse even briefly these discussions and exchanges. I would, however, like to conclude by remarking on what many consider to be an important connection between moral action and perfective end. The suggestion comes from a point that is well known by those who study Aristotle's *Ethics*: As a person is according to his appetites, so he views the end.[39] We discover in the ethical wisdom of the classical philosophers, who were deprived of all knowledge of adoptive sonship, a clue to understanding the full meaning of a Christian anthropology of sonship. To follow the way of the Lord Jesus, a person must first of all be conformed to the Lord Jesus. This conformity is fully personal insofar as it extends to every properly human capacity that man enjoys: all the powers of the soul, including and perhaps especially the powers of sense. The man who is conformed to Christ is the one who will love like Christ. In order to account for this new capacity to love completely, the theological tradition that follows Aquinas speaks about the infusion at baptism of both theological *and moral* virtues.

My pastoral experience persuades me that unless we bring people to love moral truth, especially in those situations where adhering to moral truth entails what is thought to be great sacrifice—for example, the care of pregnant rape victims and the refusal to resort to artificial forms of fertilization such as IVF—we will never persuade them to act in accord with the truth. It is my impression that even some good Catholic moral theologians are too influenced by modern moral theories and so are content to develop moral arguments. A Christian anthropology of sonship requires much more than minute attention to formal argument. Aquinas suggests what this "more" entails when he explains that the person in whom the influence of the virtues and the gifts is strong enters into a

38. Many of the articles to which I refer have appeared in *The Thomist*; e.g., Steven A. Long, "A Brief Disquisition Regarding the Nature of the Object of the Moral Act According to St. Thomas Aquinas," *Thomist* 67 (2003): 45–71.

39. For a discussion of this adage and its place in the virtue theory of Aquinas, see my *Introduction to Moral Theology*, rev. ed. (Washington, DC: Catholic University of America Press, 2013).

"semi-experiential" awareness of the divine indwelling Persons: "The Son in turn is the Word; not, however, just any word, but the Word breathing Love ... So Augustine says pointedly, 'The Son is being sent whenever someone has knowledge or perception of him,' for 'perception' points to a kind of experiential awareness and this precisely is what wisdom is, a knowing that, as it were, is tasted."[40] To this wisdom, which comprises more than the recognition of moral norms, the encyclical summons us. The whole world should be grateful for the invitation. It supplies their title to transformation.

40. See *ST* I, q. 43, a. 5, ad 2.

CHAPTER 7

AQUINAS ON THE PRIEST

Sacramental Realism and the Indispensable, Irreplaceable Vocation of the Priest

Here Father Cessario turns our attention to the indispensible vocation of the priest. Within the priest, Christ's sacramental mediation finds unique, personal expression. As head, the priest shares in Christ's government of the Church. As shepherd, he teaches the truth regarding the full reality of the moral life. As bridegroom, the priest loves those whom Christ loves and, like our Savior himself, sacrifices himself for their eternal well-being. In sum, the priest's conformity to Christ's image is unique in that he lives and dies solely that others might live forever in Christ. "To restore. To transform. To elevate. These actions represent the privilege of Christ's priesthood."

Father Cessario explains that an adequate appreciation of preaching is essential to the theology and sanctity of the priesthood. The priest's work of reconciliation is Christ's own work, and thus "the communication of divine wisdom belongs to the priest by divine right." Because sound "moral instruction remains indispensible to the happy

Originally published as "Aquinas on the Priest: Sacramental Realism and the Indispensable and Irreplaceable Vocation of the Priest," *Nova et Vetera* 8, no. 1 (2010): 1–15. Reprinted by permission.

lives of individuals," the priest's vocation is "irreplaceable." Celibacy sets the priest apart in order that he might draw others close to Christ's loving mercy. "It is worth more than one lifetime to become an irreplaceable instrument of a grace that is so indispensable," for through the Eucharistic sacrifice "we find ourselves conformed to the Risen Lord." In his eternal wisdom, God's saving work of image restoration and image perfection occurs through the instrumentality of his priests.

The Church today uses biblical language to describe the unique identity of the Catholic priest. Aquinas uses another biblical term to define the priest: mediator. He finds warrant for this usage in Letter to the Hebrews, the New Testament book that offers the most explicit instruction on the priest and on which Aquinas was one of the few medieval theologians to comment. Aquinas explores the grace to be a priest through the prism of the place that the priest occupies within the ecclesial community: Christ brings divine gifts to men, and he reconciles the human race to God.[1] Aquinas identifies mediation with the special character that the sacrament of Holy Orders confers on the priest,[2] which leads to the subtitle for this chapter: "Sacramental Realism." To understand what is real about the sacraments, we first need to recall why we need sacraments.

"Redemption is meaningless unless there is cause for it in the actual life we live, and for the last few centuries there has been operating in our culture the secular belief that there is no such cause,"[3] wrote Flannery O'Connor more than thirty-five years ago. Were she alive today, Ms. O'Connor no doubt would have dropped the qualifier "secular," for she would have discovered that not a few Catholic theologians spread the belief that there is no cause "in the actual life we live" for redemption.

This realization of our present circumstances should especially concern the priest and the seminarian. The priest discovers his *raison d'être*, his very cause for being, in the Redemption. Everything that he does is

1. See *ST* III, q. 22, art. 1.

2. See *CCC*, §1582.

3. Flannery O'Connor, *Mystery and Manners: Occasional Prose*, ed. Sally and Robert Fitzgerald (New York: Farrar, Straus, and Giroux, 1970), 33.

meant either to draw men to the Redemption or to strengthen the redeemed in their grace. Were Jesus Christ not the sole Redeemer of the world, the priesthood would represent a heartless joke. Men would give up everything in order to sustain an illusion.

It is true that even widespread beliefs, whoever sows them, about the absence of a cause for redemption cannot eliminate the Redemption won by Christ. Nor can it eliminate the need for priests. The "cause" remains whether we recognize it as a cause or not. What is more important, the Redemption won by the Blood of Christ remains whether one receives it or not. In like manner, the priesthood abides whether people recognize the need for it or not. It has been held that God will never allow the priesthood to disappear. There will always be someone on the face of the earth to hand on to a next generation what he himself has received from the Apostles.

In God's providence, the Church in the United States has not reached the point where one has to search for an authentic bearer of the apostolic tradition. Most dioceses and clerical religious institutes still celebrate priestly ordinations annually. Indeed, recent reports indicate a small increase in the number of priests and seminarians. But those who today present themselves for priestly ordination must confront the general circumstance that Flannery O'Connor has observed, even as they display by their willingness to become priests her buoyant optimism founded on a key truth of Catholic and divine faith. She expresses this conviction with the clarity of a poet: "I think that the Church is the only thing that makes the terrible world we are coming to endurable."

It belongs especially to the priest to ensure that the people of each generation recognize that the Church is the only thing that makes this terrible world endurable and that they proceed to embrace her rule, her teachings, and her sacraments. The priest accomplishes this sacred mission when, as Head, he governs effectively that portion of the Church confided to his care. He realizes this objective when, as Shepherd, he teaches clearly the full truth about the moral life. He completes this vocation when, as Bridegroom, he loves those for whose eternal well-being he has been given responsibility. Without the legitimate exercise of divine governance prefigured in the "dominion" over creation that God confided to Adam, the world would not be a better place, as the secular myth suggests; it would return to the original chaos. Without sound instruction in the moral life, the world would not discover greater freedom, as the secular myth suggests; it would, as another poet puts it, become a place of internecine warfare. Without priests who love people as Christ loves them, the world would just plain fall apart. Aquinas links the stability of the Christian religion and therefore of the world to the hypostatic union: "If," he says, "the human nature is not united to the Word in person, it would not be united at all. To hold this would be to abolish belief in the Incarnation and to undermine [*subruere*] the entire Christian faith."[4]

What does this analysis inspired by Aquinas and Flannery O'Connor say about priestly formation and those who are involved immediately in enabling it? Ms. O'Connor provides a clue to answer this question. She wrote in one of her letters, "If you believe in the divinity of Christ, you have to cherish the world at the same time you struggle to endure it." I don't know whether Flannery O'Connor had been exposed to the teachings of St. Josemaría Escrivá. But the phrase "to cherish the world" reminds me of one of his better-known essays, "On Passionately Loving the World." In any event, the message is clear: the priest must proceed with an eye to cherishing the world that he wants to redeem. He cannot lament the world. This axiom holds true however much the cause for redemption in the actual lives that people live comes startlingly to his attention. Warrant for this posture is found at the end of the creation narrative: "And so it happened, God looked at everything he had made, and he found it very good" (Gen 1:31). This goodness remains in the consummation of Christ's priesthood: for Christ, observes Aquinas who quotes Hebrews, "is a high priest of the good things that have come to be."[5]

Once the seminarian and priest begin to cherish the world, then they will discover the freedom to redeem the world. He will find the cause for redemption in the lives that people live, that is, their sins, an invitation

4. *ST* III, q. 2, a. 2.
5. See *ST* III, q. 22, a. 5, quoting Heb 9:11.

to preach to them the Good News of Jesus Christ. Above all, the priest will find new satisfaction in his vocation inasmuch as he will come to appreciate the indispensability of his Headship, his Shepherding, and his Bridal love in a world that mistakes power for authority, relativism for moral truth, and egoism for love. This noble vocation imposes grave responsibilities on those who aspire to it and who exercise what they have already received. Each must examine his conscience: does the responsible exercise of priestly authority suffer from my lack of fortitude? Does the charge to instruct in the moral life provide me with an excuse to tinker with moral truth? Finally, the tough one. Does my pledge to love as Christ loves suffer diminishment when I find myself unloved? We will be helped in this particular *examen* on priestly virtue by a final instruction from Flannery O'Connor: "There is nothing harder or less sentimental than Christian realism." Thomists surely may say the same about sacramental realism.

The priest stands as a prophet of Christian realism. Indeed, O'Connor's phrase "nothing harder or less sentimental" affords, in my view, a glimpse into the reason that only the male of the species—"male and female he created them"—are admitted to priestly ordination. Women of course also must stand as witnesses to Christian realism. But they do it differently. St. Scholastica wanted the consolation of her saintly brother for a little longer than he wanted to provide it. She prayed and God took her side. A downpour came, and St. Benedict and his monks could not return back up the hill to Monte Cassino. Gregory the Great records this incident in his *Dialogues*, his life of Benedict. He presents Scholastica as a bearer of the feminine genius *ante nomen*. Women also hold an indispensable and irreplaceable vocation in the world and in the Church. Their vocation, however, does not extend to the priesthood. Still, priest and seminarian can learn from SS. Benedict and Scholastica. We can imitate their measured, patient approach to the construction of the good. Europe was not tamed overnight. But monasteries of men and women have left their mark on our civilization. After all, without Benedictine monasteries, it would be difficult to imagine what form the Church to which priests are called to serve would take. We also would not today enjoy the same Thomas Aquinas that the Dominicans received. He came to them away from Monte Cassino.

THE PRIEST AND PREACHING IN THE CHURCH

The Church charges her bishops to preach the truth of the Gospel.[6] Preaching therefore stands at the summit of the priest's daily activities inasmuch as the preaching of the Gospel precedes the confession of faith and the enactment of the sacraments. Preaching, faith, and sacraments establish the pattern of priestly life and devotion. Because diocesan priests form first and foremost the collaborators with the local bishop, the diocesan priest bears the responsibility of communicating to the world, especially to those in his parish, divine truth. Within the limits established for him, no one else enjoys the authority to discharge this saving activity. The Church describes the task of the priest to preach divinely revealed truths about God and man as a *munus*—gift and burden. Aquinas observes that one etymology of the Latin word for priest, *sacerdos*, comes from the two Latin words *sacra* and *dans*. The priest communicates sacred things, God's things, divine gifts to the people. The background for this exegesis is found in Malachi 2:7: "The lips of the priest are to keep knowledge, and instruction is to be sought from his mouth."

The Benedictine abbot Blessed Columba Marmion (1858–1923) wrote once of the priesthood of Jesus Christ that the "privilege of this priesthood is to ensure the return of creation in its entirety to the Master of all things."[7] The thought is daunting. To return all that God made to him, the Master of all things. To restore. To transform. To elevate. These actions represent the privilege of Christ's priesthood. "The return of creation in its entirety" occurs mystically each time that a priest celebrates the Eucharist. In a way that surpasses our understanding and that is generally ignored by contemporary theology and catechesis, each Mass (whether

6. See *Lumen gentium*, §25.

7. See Columba Marmion, OSB, *Christ: The Ideal of the Priest* (San Francisco: Ignatius, 2005), 17.

a congregation is present or not) effects a change in all that exists, the material world, the spiritual world, and the composite creature, man. At the altar, the priest touches every part of creation. When he enacts the Eucharistic transformation of those material elements that come from both the earth and the work of human hands, he makes everything that God created holy. So we pray in the Third Eucharistic Prayer: "Haec Hostia nostrae reconciliationis proficiat, quaesumus Domine, ad totius mundi pacem atque salutem"—"May this Sacrifice of our reconciliation, we pray, O Lord, advance the peace and salvation of all the world."

There exists a duty incumbent on the priesthood that precedes logically if not ontologically the celebration of the Eucharist. St. Paul signals this obligation when he exclaims, "How beautiful are the feet of those who bring the good news!" The text is found at Romans 10:15. St. Paul refers to the feet of the priest, whereas the prophet Malachi refers to his lips. Both evoke a priest who brings to his people divine truth. Preaching is not ordered first and foremost to stirring up the sentiments of believers, making hearts strangely warmed. It is not ordered to supply ersatz psychological counseling on how to get along in life without too much chagrin. It certainly is not ordered to providing your hearers with an everyman's guide to the academic exegesis of the text assigned to be proclaimed on a given day in the Church of Christ. Preaching is ordered to return creation to the Master. In its entirety. This challenge is more than daunting. Just think of all the things that go wrong. Think of the mistakes people make. Think of the errors that men try to validate. No wonder the priest can never go it alone. To return everything to the Master, the priest must remain united with the Church. When the priest remains a faithful collaborator with his bishop, the "return" that preaching effects is accomplished infallibly. Again, Blessed Marmion: the "privilege of this priesthood is to ensure the return of creation in its entirety to the Master of all things."

Why is preaching indispensable for the return of creation in its entirety to the Master of all things? To answer this question, we need first to consider another: What else besides the acceptance of a common truth can ensure harmony in creation? Whence comes the model for this harmony, this reconciliation of all things in Christ? The answer is simple. The divine Wisdom. The Logos. That is why this reconciling work falls to the Catholic priest. Only he is configured to the eternal Word by reason of the ontological bond that he enjoys with the Incarnate Son. So we must conclude that the communication of divine wisdom belongs to the priest by divine right. He is, if you will, ordained to preach. Contemporary discussions about lay preaching tend to miss this important point. Strictly speaking, there is no lay preaching in the Church of Christ. Only those configured to Christ receive the divine wisdom so that they can announce the good news. No wonder the late Pope John Paul II directs that the priest "approach the word with a docile and prayerful heart."[8] The "privilege of this priesthood is to ensure the return of creation in its entirety to the Master of all things."

Preaching constitutes a burden for the priest. Restoring Babel is not easy. The Genesis (11:1–9) account of the Tower of Babel graphically illustrates the need for the "return of creation to the Master of all things" that the priesthood of Jesus Christ makes possible. "Let us then go down and there confuse their language, so that one will not understand what another says" (Gen 11:7). The collapse of Babel, note well, represents a fracture of truth only, not a division of languages. Because after Babel men did not each behold the same truth, Babel sets men one against the other. Friendship is thus destroyed. By definition, friends see the same truth. The preaching of the Gospel is not ordered to restore the human race to a common language, if one ever existed, but to restore all people to a common truth. Pastoral charity, the third burden of the priest after preaching and the sacraments, is ordered to unite the human race in one friendship. Aquinas takes pains to point out that the priesthood of Christ not only removes the *macula culpae*—that is, the stain of sin that turns hearts away from God—but also satisfies the *reatus poenae*—that is, the liability for punishment that Christ's atonement expiates.

Babel also represents the hubris of the human spirit. The specific arrogance expresses itself in the assumption that making progress justifies whatsoever human activity, even when the progress constitutes a

8. See *Pastores Dabo Vobis*, §26.

presumption against the Master of all things. Thus the word of the Lord: "nothing will later stop them from doing whatever they presume to do" (Gen 11:6). Put into the language of today, Babel reveals the penchant in the human race to relativize truth and to let political power guide the course of world events. Political power both threatens and cajoles. No one is immune from its pull. So the words in the Gospel of Mark that Christ addresses to every Christian believer take on a special meaning for the priest and seminarian: "Whoever is ashamed of me and of my words in this faithless and sinful generation, the Son of Man will be ashamed of when he comes in his Father's glory with the holy angels" (Mk 8:38). No priest should aspire to make Christ ashamed of him. For it remains the case that the "privilege of this priesthood is to ensure the return of creation in its entirety to the Master of all things."

THE PRIEST, MORAL INSTRUCTION, AND RECONCILIATION

The truth about human living and the moral guidance required to ensure that one lives a happy and godly life comes infallibly from the Church of Christ. Priests are ordained to serve as communicators of sound moral instruction. Again, Aquinas develops his theology of the priesthood from the text of Malachi, *Legem requirunt ex ore eius.*—"They shall seek the law at his [the priest's] mouth."[9] No wonder the Church reminds her pastors and bishops: "It is our common duty, and even before that our common grace, as pastors and bishops of the Church, to teach the faithful the things which lead them to God, just as the Lord Jesus did with the young man in the Gospel."[10] Moral instruction provides more than ethical guidance for individuals. The Church instructs nations about the Law of the Lord. The priest takes on the challenge of speaking the full truth about important goods such as human life, sexual activity, and the establishment of just relations among peoples and nations. Law and reconciliation. These are the occupations of the priest that Aquinas identifies as

9. *ST* III, q. 22, a. 1.
10. *Veritatis splendor,* §114.

constitutive of priestly identity, the specific mediation of the priest. We should reflect on the nature of the priestly office as one of reconciliation. For "only priests who have received the faculty of absolving from the authority of the Church can forgive sins in the name of Christ."[11]

From time to time, we discover perspectives on Christian living that expose what is difficult in Christian virtue. The reason for this exposure may be found in the Passion of Christ. The whole Christian tradition describes the Passion and death of Christ as the most difficult of those deaths suffered for the sake of righteousness. Even when it may appear that other martyrs endured harsher or more painful deaths, the saints point out that Christ's sufferings remain the most exquisite inasmuch as he is a divine person. In his human nature, Christ experiences the sufferings of the Cross to a maximal degree because of the unique sensitivity to truth and goodness that his human soul enjoyed. In the end, we confront the reality that human reason controls even the felt experience of suffering. The more refined the person, the more acute the suffering.

Why did God surrender his Son to the most acute suffering? One could hypothetically expose the same question by asking, "Why did not God avail himself of someone with reduced capacity to experience sufferings?" This of course was the case with the sacrifices and holocausts of the Old Law. The paschal lambs offered throughout the period of the Old Law did not enjoy the capacity to regret or, for that matter, to fear their fate. To reply to an objection that Christ is identified with none of the animals—buck goat, she-goat, or calf—used under the Old Law as sin offerings, Aquinas refers to Origen's Commentary on John 6:33: "although various species of animals were offered under the Old Law, the morning and evening sacrifice offered each day was a lamb. This signified that the sacrifice of the lamb, that is of Christ, was to be the consummation of all other sacrifices."[12] God sends his very own Son, "the lamb of God" (Jn 1:29). A Lenten weekday preface calls to mind the motive for this redemptive Incarnation: "As we recall [during the season of Lent] the great events that gave us new life in Christ, you [Loving Father] bring the

11. *CCC*, §1495.
12. *ST* III, q. 22, a. 4, ad 3.

image of your Son to perfection within us." The "great events" that this preface refers to include the most bitter passion and death of our Lord Jesus Christ.

The short answer to why Christ had to endure the maximal sufferings in order to restore and to perfect in us his very own image is simple to state: the sin of Adam, the sin of nature, the original sin. Put more precisely, the magnitude of this original sin requires the maximal satisfaction. As Flannery O'Connor has reminded us, people forget easily about original sin. The problem, however, is this: original sin is one problem that oblivion does not make go away. It is at this juncture of sin and redemption that I like to locate the vocation of the priest, especially the diocesan priest who is obliged to confront the effects of original sin in the people confided to his care. The prophetic burden of the Catholic priest is foreshadowed in the words of the prophet Daniel when he reminds the people of the Old Law: "Justice, O Lord, is on your side" (Dan 9:7). Daniel's prayer for mercy should ring fresh in our ears, especially because we have One greater than Daniel here. "Go and learn the meaning of the words, 'I desire mercy, not sacrifice.' I did not come to call the righteous but sinners" (Mt 9:13). Both testaments bear witness to the truth that God's justice does not pass away. Jesus had to suffer the most because of the widespread nature of sin in the world. He had to suffer most because of the attachment to sin that remains even in the baptized. He had to suffer the most because people like you and me needed the very Savior that God in his mercy sent.

There is good news in Christ's most bitter sufferings for our sins: St. Francis de Sales (1567–1622), one of the first outstanding diocesan priests of the modern period, urges that whatever the degree or nature of our sins and shortcomings, we should not judge even ourselves. "Our Saviour has bequeathed the Sacrament of Penitence and Confession to His Church, in order that therein we may be cleansed from all our sins, however and whenever we may have been soiled thereby. Therefore, my child, never allow your heart to abide heavy with sin, seeing that there is so sure and safe a remedy at hand."[13] The priest can announce this

13. St. Francis de Sales, *Introduction to the Devout Life*, part 2, chap. 19.

spiritual maxim with great profit. In fact, one could argue that a young man would want to spend his life telling people about the consolation that only Christ brings to the world and to themselves.

We are discussing the indispensable and the "irreplaceable" vocation of the diocesan priest in the life of the Church, as Pope Benedict has expressed it.[14] Moral instruction remains indispensable to the happy lives of individuals, as well as the good ordering of the societies that people form. We have reflected on what is required of the Savior of the world to rectify the disorders that sin introduces into us and into our communities. One reason for the practice of clerical celibacy is that the man who will go forth to combat Satan and his wiles needs himself a special source of spiritual strength that chaste celibacy provides.[15] Celibacy sets a man apart. Or should. The celibate priest takes the time to discover the depth of what the Gospel teaches about human happiness. He becomes an expert in beatitude. So he is able to teach with authority, an authority that comes from his priestly ordination, about the happy life. Not only is

14. "The Role of Priests Is Irreplaceable," Vatican Information Service, September 17, 2009: "This morning in Castelgandolfo the Holy Father received a group of prelates from the National Conference of Bishops of Brazil (Northeast 2), who have just completed their 'ad limina' visit. Highlighting the functions of the various members of the Church, the Pope explained how 'the particular identity of priests and laity must be seen in the light of the essential difference between priestly ministry and the "common priesthood." Hence it is important to avoid the secularisation of clergy and the "clericalisation" of the laity.' 'In this perspective,' he went on, 'the lay faithful must undertake to give expression in real life—also through political commitment—to the Christian view of anthropology and the social doctrine of the Church. While priests must distance themselves from politics in order to favour the unity and communion of all the faithful, thus becoming a point of reference for everyone.' Benedict XVI indicated that 'the lack of priests does not justify a more active and abundant participation of the laity. The truth is that the greater the faithful's awareness of their own responsibilities within the Church, the clearer becomes the specific identity and inimitable role of the priest as pastor of the entire community, witness to the authenticity of the faith, and dispenser of the mysteries of salvation in the name of Christ the Head. The function of the clergy is essential and irreplaceable in announcing the Word and celebrating the Sacraments, especially the Eucharist . . . For this reason it is vital to ask the Lord to send workers for His harvest; and it is necessary that priests express joy in their faithfulness to their identity.'"

15. At the 150th anniversary of the death of the Cure of Ars, which the Church commemorated in 2009–2010 with the Year for Priests, Benedict XVI indicated that St. John Mary Vianney "continues even now to be a model for priests, especially in living a life of celibacy as a requirement for the total giving of self, expressed through that pastoral charity which Vatican Council II presents as the unifying centre of a priest's being and actions." "Role of Priests Is Irreplaceable," September 17, 2009.

he able, but also he is bound. "It is our common duty, and even before that our common grace, as Pastors and Bishops of the Church, to teach the faithful the things which lead them to God, just as the Lord Jesus did with the young man in the Gospel."[16] But the Lord does not only teach the way to happiness; he shows us the way to happiness in his own person, as St. Thomas Aquinas says at the start of the *tertia pars* of his *Summa*. For the priest, this showing takes on special significance in the sacrament of reconciliation. Priests are indispensable and irreplaceable for forgiving sins in the name of God, which is the only real form of forgiveness. For "only priests who have received the faculty of absolving from the authority of the Church can forgive sins in the name of Christ."[17] Without this forgiveness readily available in the world, there is no imagining what will overtake the People of God and, ultimately, the human race.

THE PRIEST, COMMUNION, AND THE EUCHARIST

It is at the Eucharist that priests exercise in a supreme degree their sacred office.[18] Christ confides to his priests the most sacred of the gifts that he bestows on his Bride, the Church. There is no greater dignity on earth than the one that a man receives when he is ordained. This dignity originates not in the man's own human qualities or even in his legitimately recognized virtues, but in the ability, sacramentally established, to bring God down to earth. The priest acts in the person of Jesus Christ. This vicarious activity requires that God unite the priest to the very Person of Christ in a way that the Church describes as "ontological." That is, in his very being. "In this bond between the Lord Jesus and the priest, an ontological and psychological bond, a sacramental and moral bond, is the foundation and likewise the power for that 'life according to the Spirit' and that 'radicalism of the Gospel' to which every priest is called today and which is fostered by ongoing formation in its

16. *Veritatis splendor*, §114.

17. *CCC*, §1495.

18. See *Lumen gentium*, §28.

spiritual aspect."[19] More than anything else, this ontological bond is required because of the words that the priest alone can pronounce, "This is my body," "This is my blood." Aquinas places the priest and the Eucharist within the context of the Resurrection. When he asks whether the priesthood of Christ will remain forever, he replies to the objection that the saints no longer require the sacraments as follows: "The saints in heaven will have no further need of Christ's priestly atonement; yet they still depend on Christ, cleansed of their sins though they are, for their glory derives from him."[20]

The liturgical readings assigned to the Easter season introduce us into the grace to be a priest. The mystery unfolds on two levels. One is historical: Acts of the Apostles recounts the beginning of the Church. Therein the priest discovers his pedigree, his genealogy, his heritage: "We must obey God rather than men" (Acts 5:29). So replied Peter to the Sanhedrin when the latter tried to persuade the Apostles to stop proclaiming the power of the Risen Christ. It is from this apostolic witness that the priest finds his bearings. Because he receives from bishops what they themselves receive from the Apostles, the priest recognizes that his vocation makes no sense outside of the historical continuity that the Church enjoys with those who were witnesses to Christ's Resurrection: "The God of our ancestors raised Jesus, though you had him killed by hanging him on a tree" (Acts 5:30). As a result, the Catholic priest finds himself inserted into a sacred history. He exists because of a grace that exists outside of history. Call it resurrection time.

To live in resurrection time means that the priest can never fully explain himself in purely historical, horizontal, temporal categories. After all, what is time? It is simply a measure of motion, as we learn from Aristotle: "Tempus nihil aliud est quam numerus motus secundum prius et posterius."[21] Many things that the priest is counseled to observe reflect his unique, sacred, graced relationship to the temporal.

Celibacy of course affords the best example. The priest removes himself from the rhythms of marriage, in all their complexity, so that

19. *Pastores Dabo Vobis*, §72.
20. *ST* III, q. 22, a. 5, ad 1.
21. See Aquinas's *Commentary on Aristotle's Physics*, bk. IV, 17, no. 10.

Christ's people can encounter a man whose heart and mind are set exclusively on God, his Truth, his mysteries. People today do not talk much about celibacy for contemplation. The fact of the matter is that the Christian tradition considers it the principal reason for the bishop and priest and monk to forego marriage. Marriage is a thing of this earth. Very much of this earth. Indeed, even the most sanctified of marriages remains of this earth. Married life is pleasurable, but it is also distracting from pondering those revealed truths that can only be received in the purity of faith.

Clerical attire is another. The priest dresses differently. Black suits and collars, cassocks, sacred vestments. This apparel is not a uniform. What the priest wears provides external signs of his priestly consecration. Removing them without a clear and compelling reason creates ambiguity in the minds of the people and, in all likelihood, in the mind of the priest. Evangelical "simplicity" is another.[22] The priest lives outside the ordinary attachments of the consumer society inasmuch as he knows that his real treasure resides in a place that only the Resurrection allows entry. Ecclesial obedience also reveals that the priest cherishes his privileged relationship with the local bishop.

Once we understand the message of the Acts of the Apostles, we find ourselves in a position to say some of the things that the priest is not. In a word, he is none of those things whose existence depends exclusively on the temporal, that is, on the measure of motion. The priest is not a sociologist. Sociology represents one large effort to measure the collective motion of peoples. Informative though it may be, the priest cannot operate in sociological categories. They limit him, and eventually reduce him. This is not a hypothesis, but unfortunately the sad experience of those priests who, after the Second Vatican Council, wrongly assumed that the call to sanctify the *saeculum*, the temporal order, meant embracing mainly those categories intelligible only to the temporal order. The priest is not a politician. Politics is the art of governing the temporal order, and canon law reminds us that the priest is not a politician.[23] The one who exercises spiritual governance and headship cannot at the

22. See *CIC*, §282, para. 1.

23. See *CIC*, §285, para. 3.

same time exercise civil governance. In the modern world at least, this arrangement does not work. Historians debate whether it once worked in the periods of caesaropapism. Note that it is not the pragmatism of modern politics that alone prohibits the priest from being a politician. The reason lies in the stricture that politics puts on walking in resurrection time. No political authority enjoys access to "the one who comes from above" (Jn 3:31). The priest is not a psychological social worker. Modern psychology acknowledges solutions that are time bound. Freud is criticized for having an archaeology of the human psyche but not a teleology, an eschatology, and so no openness to transcendence. Much confusion exists about the place that psychology holds in Catholic life. This is the case because many of the words that psychologists employ are those that come from the Gospels: love, unity, peace, joy, even forgiveness, although this quality of soul is difficult for even well-trained psychologists to engender in those patients whose only hope remains here below. "The one who is of the earth is earthly and speaks of earthly things" (Jn 3:31).

The second level of the Easter mystery unfolds in St. John's Gospel. John the Evangelist. John the Divine. John whose symbol is the eagle because the ancients recognized that his revelations soar to the heights like the proverbial bird of Jove. The Gospel of John informs the priest about his true identity. The priest who dwells in resurrection time is sent to reveal the Trinity. This is the lesson that Nicodemus discovered when he asked about rebirth. No rebirth in the order of nature, nothing of the temporal, no coming twice out of the womb. The rebirth that the priest brings comes in the name of the Father, of the Son, and of the Holy Spirit. Baptism. Grace. Virtues, gifts, beatitudes. All the supernatural things—the gifts—that come from above. So the priest keeps his eyes set upon the Paschal Mystery. He looks at the things that are above where the risen Christ measures, if there exists a measure, resurrection time, "for their glory derives from him."[24]

John the Divine is also John the Celibate, which is why he receives Mary. It is also why he is the one to administer the sacraments to Mary.

24. *ST* III, q. 22, a. 5, ad 1.

There exist representations of St. John the Evangelist giving Holy Communion to Mary. The privilege of the priest that surpasses all other considerations is the Holy Eucharist. What psychologists seek to help people find, the Eucharist bestows through the hands of the priest, which is what the Church teaches. The Eucharist remains in this world the inalienable source of charity and unity. It is not a ritual act in which certain persons so inclined choose to participate. When the Mass is offered, the first beneficiary is God. He receives again the pleasing interior sacrifice of his only Son. From this sacrifice flows the graces that the world needs to survive. Peace and joy follow upon love and unity. Without one or the other, there is not a chance of any individual finding the tranquility of order or the permanent exhilaration that true joy produces in the human spirit. If there is a reason for why the diocesan priest is both indispensable and irreplaceable, the foundation for this reason will be disclosed in the celebration of the Eucharist. Without the priest, there is no Eucharist. Without the Eucharist, the world cannot survive.

The Eucharist of course exists in time. The priest receives from the bishops the power to consecrate that Christ confided to his Apostles on the night before he died. But the Eucharist belongs to both levels of the Paschal Mystery, that is, the one represented by the Acts of the Apostles as well as that represented by the Gospel of John. The Eucharist provides a pledge of eternal life. This pledge is more of a down payment than a promissory note. The more the priest shapes the Christian people with his Eucharistic caring, the more the Christian community begins to look like a group ready for heaven. The more the human community soars, if you will. Like an eagle.

Celebrating the Eucharist reveals what is unique about the Catholic priest. Eucharistizing, sacrificing, celebrating the sacrament of Christ's Body and Blood defines the man who wants to be a priest. So those who aspire to the priesthood must start by learning to love the Eucharist. Better to put oneself in the presence of the Blessed Sacrament for thirty minutes than to mull in your head, alone in your room for hours, whether one should be a priest or not. This pondering is also served by taking up the life of chaste celibacy now. Chastity in relationships to be sure. Purity, also, in conduct with one's person. Easter makes the thought that a young man can live without procuring sexual pleasure bearable. When the Lord, at night, undertakes his celebrated exchange with Nicodemus, he consoles him with the news that God's grace is both true and sufficient: "For the one whom God sent speaks the words of God. He does not ration his gifts of the Spirit" (Jn 3:34). Celibate love opens the heart of a man so that he remains as receptive as possible to the unrationed Spirit, so that a man, once ordained, abides in resurrection time, so that the priest will announce to the world the one Truth that makes it endurable.

Unchastity and impurity becloud one's vision and sully one's hands. Neither circumstance renders a man well disposed to receive the Eucharist. Mortal sins prohibit receiving the Eucharist. In this discipline that the Church establishes for Eucharistic communion, we catch a glimpse of the profound sacramentality that the Eucharist exercises in the world. In a word, the Eucharist changes us. Unlike ordinary food that we assimilate, the Eucharist is meant to assimilate us into its substance. When this happens, we find ourselves conformed to the Risen Lord. When this conformity that the sacraments of Easter, especially baptism, make possible reaches the whole world, we achieve the consummation of all things. It is worth more than one lifetime to become an irreplaceable instrument of a grace that is so indispensable. To forego wife and family is nothing compared to the supreme value that the spiritual man recognizes each time that he celebrates the Holy Sacrifice of the Mass. The Mass gives sacramental expression, so long as the Church remains a pilgrim, to the interior sacrifice of all those who belong to Christ. It is this interior sacrifice that abides forever among the saints: "Now Christ, by his passion, won the glory of resurrection, not in virtue of the sacrifice of the victim, since this was done to make reparation for sin, but in virtue of the act of worship of his by which, under the influence of his love, he submitted with humility to his passion."[25] Aquinas could have given no better description of what the Roman Catholic priest is about.

25. *ST* III, q. 22, a. 4, ad 2.

CHAPTER 8

SCHOLARSHIP AND SANCTITY

A Lesson Aquinas Teaches the Priest and Seminarian

This essay considers the relationship between the knowledge of God's truth and the sanctity of a life conformed to Christ's image. Father Cessario explains that "holiness of life" and the "embrace of the true" are not optional for the priest and seminarian. In order to illustrate this point, he summarizes the writings of the Benedictine Monk Dom Jean Leclercq on "the love of learning and the desire for God." Truth and love—theology and sanctity—are inseparable realities. "Because nothing is loved unless it is first known, the love of learning inevitably leads to the desire for God." Knowing God is of vital importance for loving God, and "the human mind is made to know the Highest Truth, and this pursuit proves impossible when we find ourselves consumed by vicious disorders." The moral virtues support the intellectual virtues. Thus moral life, asceticism, and prayer are indispensible elements within the priest's "'specific' vocation to holiness" (*PDV*, §20). These three support and enable the theological life and its proper sanctity. Finally, knowledge of the sacred Scriptures, the Church's theological

Originally published as "Scholarship and Sanctity: A Lesson Aquinas Teaches the Priest and Seminarian," *Nova et Vetera* 8, no. 2 (2010): 233–49. Reprinted by permission.

tradition, and the perennial philosophy remains an essential part of the Catholic cleric's formation in any century of the Church's history. Today more than ever, "the world needs wise diocesan priests who desire God ardently."

> It is not praxis that creates truth but truth
> that should serve as the basis of praxis.
> —Pope Benedict XVI in an
> address to Catholic educators,
> April 17, 2008

The Dominican saint and scholar whom the Church calls the Common Doctor, Thomas Aquinas (1224/25–74), instructs us that "the true is the good of the intellect; for an intellect is said to be good because it knows the true."[1] Today, however, many persons think primarily about knowledge as a tool of expediency, that is, as something that helps them to achieve an objective. While many care only about the successful, few, it seems, devote much time to pursuit of the true. For instance, college students oftentimes think of their studies as a means to attain career goals. In other words, they instrumentalize their lessons. Again today, professional and proprietary schools, courses, and programs that train people to supply services (and so find employment) tend to fare better than schools, courses, and programs that instruct in art, literature, and what we still broadly call liberal studies.

Seminaries have not been preserved from these professionalizing tendencies in higher education. Nor have seminarians been preserved from courting an instrumentalist view of human knowledge. Since the 1970s, seminary education in the United States has been influenced, I would aver unduly, by the standards and ideals set by the professional accrediting associations. Take, for example, the Association of Theological Schools, which follows a professional model of ministry broadly construed to accommodate its ecumenical constituency. Tensions inevitably arise; for example, between the requirements of practical learning based

1. Thomas Aquinas, *Summa contra Gentiles*, trans. Anton C. Pegis (Notre Dame, IN: University of Notre Dame Press, 1975), bk. 1, ch. 71.

on the supervised social work model and the liberal studies traditionally offered to clerics.

The English word "clerisy" gives us a clue about the origin of the word "cleric": clerisy means a distinct class of learned or literary people. Since the development in the sixteenth and seventeenth centuries of seminaries, Catholic clerics have been formed to become learned and literary men. The Church underwent a hard lesson at the time of the Protestant Reform, illustrated in a famous dispute between Catholics and reformers held at Lausanne in 1536. Not one Catholic cleric could be found to answer the humanist reformers' objections that, because the word "sacrament" could not be found in the New Testament, the sacraments must represent superstitious historical accretions to Christianity.[2] Because no priest was able to deal with the issue, a Catholic doctor volunteered to reply. He explained that the whole New Testament was about sanctifying the mind—*sacra mens*—and so the text refers throughout to sacraments that make the soul holy. The Greek scholars scoffed, and the Swiss Canton of Vaud passed over to the reform of Zwingli and Calvin.

The word "liberal" in the phrase "liberal arts" comes from the Latin for "free." Historically, then, liberal studies were meant for those citizens who enjoyed the leisure to think, even though thinking about the traditional liberal arts—for instance, the Trivium, grammar, rhetoric, dialectics—involves forms of doing—that is, language, oratory, and logic.[3] Roughly until the high Middle Ages, those other than nobles and rich persons who received a liberal education were almost exclusively Catholic clerics. Priests became the learned men in the street. The Church made them free for this purpose. Other persons who were not free enjoyed no leisure and so were obliged to engage in servile work to ensure their livelihood. They received an education in *technē*. That is, they

2. For further information, see Eric Junod, *La dispute de Lausanne 1536: La théologie reformeé après Zwingli et avant Calvin*, Bibliothéque Historique Vaudoise 90 (Lausanne: Bibliothéque Historique Vaudoise, 1988).

3. The Trivium, the *artes sermocinales*—grammar, rhetoric, and dialectic (language, oratory, logic)—and the Quadrivium, the *artes reales* or *physicae*—arithmetic, geometry, astronomy, and music. The arts admittedly were considered perfections of the practical intellect (*recta ratio factibilium*), whereas prudence the *recta ratio agibilium*.

were taught how to accomplish certain tasks but not how to think about the highest principles or causes of the effects that they produced. Today, even the highest form of technological expertise ordinarily finds its rationale in a task-ordered making of things, whether they be microchips or spaceships.

Cardinal Newman reminds us that we proceed at great peril when we forget that the perfection, the good, of the human intellect is the possession of the true and not the attainment of whatsoever bits of learning, including the acquisition of practical knowledge useful for solving a here-and-now problem.[4] When we fail to reach out for the knowledge of the Highest Truth, the stakes become very high inasmuch as the human person stands to lose what is most important in human life. The Church speaks clearly to the point: "When the sense of God is lost, the sense of man is also threatened and poisoned, as the Second Vatican Council concisely states: 'Without the Creator the creature would disappear ... But when God is forgotten the creature itself grows unintelligible.'"[5] In other words, the human race risks losing the truth about what it means to be human. Perhaps more today than in Newman's period, what is at stake is not only how to achieve the best form of education but also how to preserve the dignity of the human person. T. S. Eliot (1888–1965) was once asked what future he foresaw for our civilization. He replied, "Internecine fighting ... People killing one another in the streets."[6]

Aquinas clearly grasped the connection between knowledge and the good of persons. He replied to those who used the text of 1 Corinthians 8:1, "Knowledge puffs up," as a weapon against those clerics who devoted themselves to study by saying that "the text applies when science is without love."[7] In other words, knowledge inflates with pride only when knowledge is separated from the embrace of the good. We return to Aquinas's notion of what perfects the human intellect: "an intellect is said to be good because it knows the true."[8]

4. For one example, see Cardinal John Henry Newman, *The Idea of a University* (London: Longmans, Green, 1907), discourse 6, and note 21 below.

5. Pastoral Constitution on the Church in the Modern World, *Gaudium et spes*, §36, as cited in *Evangelium vitae*, §22.

6. Stephen Spender, "Remembering Eliot," *Sewanee Review* 74 (1966): 69.

7. *Contra impugnantes*, §11.

8. *ScG* I, ch. 71.

When one considers the high mindedness of Enlightenment thinkers, especially the continental ones, social critics and intellectual historians should regard our contemporary cultural circumstances as ironical. Who would have thought that "Dare to know"—*Sapere aude* (a phrase borrowed from Horace)—would have led eventually to a generation of twenty-first-century Westerners whose highest aspirations may include something so banal as manipulating Facebook?[9] Even when we consider the legitimate progress made in human knowing, such as computer technology and space exploration, the fact remains that the instrumentalization of human knowledge leaves the human person at a great disadvantage. If the only thing a person can do successfully is deploy knowledge to achieve practical results, there develops something incomplete in the person's character. Technocrats forget about loving the true. Thus we encounter the well-known stereotypes of the computer geek without the social skills to make friends or of the astronaut driven to senseless jealousy within a love triangle. In these examples and in other familiar figures from our culture, it is difficult to discover human persons in whom one finds verified the Thomist principle that "an intellect is said to be good because it knows the true." To put this otherwise, we discover smart but not wise people. "Wisdom," says Aquinas, "differs from mere science in looking at things from a greater light."[10]

We learn from what Aquinas teaches us about the divine image in man that nothing short of God fully satisfies the human mind.[11] The intellectually deprived children of educational programs dedicated to the acquisition of information or the aggregation of skills do not suffer definitive lobotomies. Their intellects still want to look at things from a greater height. They remain made in the image and likeness of God, and so by nature desire to know what is true. Indeed, to know the Highest Truth. Herein lies the challenge of Catholic seminary education. Seminarians must learn how to communicate sacred truth to people who have for-

9. See Horace, *Epistles*, I, 2, 40: "Boldly undertake the study of true wisdom: begin it forthwith."

10. *ST* II-II, q. 51, a. 4.

11. See my "Sonship, Sacrifice, and Satisfaction: The Divine Friendship in Aquinas and the Renewal of Christian Anthropology," *Letter and Spirit* 3 (2007): 71–93 (chap. 4, this volume).

gotten that truth alone satisfies the human creature. For the priest, the stakes are high. He must preach about the Highest Truth. About God. Otherwise, he falls under the stricture St. Paul enunciates: "If I preach the Gospel, this is no reason for me to boast, for an obligation has been imposed on me, and woe to me if I do not preach it" (1 Cor 9:16). Aquinas helps us to see the urgency behind the preaching act: "A man cannot believe unless the truth be proposed to him."[12]

The depreciation of the human good illustrates only one dimension of the difficulties that arise in a world saturated with *technē*. A concomitant result of the modern penchant to regard knowledge only as instrumental to the achievement of created objectives involves the eclipse of God from the conscious activity of human knowing. God becomes a hypothesis that is no longer useful. It is easy to assess the dimensions of this eclipse. When was the last time you heard someone immersed in *technē* talk about the contemplative life? Religion maybe, but not contemplative prayer. The secular philosophical currents of the modern period account largely for the present-day penchant to push God to the margins of thinkable objects. Seminarians study these movements and ideas in their philosophy and theology courses. At the same time, the best professors will instruct their students that the great Christian tradition does not accept the extraordinary myopia that displaces God from the apex of the intellectual life. Hegel's Absolute Spirit or Idea. Tillich's Ultimate Concern. Whitehead's Process. To discuss why God evaporates in modern philosophy and even from some contemporary theology belongs to another essay. But the fact is incontestable. For instance, not everyone who exegetes sacred Scripture shares the premise that Catholics do, namely, that God speaks. Thus divine revelation. Many advance the view that the sacred Scriptures represent man-made expressions of the legitimate aspirations of the human race. Call them, if you will, Neo-Feuerbachians.

Thomas Aquinas would find the modern proclivity to marginalize God a strange turn of events. To return to a point already made: he built his whole practical theology, his moral theology, upon the premise that

12. *ST* II-II, q. 1, a. 9.

"there can be no complete and final happiness for us save in the vision of God."[13] When Aquinas speaks about a vision of God, he is not referring to a sense vision, obviously. Rather, he means the human mind's capacity "to come through to the essence itself of the first cause" of all things that exist.[14] He is talking plainly about God, the maker of heaven and earth. In fact, Aquinas advances the startling claim that "all conscious things implicitly know God in everything they know."[15] Contemplative knowledge of God cannot be instrumentalized. The proof for this axiom is easy to state: nothing exists "beyond" God. So the saints commonly teach that only in God do our souls find rest. They have "come through to the essence itself of the first cause." The saints should be allowed to set the functional objectives for clerical education. The holy men and women who have done God's will throughout the ages demonstrate the Thomist axiom that theology forms a science of faith.

The classical theologians of the Christian era were not loath to borrow from ancient philosophy in order to enlarge upon and to express the truths of faith. It has been said that Aquinas baptized Aristotle. This long-accepted practice is discussed in the 1998 encyclical letter of Pope John Paul II, *Fides et ratio*. The pope in fact refers to the figure of St. Thomas Aquinas, saying: "Although he made much of the supernatural character of faith, the Angelic Doctor did not overlook the importance of its reasonableness; indeed he was able to plumb the depths and explain the meaning of this reasonableness."[16] Aquinas, it should be emphasized, does not obscure the truths of faith by preparing for them or examining them in light of the conclusions of ancient philosophy. He rather scrutinizes what is held by faith with the help of the philosophy available to him. So when Aquinas tells us that our highest and most perfect fulfillment lies in a knowledge that remains entirely without further usefulness, he reflects what Christian teachers have taught from the beginning. In fact, Aquinas actually builds upon an important element of divine revelation: "God, infinitely perfect and blessed in himself, in a

13. *ST* I-II, q. 3, a. 8. See also my *Introduction to Moral Theology*, rev. ed. (Washington, DC: Catholic University of America Press, 2013).

14. *ST* I-II, q. 3, a. 8.

15. *De veritate*, q. 22, a. 2, ad 1.

16. *Fides et ratio*, §43.

plan of sheer goodness freely created man to make him share in his own blessed life."[17]

In order to see the importance of knowing the true God and coming to share in his own blessed life, one may start with the New Testament. Recall for a moment what St. Paul says at the beginning of the Letter to the Romans about the natural knowledge of God: "For what can be known about God is evident to them, because God made it evident to them" (Rom 1:19). St. Paul refers of course to those who were without the benefit of the divine revelation made to Abraham, Isaac, and Jacob. The first chapter of the Letter to the Romans goes on to explain that those who failed to draw the right conclusions about God the creator of all things quickly fell prone to committing forms of immorality that brought them special shame: "And since they did not see fit to acknowledge God, God handed them over to their undiscerning mind to do what is improper" (Rom 1:28). The warning remains valid for us. St. Thomas, commenting on the text of Romans 13:12—"The night is far spent, the day is at hand"—says, "The entire stretch of our present life may be compared to night, because of the darkness of ignorance lying heavily on it; the state of future happiness today, for God's brightness shines on the blessed."[18]

The biblical and Thomist texts capture the theme of our discussion: holiness of life and embrace of the true. The theme merits special attention from seminarians. The priest above all must strive to offer a perspective that allows his parishioners to gain a glimpse of the whole, of a vision of life that encourages the sanctification of the intellect. "Wisdom," Aquinas again reminds us, "differs from mere science in looking at things from a greater light."[19] Cardinal Newman offers the same advice. He urges educators to give students perspective: "If one leads students to the mountaintop, so that they see all the surrounding territory, then they may go back and work in detail at some specific spot of the valley. But they will never forget that vista from the top of the mountain; all their work will have reference then to the whole terrain."[20] The seminarian

17. *CCC*, §1.

18. *On the Epistle to the Romans*, xiii, lect. 2.

19. *ST* II-II, q. 51, a. 4.

20. See Newman, *Idea of a University*, discourse 6, section 7, 139, 140: "I say then, if we

who has scaled the top of the mountain will, as a priest, know how to lead others there. That is, he will have gained a glimpse of God's brightness that shines on the blessed, at least as much as this is possible in the present life, and then may allow this blessed light to illuminate every other aspect of human life. This illuminating glimpse escapes those who spend all their time in the valleys.

THE LOVE OF LEARNING AND THE DESIRE FOR GOD

In the academic year 1955–56, a distinguished Benedictine monk, Dom Jean Leclercq, gave a series of lectures at Sant' Anselmo, the Benedictine college in Rome. He pointed out that in the twelfth century there were two kinds of preparatory schools, a school for monks and a school for clerics, that is, those who were destined to serve as diocesan priests. These latter studied in what was called the "exterior" school, a room not within the monastic enclosure. They received instruction in the seven liberal arts, the Trivium and the Quadrivium, which would prepare them for when they later attended schools of theology, often located near a cathedral. Monks, on the other hand, were educated differently. They were instructed individually in "interior" schools under the guidance of an abbot, a spiritual father, through the reading of the Bible and the Fathers, within the liturgical framework of the monastic life.[21]

---

would improve the intellect, first of all, we must ascend; we cannot gain real knowledge on a level; we must generalize, we must reduce to method, we must have a grasp of principles, and group and shape our acquisitions by means of them. It matters not whether our field of operation be wide or limited; in every case, to command it, is to mount above it. Who has not felt the irritation of mind and impatience created by a deep, rich country, visited for the first time, with winding lanes, and high hedges, and green steeps, and tangled woods, and every thing smiling indeed, but in a maze? The same feeling comes upon us in a strange city, when we have no map of its streets. Hence you hear of practised travellers, when they first come into a place, mounting some high hill or church tower, by way of reconnoitring its neighbourhood. In like manner, you must be above your knowledge, not under it, or it will oppress you; and the more you have of it, the greater will be the load." This citation of Newman's words comes from an address delivered by Louise Cowan at Thomas More College, Merrimack, New Hampshire. See the college's *Newsletter* 14, no. 3 (March 1997): 6–9.

21. Jean Leclercq, OSB, *The Love of Learning and the Desire for God: A Study of Monastic Culture*, trans. Catherine Misrahi (New York: Fordham University Press, 1974), 3.

We get a glimpse of this monastic pedagogy from the prologue of St. Bernard to his sermons on the Canticle of Canticles, where he addresses the young monks with these words: "The instruction that I address to you, my brothers, will differ from those I should deliver to people in the world, at least the manner will be different."[22] St. Bernard proceeds on the assumption that the monks already find themselves disposed to love the sacred text, and so he can speak to them not as searchers for but as lovers of what is true.

By referring to the provocative essay of Dom Jean Leclercq it is not my intention to comment on the distinctions that he introduces between scholastic and monastic theologies. Still less do I want to lend credence to the view that one should drive a wedge between professional studies for ministry and monastic studies for consecrated persons. The fact of the matter is that St. Thomas Aquinas has taught us how to combine both the salutary emphases of the monastic tradition with the reasoned argumentation that later developed within the scholastic tradition. It also has been argued that the birth of scholasticism was inevitable once ancient philosophy, especially Aristotle, became known to the universities of Europe from the twelfth century. In any case, Aquinas never lost sight of the importance of the affective theology that St. Bernard urged upon his monks. Aquinas's treatment of the gifts of the Holy Spirit, especially the gift of wisdom, affords a good example. Or we can turn to the *Summa contra Gentiles*, where Aquinas explains that "our intellect . . . extends to the infinite in understanding . . . But this ordination of the intellect would be in vain unless an infinite intelligible reality existed."[23] In other words, because nothing is loved unless it is first known, the love of learning inevitably leads to the desire for God.

Yearning is never absent from Aquinas's theology, although he admittedly prefers to express the affective movement of the soul in a way that one may call "intellectualist" rather than emotional. In any case, I return to the more than fifty-year-old lectures of Dom Leclercq to defend

22. Bernard of Clairvaux, "On the *Song of Songs* I," in *The Works of Bernard of Clairvaux*, vol. 2, trans. Kilian Walsh, OCSO (Spencer, MA: Cistercian, 1971), Sermon 1, "On the Title of the Book," 1.1; as cited in Leclercq, *Love of Learning*, 5, 6.

23. *ScG* I, ch. 43.

a thesis that today may be considered in some quarters quite controversial, namely, that every authentically Christian approach to knowledge remains monastic in character. This means that all learning is fundamentally contemplative. Study proceeds successfully only within the establishment of a real contact with God. This thesis holds especially true for the training of diocesan priests. Although things may have been different in St. Bernard's day, the fact of the matter is that in the reforms that followed upon Trent, reforms that still more or less inspire programs of priestly formation, the distinction between the exterior and interior classrooms was dissolved. All priests are expected to receive an affective training in theology. We call it human, spiritual, intellectual, and pastoral training.

St. Bernard of Clairvaux (1090–1153), as we have seen, exemplifies the monastic style of doing theology. He displays a surprisingly modern emphasis on experience. To return to his Prologue, Bernard says of the Old Testament book, the Song of Solomon, or the Canticle of Canticles: "Only the touch of the Spirit can inspire a song like this, and only personal experience can unfold its meaning. Let those who are versed in the mystery revel in it; let all others burn with desire rather to attain to this experience than merely to learn about it."[24] It would be a supreme anachronism to interpret St. Bernard's emphasis on experience according to the contemporary and fashionable but still Marxist-inspired views of experience. When people today talk about experience as a locus for learning, they usually proceed on the supposition that knowledge develops only from below, from the bottom up, so to speak, and that the task of the inquirer is to immerse himself as much as possible into the rhythms of the materialist evolution that governs the universe. On the contrary, St. Bernard held and expressly taught that in the knowledge of divine things, such as the text of a biblical author, it is God who really does the teaching. St. Bernard's understanding of experience approaches an affective knowing, an *amata notitia*. Really, an affective beholding. Aquinas later would take up this same point, observing that there is something of love in knowledge and something of knowledge in love:

24. Bernard, "On the *Song of Songs*," Sermon 1, 6.11.

"love of the word [*dilectio verbi*] ... is a beloved awareness [*amata notitia*]."[25] He learned this principle from his study of the divine persons of the Trinity.

Jean Leclercq recapitulates what St. Bernard emphasizes about the nature of monastic learning: "Just as there is no theology without moral life and asceticism, so there is no theology without prayer."[26] Prayer is the way that we let God instruct us. Bernard of course shifts the movement of learning from the one who seeks (*quaeritur*) knowledge to the one who desires (*desideratur*) to know, and from what is to be known (*sciendum*) to what is to be experienced (*experiendum*). The moral life. Asceticism. Prayer. These qualities of life still mark the monastic culture that sets the standard for all authentic learning.

In order to develop his thesis about the evolution of monastic culture in the West, Dom Jean Leclercq conducts his reader on a tour of the history of monasticism from the beginning to the dawn of the High Middle Ages. He begins with St. Benedict and St. Gregory the Great, and goes on to show how their program of study, contemplation, work, and loving God within the context of a virtuous life was spread throughout Europe by Benedictine missionary monks during what we call the Carolingian period. The love of learning and the desire for God did not create theocracies. The Christianization of Europe did not require the complete suppression of pagan literature and wisdom. Even before the thirteenth century, the monk Rabanus Maurus (ca. 780–856) wrote, commenting on the provision of Deuteronomy 21:10–13 that allows an Israelite to marry a pagan woman in time of war, "That is what we customarily do, and what we ought to do, when we read pagan poets, when the books of worldly wisdom fall into our hands. If we meet therein with something useful, we convert it to our own dogma [*ad nostrum dogma convertimus*]."[27] It is worthwhile to note that the methodology that Aquinas developed when he read the works of Aristotle may not have been

25. *ST* I, q. 93, a. 9, ad 4: "Ad quartum dicendum quod dilectio verbi, quod est amata notitia, pertinet ad rationem imaginis; sed dilectio virtutis pertinet ad similitudinem, sicut et virtus."

26. Leclercq, *Love of Learning*, 7.

27. Rabanus Maurus, *De clericorum institutione* III, 18 (PL 107: 396); as cited in Lerclercq, *Love of Learning*, 60.

as innovative as certain researchers sometimes claim. The Angelic Doctor was perhaps developing lessons that he had learned while a young student in the Benedictine Abbey of Monte Cassino. He took Aristotle's philosophy and converted it to Catholic doctrine. In more areas of Catholic thought than is commonly acknowledged, the Church has canonized this conversion.

The great heritage of classical Christian culture recognizes that on the one hand learning is necessary if one is to approach God and to express what is discovered about him, while, on the other hand, literature must be continually transcended and elevated in the striving to attain eternal life. Leclercq speaks about "devotion to heaven."[28] The principal literary sources of monastic culture are those that still occupy our attention. Of course, because the contributions of the scholastic and the later doctors of the Church were not yet available to them, the monastic tradition was founded upon the patristic heritage. But if we enlarge the patristic tradition to include the later scholastic and theological tradition, such as Thomism, then we can say that this body of literature, along with the sacred Scriptures as well as classical literature, a category that can be expanded to include modern classics, remains the source of Christian learning. We see this rule maintained in our seminaries and programs of ongoing formation. Catholic seminary education revolves around three foci: Bible, tradition, and philosophy. Mention needs also to be made of the Liturgy as the place where the sacred Scriptures and the writings of the Fathers and the doctors of the Church are first received and where one gives the assent of faith to what these *documenta fidei* contain. In short, then, what has contributed to the shaping of monastic culture and to the intellectual tradition of the West continues to set the perennial norm for the training of priests. Dom Leclercq urges us to answer the question whether other disciplines taught in Catholic seminaries can contribute to the preaching of the Gospel without seminarians standing squarely on the foundations of monastic culture.

When he describes the flowering of monastic culture in the early Middle Ages, Leclercq completes his essay "Love of Learning and the

28. Leclercq, *Love of Learning*, chap. 4.

Desire for God." This history is well documented. The general storyline is well known: monastic schools gradually gave way to the development of the universities. Although some monks participated in the evolution of European education, the most famous actors from the thirteenth through the fifteenth centuries were drawn from among the friars, and after the sixteenth from the Jesuits and those congregations of religious men who followed their example. It is not possible at this juncture to trace the history of the effect of the sixteenth-century reform and of the new humanism that developed after Erasmus of Rotterdam wrote in 1509 his *Praise of Folly*. The Dispute at Lausanne provides an instructive and perhaps indicative anecdote, however. All in all, we can conclude that the Church has undergone a more difficult time sustaining her seminaries in the last 400 years than she experienced during the first 1,600 years of her existence. Take another example: the French school of priestly formation that dates from the seventeenth century suffered the outrageous assault of the French Revolution. Instead of surveying the history of seminary education in the modern period, I would like instead to return to an important lesson that the monastic experience continues to teach seminarians—the importance that holiness of life holds in the advancing toward knowledge of the truth.

HOW TO DEVELOP A CLERICAL HEART?

One of the most important texts in *Pastores Dabo Vobis* is found at numbers 19 and 20 when the text discusses the spiritual life of the priest. It speaks about a "'specific' vocation to holiness," or more precisely of "a vocation based on the Sacrament of Holy Orders, as a sacrament proper and specific to the priest, and thus involving a new consecration to God through ordination."[29] We can discover the foundation for this specific form of priestly holiness in the pattern that has been called monastic. *Pastores Dabo Vobis* confirms that the relationship of holiness to learning remains as true today as it did during the decades when monastic culture was transforming old Europe.

29. John Paul II, Post-Synodal Apostolic Exhortation, *Pastores Dabo Vobis*, §20.

I would like to comment briefly on how to apply to seminarians the principles that monastic culture placed at the center of all human life and learning. They are six altogether. The first group addresses issues of personal discipline. They include the moral life, asceticism, and prayer. The second group specifies the texts that undergird liberal studies, namely, the sacred Scriptures, works of theological learning, and philosophical texts.

PERSONAL DISCIPLINE

The Moral Life

It was St. Gregory the Great in his commentary on the Book of Job, known as the *Moralia*, who for the first time presented to the Christian West a pattern of life based on the virtues and vices. Aquinas put systematic order into Gregory's text. As the Dominican scholar Servais Pinckaers has pointed out, a virtue-based program for Christian living found antecedents in the earlier Fathers, especially in St. Augustine, and continued to provide the model for giving pastoral care until the mid-sixteenth century.[30] It was around the time of the Council of Trent that an alternate model for doing moral theology, what is known as casuistry, arose. The virtues of the Christian life are seven: faith, hope, charity, prudence, justice, fortitude, and temperance. It would be impossible to sketch even briefly the material content of these theological and moral virtues.[31] Suffice it to observe that it constitutes a high-risk experiment to develop the intellectual virtues without the moral virtues. There are many examples that demonstrate this point: the expert in accounting who does not love justice. Possible outcome: embezzlement. The humanist who is a womanizer. Possible outcome: self-destruction. The seminarian who is lazy. Possible outcome: pastoral neglect. The seminarian who abets unchastity. Possible outcome: too tragic to think about. When the moral virtues are not functioning in the way that they should, which is not to affirm that every sin results in the loss of a virtue, the intellectual

30. See Servais Pinckaers, OP, *The Sources of Christian Ethics*, trans. Mary Thomas Noble, OP (Washington, DC: Catholic University of America Press, 1995).

31. See my *Virtues, or the Examined Life* (New York: Continuum, 2002).

life falters.[32] The human mind is made to know the Highest Truth, and this pursuit proves impossible when we find ourselves consumed by vicious disorders. Or, to return to St. Bernard, the attainment of the Highest Truth requires a passionate desire to embrace the true.

Asceticism

The high calling that is the priestly vocation requires of each priest and seminarian a special discipline of the senses. The seminarian and priest are required to think seriously about the ascetical life, to reflect on an organized pattern of self-denial. Asceticism is not reserved to monks and religious fanatics. Of course, the choice of ascetical practices, especially for the beginner, requires wise counsel. Saints in the past have been reprimanded for their youthful indiscretions. One can offer a short reason for adopting some ascetical practice, such as observing the fasts that occur throughout the Church's year or sacrificing one's own pleasure in order to help others in need or to step back from even legitimate entertainments, such as music, computer games, and television. The effects of original sin leave us prone to sin. St. Augustine devoted extensive reflection to the vice of *curiositas*, the vice that prompts us to look around unnecessarily. So our movements require vigilant watching. We facilitate this self-discipline by fasting, almsgiving, and voluntary works of self-denial. One of the most unhappy examples of the hermeneutics of discontinuity after the Second Vatican Council is the wholesale abandonment of ascetical practices, fasts, vigils, acts of personal sacrifice, in favor of what was falsely presented to represent their legitimate substitutes. In short, these alternatives included nonburdensome activities such as fulfilling one's ordinary duties or performing those everyday works of charity that characterize Christian life. Ascetical practices are especially urgent in circumstances when temptations are strong, such as happens with Internet pornography and other illicit satisfactions of the concupiscence of the eyes. Because there are so many instances

32. For a discussion of the unity and the connection of the moral virtues, see my *The Moral Virtues and Theological Ethics*, 2nd ed. (Notre Dame, IN: University of Notre Dame Press, 2008).

when sinful self-satisfaction is forbidden, the Christian life requires that one become accustomed to self-denial.

Prayer

The third and principal element of monastic culture is prayer. It is not often remarked that the pattern of the Church's official prayer has been set for many centuries. This pattern was developed normatively in the monasteries. Take for example the Liturgy of the Hours or its adaptation for the laity that is found in the monthly *Magnificat*. The praying of psalms and canticles and readings from the Bible forms the background for Catholic worship. The concrete expressions that these prayers adopt are each monastic in origin. The seminarian may not dispose of the time or schedule to take up the rhythm of monastic hours. He must, however, establish a regular rhythm of prayer at certain set hours. Prayer without times for prayer evaporates. Indispensable moments in this rhythm are morning, evening, and before retiring. Eventually, the seminarian must learn to embrace the complete Liturgy of the Hours. Contemplative prayer indispensably complements this commitment.

The practices of prayer that the *Catechism of the Catholic Church* recommends are vocal prayer, meditation, and contemplative prayer. The latter form St. Teresa of Avila describes as "a close sharing between friends; it means taking time frequently to be alone with him who we know loves us."[33] I strongly encourage seminarians to read closely what the *Catechism* has to say about contemplative prayer in numbers 2709–19. Indeed, I encourage seminarians to read again the whole of Part Four of the *Catechism*, which is devoted to Christian prayer. The monastic culture confirms that learning and prayer go hand in hand. Prayer is the place where desire is enkindled. Remember what St. Bernard told his monks: "Let those who are versed in the mystery revel in it; let all others burn with desire rather to attain to this experience than merely to learn about it."[34] Burning. Desiring. Experiencing. These activities,

33. St. Teresa of Jesus, *The Book of Her Life*, 8, 5; as cited in *CCC*, §2709.
34. Bernard, "On the *Song of Songs*," Sermon 1, 6.11.

when they have God for their object, transpire only within the context of regular, personal prayer.

LIBERAL STUDIES

The other feature of monastic culture that Dom Leclercq draws to our attention is the program of monastic studies that was built around the Bible, the writings of the Fathers of the Church, and the philosophical texts considered suitable for monastic studies. This is not the occasion to comment on curriculum development. At the same time, the list of subjects that seminarians are required to master makes it clear that they can only complete the program to the extent that they develop the habit of recollection. At this juncture note the congruity between the features of monastic life and the program for priestly formation: human formation, asceticism, spiritual formation, prayer. Human and spiritual formation, the life of virtue. Intellectual formation, study. We should further note the importance that the monastic tradition attaches to the study of the Bible, the tradition, and philosophy.

The Bible

One may question whether St. Bernard would have been able to encourage his monks to read the *Canticle of Canticles* had he known about the requirement of higher exegesis, as it is called. I expect that seminarians are accustomed to reading prayerfully the sacred Scriptures without too much reliance on scientific Scripture studies, at least the first time through. One of the sad results of modern Scripture studies manifests itself in the pulverization of the sacred texts. As one of my friends likes to remark, the commentaries keep getting bigger and bigger. The reason for this obscurantist development is closely linked to the requirements of academic institutions that put a premium to research. In any case, Pope Benedict has remarked on what he calls canonical exegesis. One feature of this method is to read all the sacred Scriptures together. In other words, there is an effort afoot to put Humpty Dumpty back together again. Pope Benedict's own book on Jesus Christ tries to implement the principles of this canonical exegesis. My recommendation to seminarians is that they read the sacred Scriptures with confidence and devotion. The text of St. Bernard on the *Canticle* returns with special aptness: "Only the touch of the Spirit can inspire a song like this, and only personal experience can unfold its meaning."

Tradition

No seminarian can ignore the patristic and scholastic traditions and at the same time succeed in his priestly office. There always lingers the temptation to adopt the encyclopedic view of knowledge. Only what is up-to-date is true. I refer to this approach to learning as romantic evolutionary. It is romantic because it places without sufficient warrant a premium on what is the latest. It is evolutionary because it assumes that things keep getting better. The fact of the matter is that many good books are old books. To read St. Athanasius's *On the Incarnation* is worth more than reading almost any of the one hundred books written about Christ since 1900. The same may be said for St. Thomas Aquinas. I made this case in my book *A Short History of Thomism*.[35] One witness from the Thomist tradition who helps us understand the importance of seeing things from the perspective of the whole is the French Dominican author A. G. Sertillanges, who wrote a short classic translated into English as *The Intellectual Life*. Sertillanges helps us grasp why holiness and learning must go together. He writes: "Great men seem to us men of great boldness; in reality they are more obedient than others. The sovereign voice speaks to them. It is because they are actuated by an instinct which is a prompting of that sovereign voice that they take, always with courage and sometimes with great humility, the place that posterity will give them—venturing on acts and risking inventions often out of harmony with their time and place and even incurring much sarcasm from their fellows. They are not afraid because, however isolated they

35. Romanus Cessario, OP, *A Short History of Thomism* (Washington, DC: Catholic University of America Press, 2005).

may appear to be, they feel that they are not alone. They have on their side the power that finally settles everything. They have a premonition of their empire to come."[36] He refers to those persons who give themselves over to the Bible, the tradition, and philosophy.[37]

Philosophy

The importance of philosophy and the classical disciplines that support it, including the classical languages, is central for seminary formation. The Church is taking back some of the ground lost in the 1960s and 1970s, when it was thought that human sciences may replace philosophy. If you cannot distinguish, you are left with no alternative but to deny or affirm. To always deny results in recalcitrance. To always affirm makes you a dupe. Today it is not easy to choose the kind of philosophy that one should read. Again, I recommend that one follow the tutelage of St. Thomas Aquinas. The reason for this suggestion is not partisanship. The suggestion follows the urging of Pope John Paul II in his encyclical letter that I have already cited, *Fides et ratio*. Aquinas calls for a philosophy that merits the name of metaphysical realism. "If I insist so strongly," writes the pope, "on the metaphysical element, it is because I am convinced that it is the path to be taken in order to move beyond the crisis pervading large sectors of philosophy at the moment [1998], and thus to correct certain mistaken modes of behavior now widespread in our society."[38]

36. A. G. Sertillanges, OP, *The Intellectual Life: Its Spirit, Conditions, Methods* (Westminster, MD: Newman Press, 1959), xi–xii.

37. We call them recognized spiritual authors. Dominican Father Reginald Garrigou-Lagrange, OP (†1964), in his monumental work *The Three Ages of the Interior Life* (Rockford, IL: TAN, 1989), 249–50, provides a list of the saints and other spiritual giants whose works "we should not ignore" because "these works, though not composed under infallible inspiration, were written with the lights and the unction of the Holy Ghost." Garrigou-Lagrange's list of indispensable authors reads as follows: "The chief spiritual works of St. Augustine, St. Jerome, Cassian, St. Leo, St. Benedict, St. Gregory the Great, St. Basil, St. John Chrysostom, Dionysius, St. Maximus Confessor, St. Anselm, and St. Bernard. Very useful also is an acquaintance with what most concerns the interior life in the writings of Richard of St. Victor, Hugh of St. Cher, St. Albert the Great, St. Thomas Aquinas, St. Bonaventure. Profit may always be drawn from the *Dialogue* of St. Catherine of Siena, the works of [John] Tauler, and those of Blessed Henry Suso, Blessed Angela of Foligno, Blessed John Ruysbroeck, Thomas à Kempis, the probable author of *The Imitation.*"

38. John Paul II, *Fides et ratio*, §83.

This warning from Pope John Paul II brings us back to where we began: holiness and learning. It would surprise me to discover that Pope Benedict XVI had not read Jean Leclercq's book. Whether he read it or not, Pope Benedict agrees with Leclercq on the contribution that St. Benedict made in establishing the Christian intellectual roots of Europe. These Christian roots mean a great deal to the pope, and they should also to us. So I urge seminarians to take up the essay of Dom Jean Leclercq and to discover the monastic culture that is required for seminarians to lead a happy life, and to realize the priestly vocation, the seed of which God has placed in seminarians. Marriage is noble and essential for the well-being of the human race. Consecrated or religious vocations adorn the Church with special witnesses to the consuming power of God's face. But neither the Church nor the world can survive long without priests. So I conclude by encouraging seminarians to fulfill the role that clerics played in creating Western civilization. The world needs wise diocesan priests who desire God ardently. So, as Pope Benedict XVI reminded priests and deacons: "Let us be the first to demonstrate the humility and purity of heart which are required to approach the splendor of God's truth. In fidelity to the deposit of faith entrusted to the Apostles (cf. 1 Tim 6:20), let us be joyful witnesses of the transforming power of the Gospel!"[39]

39. Benedict XVI, "Homily at the Mass at Saint Patrick's Cathedral," April 19, 2008.

CHAPTER 9

ON BAD ACTIONS, GOOD INTENTIONS, AND LOVING GOD

This essay is perhaps one of the most important chapters in *Theology and Sanctity*. It reflects the themes considered previously, and it outlines their moral significance and integral unity. Father Cessario reminds us that moral truth—like all truth—is based upon God's knowledge of reality: "how God knows the world to be." This, the eternal law, is the foundation of everything the Church teaches about the morality of human happiness. "Good moral theology, then, describes a happy life that God himself makes happy, and so a life that conforms fully to the requirements of the Gospel." Here the importance of "personhood" noted in chapter 6 reemerges. Because "personhood explains the highest perfection of an individual human nature," "it is the human person who possesses a nature, and whose good is deployed, articulated, and perfected through the ordering of that nature." The human person does not create for himself the contours of his own happiness and fulfillment. "Realist theology, therefore, seeks to contemplate an immanent wisdom in the universe and in salvation, reflecting the ordered wisdom of the divine plan for creation."

Originally published as "On Bad Actions, Good Intentions, and Loving God," *Logos* 1, no. 2 (1997): 100–124. Reprinted by permission.

In his eternal wisdom, God simultaneously created and ordered reality—both natural and moral—according to certain laws that indicate what perfects the human person (and what does not). As with all things, God creates human happiness and has shown the way through which it is achieved (or frustrated). Thus Father Cessario argues that authentic Catholic moral theology reflects the "moral realism" that arises from an adequate consideration (and appreciation) of the natural truth we encounter in created reality and the divine truth God in his loving mercy reveals to us. Moral truth and human freedom are not paradoxically paired in the Christian life. The latter essentially depends on the former. Rational conformity to the true good is an indispensible part of man's movement toward his final end—God himself. Thomistic moral theology is "at once" both realist and personalist.

The expression "Heaven on earth, Heaven in faith" comes from the pen of Blessed Elizabeth of the Trinity (1880–1906). The words describe the overall theme of a ten-day retreat that she composed shortly before her death for the benefit of her younger sister Marguerite, known as Guite (1883–?), who was a housewife and mother of two children.[1] It might seem odd to begin a chapter about Aquinas's teaching on the happy life by turning back to a cloistered nun of Carmel who died an early death at the beginning of the twentieth century. Still, Elizabeth of the Trinity, I believe, illumines what Christians believe about the ultimate happiness of the human person. That is, she reminds us about our true goal or end. Her message is simple: Heaven is our goal. For Elizabeth, a woman who dedicated her adult life to prayer and sacrifice in union with Christ, the happy life is one that rests only in God.

In my view, Elizabeth's spiritual writings can help our contemporaries better realize what makes for a happy human life. And they must understand this. For without taking account of what makes us happy, no one is able to provide a compelling account of the Christian moral life. Again, Elizabeth's message is a simple one: God makes us happy. But there's

1. See Aletheia Kane, OCD, trans., *Complete Works of Elizabeth of the Trinity*, vol. 1, *Major Spiritual Writings* (Washington, DC: ICS, 1984), 90–91, for an explanation of how the two themes form part of Elizabeth's "last retreat."

more. The Father of our Lord Jesus Christ is enormously generous to his adopted children. To the extent that the Christian believer lives the truth here and now, he or she does not have to wait until death in order to experience the happiness of God. Rather, through faith, heaven begins right here on earth. We see, then, that Elizabeth's final retreat prepares us for the already and the not yet: "Heaven on Earth, Heaven in Faith."

Because God's own knowledge about himself grounds the truth about the moral life, moral theology is an exercise closely associated with the theological virtue of faith. I sometimes tell my students that the study of moral theology enables one to discover "how God knows the world to be." Of course, I mean by "world" the properly human world of our beliefs and desires, our intentions and actions. You may recognize a particularly Dominican emphasis in this way of expressing what moral theology is about. We are looking for the truth about God's creative knowledge of the world. For, as the English Dominican Thomas Gilby once said, "the *ratio* which measures moral action is the manifestation of God's mind in revelation, the Logos, not just a rule that can be discovered by rational reflection on experience."[2] Good moral theology, then, describes a happy life that God himself makes happy, and so a life that conforms fully to the requirements of the Gospel. This explains why Aquinas refers to the *nova lex Evangelii*—the new law of the Gospel, a term that Luther, we are told, avoided.[3]

We can express Aquinas's position another way. Moral theology defines the "truth of life." Because truth is known only by the intellect, the moral theologian should be less occupied with discerning, let alone looking for ways to enforce, the dictates of the divine will, and more concerned to discover the rule and measure for human actions that have their origin in the divine intelligence.[4] Our own experience affirms this: the truth per-

2. Thomas Gilby, OP, *Principles of Morality*, vol. 18 (1a2ae.18–21), *St. Thomas Aquinas, Summa Theologiae* (New York: McGraw-Hill, 1966), 154.

3. My authority is Denis R. Janz, *Luther on Thomas Aquinas: The Angelic Doctor in the Thought of the Reformer* (Stuttgart: Franz Steiner Verlag, 1989), esp. 62–65.

4. See *ST* II-II, q. 109, a. 2, ad 3: "Truth of life is the kind of truth by which something exists as true not by which someone speaks what is true. Like everything else one's life is called true on the basis of its reaching its rule and norm, namely divine law; by measuring up to this, a life has uprightness. This is the kind of truth or uprightness common to every virtue."

suades; threats paralyze. Studying the history of theology reveals, moreover, that voluntarist ethics are notoriously unsuccessful. Much that Luther objected to in late medieval scholasticism, for instance, stems from the truncated anthropology of the nominalist theologians. But to the extent that the divine rule and measure (*regula et mensura*), which is properly associated with the *Eternal Logos*, governs human actions, our lives reflect the truth or rectitude that is common in all the virtues and to which the Gospel commits us. The question of how one achieves this rectitude of life—*rechtfertigung* or justification—should not be confused with what actually constitutes this state as one of blessedness.[5]

In order to address the sources of confusion within contemporary religious ethics, it is important that we further clarify the presuppositions of that realist moral theology implied by the "new law of the gospel."[6] Then we may turn straightforwardly to the particular confusions that serve to *vitiate* moral realism regarding the *lex nova*.

THREE PRESUPPOSITIONS FOR A REALIST MORAL THEOLOGY OF HAPPINESS

Three presuppositions underlying Aquinas's teaching are especially crucial for understanding his account of morality and human happiness. These presuppositions concern human language, creation in wisdom and love, and God's heaven. It is these themes that provide the immediate theological coordinates enabling one to situate Christian moral thought within the wider framework of theology conceived as a divine science. These themes are presuppositions not in the sense of arbitrary starting points or postulates, but rather articulate the contours of that eternal law in which all theological wisdom must participate if it is to be worthy of the name.

5. See "Report of the Third Phase of Lutheran/Catholic International Dialogue—Church and Justification: Understanding the Church in the Light of the Doctrine of Justification," in *The Pontifical Council for Promoting Christian Unity*, Vatican Information Service 86 (194/II-III): 128–88.

6. For an extended consideration of "moral realism," see my *Introduction to Moral Theology*, rev. ed. (Washington, DC: Catholic University of America Press, 2013), 1–49.

Thus, situated in relation to that divine wisdom which is the exemplar of every good and the foundation for human order, each of these abovementioned ideological coordinates ratifies the "essential connection between the moral value of an act and man's final end."[7] (Parenthetically, one should add that we need to speak about "man's final end" because each member of the human race is ordered to one and the same goal—heaven. If we say "a person's final end," we perhaps preserve some type of teleology, but we lose the explicit reference to the common goal for all human persons.)

Because morality is often associated with reward and punishment, one expects to hear moral theologians speaking about heaven. But among the emphases and schools that typify moral theology, two divergent schools are particularly important for their implications regarding the nature of human beatitude. The first school, represented by casuist moral theologians, treats heaven largely as a reward for right conduct. Within this framework, the ideological relation of beatitude to the unfolding life of grace and virtue is largely unstressed, rendering human happiness almost an extrinsic denomination with respect to morality. Enthusiasts of this school, both Catholic and Protestant alike, have even made heavenly reward (or its absence) part of the divine game of chance into which men were cast willy-nilly.

The second school is that to which St. Thomas Aquinas belongs. This approach begins with heaven as the starting point for a contemplation of the moral life. One recalls that in the *Summa Theologiae* the article explaining why man's happiness is the vision of God's very essence comes at the very beginning of the *secunda pars* (I-II q. 3, a. 8). Contemporary Roman Magisterium follows Aquinas. In the encyclical *Veritatis splendor*, for example, the methodological option is clear from its opening lines, "Teacher, what good must I do to have eternal life?" (Mt 19:16).[8]

Of course, there is a sense in which heaven comes both first and last in the Christian life. To express the matter in the philosophic parlance of St. Thomas, in the moral life heaven comes first in the order of intention but last in the order of execution. This does not mean that we are moved

7. *Veritatis splendor*, §72.
8. Ibid., §8.

to action exclusively by thinking about heaven. Rather, we are moved by heaven itself according to our divine constitution as rational creatures.

As we will explore further, this is indeed one crux upon which the interpretation of the natural moral law has faltered at the hands of both Catholic and Protestant commentators alike. For natural law is not a zone of human autonomy from the divine governance but rather is itself one mode of that divine governance. Deferring this discussion until later, however, one may note the insight of an earlier commentator on the Christian moral life. Commenting on the role of good ends in life, the Renaissance Thomist commentator Cardinal Cajetan observes that we want real health, real knowledge, a real bath—and, I will add, the real God—not just the thought of them.[9] Whatever their disputes at the Augsburg meeting in 1518, both Luther and Cajetan surely could have agreed on this foundational teaching of the Christian life. This realism about our common divine end revealed in Christ contextualizes our theological discussion of human happiness. Let us now look at each of the three presuppositions in turn.

THEOLOGICAL LANGUAGE AND THE LOGIC OF THE INCARNATION

Our first consideration is the nature of theological language, or the language of faith. Along with other witnesses available in the Christian tradition, conciliar definitions demonstrate that the Church exercises supervision over the use of language, especially descriptive language, in theology. The *Catechism* employs a forceful analogy: "As a mother who teaches her children to speak and so to understand and communicate, the Church our Mother teaches us the language of faith in order to introduce us to the understanding and the life of faith."[10] What holds true for the speculative truths of faith is also true for morals, which encompass the practical truths of the Christian religion.

The language of faith teaches us about living the life of faith. This

9. See his commentary on *ST* I, q. 5, a. 4.
10. *CCC*, §171.

dynamic flows from the logic of the Incarnation: human words can reveal the truth about the Word made flesh, and so conform us to Christ. The believer is obliged, then, to employ the language of faith, and to do so, moreover, with a confidence that comes from his own personal adherence to the truth. In morals, the language of faith expresses not only the commandments and the teachings of the Church, but also the vocabulary of the virtues, which translates what the Church teaches into the everyday, and easily recognizable, circumstances of human life.

In moral theology, the language of faith embraces the fact that the Church can formulate "general statements in morals, founded on the nature of human activity, that have meaning which can be verified without being bound up with an example."[11] In the encyclical *Evangelium vitae*, the pope uses language in exactly this way; for example, he confirms that "euthanasia is a grave violation of the law of God" (§65). Just as the Church confesses the Trinity and the Incarnation, so she teaches that "there are certain specific kinds of behavior that are always wrong to choose, because choosing them involves a disorder of the will, that is, a moral evil."[12] We can identify these specific kinds of behavior through a proper use of descriptive language, and so communicate to the People of God moral truths that are as integral to the Christian faith as the articles of the Creed.

In order to give some examples of acts that are wrong "by reason of their object," *Veritatis splendor* refers to a text from the Second Vatican Council's Pastoral Constitution on the Church in the Modern World, *Gaudium et spes*, which lists homicide, genocide, abortion, euthanasia and voluntary suicide, mutilation, physical and mental torture, and so forth. Aquinas would recognize this practice as fully consonant with his own understanding of how a Christian theologian can use human language when speaking about morality.

11. Gilby, *Principles of Morality*, 170.

12. *Veritatis splendor*, §78, citing *CCC*, §1761. Note that the English translation in the *Catechism* differs slightly from the official English version of the encyclical: "There are concrete acts that it is always wrong to choose, because their choice entails a disorder of the will, i.e., a moral evil."

CREATION, ETERNAL LAW, AND NATURAL LAW

The second consideration is that of creation in wisdom and love. One of the grounds for the Church's confidence that she can identify certain specific acts as morally bad is the Christian attitude toward creation. As we know from the classic textbooks of theology, creation, even though it enjoys its own native intelligibility apart from divine revelation, still constitutes a category for Christian theology. This means that there are some things that neither philosopher nor scientist can tell us for sure about creation, for example, that the world has a beginning in time.

Because nothing exists that God did not create, "each creature possesses its own particular goodness and perfection."[13] Thus in morals we evaluate human actions according to the way that they promote—or detract from—the goodness and perfection of the human creature. This is but one implication of the Catholic tradition's affirmation that natural law and revealed law have one and the same God as author. One observes the crystaline locution of Pope John Paul II in *Veritatis splendor*, §45: "Even if moral-theological reflection usually distinguishes between the positive or revealed law of God and the natural law, and, within the economy of salvation, between the 'old' and the 'new' law, it must not be forgotten that these and other useful distinctions always refer to that law whose author is the one and the same God and which is always meant for man."

By contrast with this rich appreciation of the divine source of the moral order, some moral thinkers seem to suppose that it is solely the human intellect that turns the water of human *inclinatio* into the wine of *lex*. But St. Thomas, in accord with the selfsame tradition articulated in *Veritatis splendor*, insists that natural law is law only because it participates in the eternal law.[14] Natural law is not, then, an independent principate beyond the divine jurisdiction, nor are divine norms of human conduct coercive of the human conscience. Rather, natural law itself is

13. *CCC*, §339.
14. *ST* I-II, q. 91, a 2.

a mode of the divine governance promulgated from the creation and measuring the good of the human creature according to the very nature of the human person. St. Thomas is fond of a philosophic maxim that "the received is in the receiver according to the mode of the receiver."[15] Hence the governance of the moral law is participated by rational creatures rationally and freely. But this rational and free participation can by no means substitute for, nor should it occlude, the divine source, authority, and indeed majestic wisdom of the natural law.

Yet despite the Church's traditional reliance on nature as a category for morals, in certain quarters it is still unfashionable to speak about nature and grace. I am thinking specifically of two theological schools, both of which are influenced by German idealism. On the one hand, there are those who follow the transcendental theology of Karl Rahner: these, in the words of one leading theologian, "cannot provide a description or analysis of the natural order at the theoretical level which is not dependent upon, or does not require appeal to the supernatural order."[16] And on the other hand, there are those inspired by the theological aesthetic of Hans Urs von Balthasar: these usually share his mistrust of natural theology and think about nature, especially in moral theology, as a prebiblical category. Given the widespread influence of these two giants of twentieth-century Catholic theology, we are not surprised to discover that contemporary moral theologians speak hardly at all about the acquired and infused virtues. The historian of doctrine must view this circumstance as an anomaly.

It was not always so. Recall that Aquinas argued that Christian theology must speak about two classes of virtues in order to take full account of the requirements of the divine law, which is both natural and evangelical. One commentator puts it clearly: "The moral virtues infused by God lead the powers of the soul from their pursuits within the earthly city to a fellow-citizenship with the saints in heaven ... Yet the lower [natural virtue] is not cast aside, but rather is contained in the higher

15. *ST* I, q. 84, a. 1.

16. The descriptive phrase comes from J. A. Di Noia, OP, "Karl Rahner," in *The Modern Theologians: An Introduction to Christian Theology in the Twentieth Century*, vol. 1, ed. David F. Ford (Oxford: Basil Blackwell, 1989), 200.

[evangelical virtue], and is a condition for it, for a purely supernatural man or a purely supernatural human act is strictly speaking a contradiction in terms."[17]

There is an important truth here. Christian theology proclaims the biblical distinction between God and the world. But if we do not also affirm some analogical continuity between the world and God, then recent intellectual history bears abundant witness that we risk either divinizing the world or collapsing into nihilistic despair.[18]

Because the believer knows that God created in wisdom and love, no Christian should engage in the popular suspicion about the reliability of nature as a theological category. So, despite the strong prejudice found in many modern theologians against using nature as a theological category, contemporary Catholic thought reaffirms the classical natural law tradition. It was Father Bernard Lonergan who reminded us that the Church always opts for the *lectio difficilior*. To cite one example, *Veritatis splendor* argues for the universality of the moral law on the basis of a common human nature: "The separation which some have posited between the freedom of individuals and the nature which all have in common, as it emerges from certain philosophical theories which are highly influential in present-day culture, obscures the perception of the universality of the moral law on the part of reason."[19]

Were he alive today, Aquinas would have said the same thing. In order to show the truth ingredient in human actions, Aquinas drew upon natural law, but without thereby slighting either the fully personal quality of each meritorious good act or the sovereign divine dominion. We should heed Aquinas's lesson. To the extent that Christian believers fail to take the natural law seriously, they are constrained either to rely unduly on the Church's authority as moral teacher—thus abstracting this

17. W. D. Hughes, OP, *Virtue*, vol. 23 (1a2ae.55–67), *St. Thomas Aquinas, Summa Theologiae* (New York: McGraw-Hill, 1969), 247–48.

18. See Edward T. Oakes, SJ, *Pattern of Redemption: The Theology of Hans Urs von Balthasar* (New York: Continuum, 1994), as cited in Aidan Nichols, OP, "The Century's Greatest Theologian," *Crisis* 13 (1995): 47–48: "the refusal to make the (analogical) distinction between God and the world ... results in either an attempt to effect a complete transfiguration of the world and a divinization of the earth (Marx) or a pure collapse into nothingness and nihilistic despair."

19. *Veritatis splendor*, §51.

authority from the wider economy of providence and salvation—or to compromise the truth.

It will be helpful to reiterate Aquinas's preferred definition for natural law: it is "a sharing in the eternal law by intelligent creatures."[20] Remember my Dominican description of the eternal law: "how God knows the world to be." Realist theology, therefore, seeks to contemplate an immanent wisdom in the universe and in salvation, reflecting the ordered wisdom of the divine plan for creation.[21] This stands in contrast to the characteristic tendency of voluntarism to find ready-made solutions for theological difficulties by a simple appeal to the will of God. The voluntarist is not arrested by that divine wisdom causally manifest in creation and extending even to the very present moment of the divine providence.

Three features of natural law are pertinent to our present inquiry. First, natural law is a moral, not a reductively physical, category. When Aquinas speaks about the nature of the human person, he refers to "the person himself in the unity of soul and body, in the unity of his spiritual and biological inclinations and of all the other specific characteristics necessary for the pursuit of his end."[22] Recall that Aquinas considered that personhood explains the highest perfection of an individual human nature. Second, from this personalist understanding of common nature, it follows that natural law is a precept for human acts, and so considers their purposes (ends) directly: "therefore this law cannot be thought of as simply a set of norms on the biological level."[23]

For example, medical interventions affecting the natural order of human processes do not merely as such violate natural law. But procedures that vitiate specifically human capacities, and invert the ordering of human nature to its good, do more than simply affect some putatively neutral biological processes. For instance, the vitiation of human sexuality—whose unitive and procreative ordering defines a horizon of good for the

20. *ST* I-II, q. 91, a. 2. The *Catechism* (§1955) uses another definition, one taken from a less well-known work, the *In Duo Praecepta Caritatis et in Decem Legis Praecepta: De Dilectione Dei*, prologue.

21. I am relying here on Colman O'Neill's account in *Sacramental Realism: A General Theory of the Sacraments* (Wilmington, DE: Michael Glazier, 1983), esp. 101ff.

22. The text actually is found in *Veritatis splendor*, §50, but it represents Aquinas's view.

23. *Veritatis splendor*, §50, quoting the CDF Instruction on "Respect for Human Life in Its

person—contravenes the natural law. Thus, while it may be a moral good to use a feeding tube on a patient who cannot swallow, for example, it is never a moral good to resort to artificial insemination. And this follows, because whereas the first instance is an auxiliary means whereby the self-same good of nutrition is achieved, in the second case the body/spirit unity of the person by its very nature precludes a surrogate or impersonal achievement of the unitive purpose of human sexuality.

It is the human person who possesses a nature, and whose good is deployed, articulated, and perfected through the ordering of that nature. Hence we can never treat the biological structure of the person as a structure whose teleologies are neutral with respect to the moral good. This is indeed at some points manifest: for who supposes that the prohibition on wrongful homicide is intelligible apart from the good of life as not only a given state of organic matter, but also a state of such matter that is objectively ordered to the whole universe of ends perfective of the person? One must beware the supposition that anything articulated in the argot of science is by that fact merely instrumental or neutral for the person. For this supposition reflects nothing other than a false anthropology that denies the unity of human nature.

Third, because natural law is the participation of the human being in the eternal law, natural law establishes a rule for moral movements "from within." For Aquinas, Christian morality is never heteronomous, but rather an exercise in participated theonomy. The first moment of this theonomy is constituted by the natural law as promulgated in creation. It is the natural law that provides the ground and dynamism for virtuous actions, including those who are uplifted within the life of grace. However weakened is the inclination to virtue after the Fall, the essential properties and tendencies of human nature remain—elsewise to be in grave sin would be not only to be inhumane, but literally not to be a human person. Hence the inclinations divinely impressed upon human nature underlie both the acquired and the infused virtues.

Origin and on the Dignity of Procreation *Donum Vitae*," February 22, 1987, and alluding also to Pope Paul VI's encyclical letter *Humanae vitae*, July 25, 1968.

THE NEW TELEOLOGY: MORAL THEOLOGY WITH HEAVEN AS ITS GOAL

We have considered the language of faith and the divine creation in wisdom and love. A final presupposition for our discussion is heaven. When we mention the infused virtues, we introduce the topic of grace. As I have already mentioned, beatitude comes first in the moral theology of Aquinas, not so much as a reward as an incentive. When the saints make heaven a starting point for moral theology, they ensure that we have a correct understanding about happiness. Although the truly happy person does experience a sense of contentment, Christian happiness is not to be confused with subjective feeling. In order to stress that "happiness" means a godly perfection, I think that we should make more use of the theological term "beatitude." Beatitude, which refers in the first place to God's own happiness, connotes that the end of the Christian life is the same as the origin of the Christian life. Aquinas's whole *Summa* constitutes an essay that places the human creature, whom we designate "man," as one set between God and God. This approach depicts the entire drama of creation and salvation in terms of *exitus* and *reditus* with respect to God.[24]

Personal fulfillment for the Christian means loving God, and that is something that only God can move us to do. As important as leading a good life is for the Christian religion, a good moral life is never an ultimate end in itself. Loving God, however, is. Christian morality points to something beyond morals, beyond ethical considerations. Heaven is God, who alone can fulfill the ultimate destiny of each human person. Theories of ethical objectivity that forfeit metaphysical objectivity suffer from an emaciated account of the good for this very reason: there are natural moral obligations to God, the provident Creator. Lacking appreciation of the divine origin and end of the moral life, such metaphysically eviscerated teachings fail to do justice to the actual moral richness

24. Christian theology must retain the word "man" in order to describe the vocation to holiness. It should be clear that the vocation belongs to everyone who possesses a human nature and is not a matter of personal choice. Fulfillment is personal, but the vocation is communal.

and depth of human agency. Of course, I am thinking of Kant and of all other accounts of the ethical life that begin by severing morality from its speculative and theistic foundation. One cannot deny the intelligibility of being without suppressing at least some significant quantum of the intelligibility of the good.

We may summarize the three presuppositions, with special reference to the happy life, in this way: (1) Aquinas possesses great confidence that ordinary language is capable of communicating authentic knowledge about divine truth, even in matters of personal morality; (2) he accepts the natural law as the Creator's "very good work" and so recognizes the capacity of human reason to discover theological meaning in the created order, especially in human nature; and (3) the Angelic Doctor presents the Christian moral life as man's response to the call to beatitude, so that Christian morality is always a matter of rightly formed desire of the sort that Christ himself encourages in the Sermon on the Mount.

In their own ways, human language, creation in wisdom and love, and God's heaven each fall within the logic of the Incarnation. They all contribute to the development of a Christocentric moral theology. Spiritual realism demands this. Why? No moral theology can ignore the Gospel text where Christ assures us that those who love the members of his Body are really loving him (see Mt 25:40).

THREE MUCH-MISUNDERSTOOD ISSUES ABOUT THE HAPPY LIFE

The abovementioned features of Christian moral theology are surely familiar. They suggest a critique not only of the legalism that Luther despised, but also of the inadequate solutions that were suggested in the immediate aftermath of the Second Vatican Council (1962–65). It remains for us to look at three much-misunderstood issues about a happy life. I hope that the lengthy prologue of my three presuppositions will now prove its worth. These presuppositions should provide us the theological light we need in order to understand bad actions, good intentions, and loving God. For these presuppositions or theological coordinates situate moral theology within the larger picture of that *sacra doctrina* that God communicates to the saints, both on high and here below.

FIRST MISUNDERSTANDING: BAD ACTIONS THWART NOT ONLY HUMAN FLOURISHING, BUT ALSO DIVINE COMMUNION

In order to understand why bad actions thwart human flourishing, we must first know what makes an action bad. The easy answer is to say that what makes a bad action bad is that it contravenes a moral law. That's what a voluntarist would say. Moreover, so far as it goes, and in precision from the specifically voluntarist thesis that reduces wisdom to will, it reflects part of the truth. But Aquinas, drawing on the teaching of St. Augustine, offers a more profound explanation of what makes an action bad. Augustine had defined a bad action as "an utterance, a deed, or a desire contrary to the eternal law."[25] What makes an action bad, then, is that this action runs contrary to "how God knows the world to be." In the Christian theological tradition, the eternal law shapes the whole fabric of morality: the lawfulness of the natural law, its normativity, derives from its character as a participation in the eternal law. And this eternal law is not an arbitrary volition—within St. Thomas's analysis—to say that the divine will is not specified by the divine wisdom is indeed blasphemy. One wonders whether the sixteenth-century reformers would have driven such a sharp wedge between Law and Gospel if this truth about the eternal law had been better understood in the period of late medieval scholasticism. Nominalist decadence and voluntarist reductionism combine to occlude this essential element of the doctrine of natural law: that the normativity of the natural law derives from its promulgation at creation by the divine governor of the commonwealth of being, whose supereminent directive wisdom it authoritatively manifests.

Insofar as the Church defines natural law as a participation in the effective ruling design whereby God governs creation, authentic natu-

25. *CCC*, §1849, citing St. Augustine's *Contra Faustum*, 22 (PL 42:418). Aquinas refers to this text in *ST* I-II, q. 71, a. 6.

ral law theory is quite different than the "Book of Nature" theories developed by Enlightenment thinkers. The Enlightenment rejected divine revelation as an authoritative source of truth, so it sought to ground its version of religious truth in rationality and science (to which the men of the Enlightenment, as Alasdair MacIntyre has reminded us, gave the most unquestioned adherence).[26] As I have already mentioned, natural law is not a substitute for divine revelation, but rather another expression of divine wisdom.[27] The harmonies of grace and nature run all through the moral theology of Aquinas. Listen to him reply to a student's question: "we are bound to affirm that the blessed see God's very being. Happiness is the ultimate achievement of rational nature."[28] Where the Enlightenment sought to define nature as separate from divine dominion, St. Thomas's metaphysical realism discerns the utter dependence of finite being—whose existence is not *causa sui*—upon God. Hence any effort to separate nature from God's providential governance signifies a loss of metaphysical rationality—a loss whose reverberation resonates throughout the diverse moments both of modernity and postmodernity.

Bad actions, which contravene the order of right reason, fail to embody the divine wisdom and goodness. This is to say that they actively impede and war against the ultimate achievement—the final good—of rational nature. Today, some writers give the impression that the foundation for moral good is something arbitrary. So recall that, for Aquinas, moral good shares in the nature of the good, which is a transcendental property of being. The good, for Thomas, is being as appetible or desirable: to be is in some respect to be good. The specifically moral good is a good-to-be-done (*bonum faciendum*)—for the good embraced by man's initial state of being requires development and articulation through many actions in order for human nature to achieve its consum-

26. See his *Three Rival Versions of Moral Enquiry* (Notre Dame, IN: University of Notre Dame Press, 1990), 23ff.

27. See *Veritatis splendor*, §40: "The moral law has its origin in God and always finds its source in him: at the same time, by virtue of natural reason, which derives from divine wisdom, it is a properly human law. Indeed, as we have seen, the natural law 'is nothing other than the light of understanding infused in us by God,' whereby we understand what must be done and what must be avoided."

28. *Quodlibetal Question* 10, q. 8, a. 1.

mate state of being and good. Only in God are being and good absolutely identical.

The moral good is concerned with choices (*ex voluntate deliberata*). The good-to-be-done is held in the mind with evidence for its existence and nature, and according to a measure, norm, or law.[29] Once it is affirmed that the highest measure for moral good is the eternal law, then we can identify other authentic expressions of law that ensure proper guidance for human activity in different spheres of Church and world.

What many people fail to understand is that the morality of human acts is a quality intrinsic to them. Good actions by nature and definition are related to the divine Good and the good, which are its participations. This is the substance of Jesus's reply to the rich young man of the Gospel, of which Pope John Paul II makes such good use in the first chapter of *Veritatis splendor*. To speak of actions as neutral appendages to inner states radically misconstrues the nature both of intention and of choice. We are thus reduced to speaking about external actions as if they were on a par with the circulation of the blood, the beard's growing, the ear's hearing, or a spasm of the limb.[30] More to the point, to construe human behavior in this way threatens the Christian believer's attainment of happiness.

Bad actions do not and cannot perfect the good of the human person; in other words, they are always harmful to us. This is to say that bad actions not only fail to embrace the good, they actually cause positive harm to the human person. Minimalizing moral theology that thinks only in terms of what is allowed and what is forbidden frequently misses this point, causing neurosis in the conservative and injury to the liberal. Because true freedom flows from "communion of life with Christ,"[31] no injury is done the believer by the truth that "there are certain specific kinds of behavior that are always wrong to choose, because choosing them involves a disorder of the will, that is, a moral evil" (§78).[32] Moral evils erode the good of the person, and at the same time they impede

29. See Gilby, *Principles of Morality*, 163ff.

30. I have adapted these words from Ralph McInerny, *Ethica Thomistica: The Moral Philosophy of Thomas Aquinas* (Washington, DC: Catholic University of America Press, 1982), 85ff.

31. See *Veritatis splendor*, §16.

32. This text is found in *CCC*, §1761.

that good of charity that is the ultimate perfection of the will. Because they destroy charity, bad actions thwart not only human flourishing but also divine *communio.*

SECOND MISUNDERSTANDING: WHEN AN ACTION IS BAD, GOOD INTENTIONS CANNOT PAVE THE "WAY" (JN 14:6), THEREBY RENDERING IT PERMISSIBLE

Because human acts are freely chosen in consequence of a judgment of conscience, they can be morally evaluated. Aquinas rules out concrete moral neutrality: "All activity of human beings which proceeds from deliberate reason must needs be good or bad in the individual case."[33] So the *Catechism* states clearly that human acts "are either good or evil."[34] When an action is evil or bad, good intentions cannot make it serve the purpose of salvation. There is scarcely a serious Roman Catholic theologian who would defend the thesis that good intention can render evil acts to be condign for salvation. Still, the view that personal meaning, desire, and purpose give a human action its ultimate moral determination has become widely held. Frequently an appeal to the outcomes of a given action, whether clearly foreseen or unforeseeable, has figured in this "teleologistic" approach to morals.[35] Aquinas's teleology, however, is about an act's inner perfection, not about its consequences, just as his view of freedom is about excellence, not expediency.

It would require a special series of lectures to give a complete account of Aquinas's teaching on the "object" of the moral action.[36] *Veri-*

33. *ST* I-II, q. 18, a. 9. In the preceding article, Aquinas affirms that one can speak about morally neutral acts according to their species when an action, such as picking up a blade of grass, does not include anything that immediately affects the perfection of the rational creature.

34. *CCC*, §1749.

35. Among other objectives, *Veritatis splendor* was written to clarify this crucial issue in moral theology. In its official English version, the adjectival form of teleologism is rendered "teleological." It would have been better to translate it "teleologistic," so as to maintain the difference between "teleology," which is good, and "teleologism," which is bad.

36. For extended considerations of the nature of the moral object, see Steven A. Long, *The Teleological Grammar of the Moral Act* (Ave Maria, FL: Sapientia Press, 2007), and "Natural Law, the Moral Object, and *Humanae Vitae,*" in *Ressourcement Thomism: Sacred Doctrine, the*

tatis splendor does an admirable job of summarizing Aquinas's teaching: the object of a given moral act "is the proximate end of deliberate decision which determines the act of willing on the part of the acting person" (§78). Aquinas himself recognized that the acting person had to choose an action that is capable of being ordered to its ultimate end. This is why Aquinas argues against the case of Robin Hood:

> it often happens that man acts with a good intention, but without spiritual gain, because he lacks a good will. Let us say that someone robs in order to feed the poor: in this case, even though the intention is good, the uprightness of the will is lacking. Consequently, no evil done with a good intention can be excused. "There are those who say: And why not do evil that good may come? Their condemnation is just" (*Rom* 3:8).[37]

Aquinas teaches us that ends—what we are translating as "intentions"—play a decisive role in the Christian life. There are two things that need to be said: on the one hand, good intentions cannot turn bad actions into good ones, and on the other, bad intentions can make otherwise good actions bad. In the case of the bad action, it must be emphasized that the will is already corrupted by engaging in the evil action, so that no intention whatsoever can bring about spiritual gain. I call this moral realism.

In order to see why these conclusions do not put a heavy burden on the shoulders of the Christian believer, we would do well to recall a general premise of the moral life. We know that the Christian tradition thinks about moral theology as an analysis "of the journey to God of reasoning creatures." God, though infinitely perfect and happy in himself, created man to share in his happiness; owing to the existence of sin, he even sent his Son into the world for our salvation. Christ, through the action of the Holy Spirit, invites everyone to participate in divine beatitude. For this reason, Jesus identifies himself as "the Way" (Jn 14:6). Hence one description of moral theology rightly makes it the science of reaching God. The first non-gainsayable premise of the science is: "Only the act in conformity with the good can be a path that leads to life."[38]

Sacraments, and the Moral Life, ed. Reinhard Hütter and Matthew Levering (Washington, DC: Catholic University of America Press, 2010), 285–311.

37. *Veritatis splendor,* §78. The text comes from Aquinas's *De duobus praeceptis legis,* a. 1

38. This particular formulation comes from *Veritatis splendor,* §72.

What Aquinas holds about personal intentions flows from this premise:

> The reason why a good intention is not itself sufficient, but a correct choice of actions is also needed, is that the human act depends on its object, whether the object is capable or not of being ordered to God, to the One who "alone is good," and thus brings about the perfection of the person.[39]

To claim that there are good and bad actions, and that no alchemy of good intentions turns a properly identified bad action into a morally acceptable, if perhaps regrettable, good one is not to replace the Gospel of mercy with a standard of moral rigorism. Instead, as Luther himself pointed out, truly evangelical preaching about moral goodness should lead the hearer of God's Word to a transformed life, to new life in Christ. Good catechesis will present its moral instruction as a long catechesis on the "newness of life." On what authority? The reference is to St. Paul: "We were buried therefore with him by baptism into death, so that as Christ was raised from the dead by the glory of the Father, we too might walk in newness of life" (Rom 6:4). If we follow the logic of St. Paul, newness of life means a life transformed in Christ. And by God's gracious design, this gift comes through baptism at the very beginning of our Christian pilgrimage.

THIRD MISUNDERSTANDING: LOVING GOD MEANS OBSERVING THE CHRISTOLOGICAL FORM OF THE MORAL LIFE, NOT COMPROMISING IT

Because the form of the moral life is irreducibly Christological, Christian morality is not an engagement only for the perfect. Jesus came to save sinners. Truth himself never requires us to deny sin. Nor, therefore, should sin make us look for empty rationalizations or compromising strategies. We know that the disordered effects of sin remain even

39. Again, see *Veritatis splendor*, §78.

in the baptized. There is only one grace of the Immaculate Conception, and by divine dispensation this grace belongs only to the Virgin Mother of God. Christian moral theology, then, should provide both instruction for living a holy life and consolation for times of failure and temptation. It helps to recall that God is never embarrassed by sin. God's attitude toward sin is one of forgiveness, yes, but even more so one of restoration. Thus Aquinas teaches that the principal purpose of the Incarnation and the sending of the Holy Spirit is to accomplish the image restoration and image perfection of those who are predestined for holiness.

In order to preach this message of divine love, the moral theologian must know the reason God allowed sin to gain entrance into the world. His purpose in permitting sin is best expressed in the words of the Easter Exultet: *O felix culpa!* The Church knows that to say this strikes unaided human reason as odd, which is why she places this truth of faith at the heart of the celebration of the Paschal Mystery. St. Ambrose captures the significance of this truth for the life of the individual believer when he writes, "My guilt became for me the cause of redemption, through which Christ came to me."[40]

Jesus remains at the center of the Christian life. He is the one who shows us the Way, teaches us the Truth, and communicates Life itself. In my view, the moral teachings of both the Scriptures and the Christian tradition are best enshrined in the language of virtue. Moral virtue ensures a good action, both its end and its intention, no matter what the given circumstance of the action may be. In a complete Christian life, all the virtues work toward the perfection of human flourishing and, when we include the theological and infused virtues, *beatitudo*. What is perhaps most significant, Aquinas held that all these virtues make the Christian believer look like Christ, who is the source of all holiness in the Church. There is no other way to achieve the holiness that comes from loving God than by attaining "to the measure of the stature of the fullness of Christ" (Eph 4:13).

40. See his *Jacob and the Happy Life*, bk. 1, ch. 6, no. 21.

THE MORAL LIFE: AT ONCE REALIST AND PERSONALIST

Because both human language and visible creation serve as instruments for communicating divine truth, Christian theology can boast of being at once personalist and realist. First, Christian theology is eminently personalist: it develops out of a word of personal address, which terminates in the act of faith, and perfects the human person by drawing him or her into a communion of persons. Pope John Paul II frequently refers to the *communio personarum* as a way of expressing the reality of the Church at all of its levels. In his mind, this coming together in unity and love represents the highest expression of personal being in the world.

Second, Christian theology is eminently realist: the perfection of persons entails the perfection of human nature. Only God is a pure person; in fact, God is three persons in one nature. Both angels and men share in the perfection of personhood, but they are persons of a nature, of specifically different natures, to be sure. Man alone is the creature caught between time and eternity, between spirit and matter, and so the human person depends on created things for his or her well-being. All this adds up to an important truth: moral realism takes seriously the inner formation of man's being and acting by nature and grace, even though our final transformation consists only in love.

ONE NATURE AND MANY PERSONS: HUMAN NATURE AND PERSONHOOD

Because each person on earth shares a common human nature, the irreducible uniqueness of the person—what some have called its mystery—subsists in a nature whose perfection is the same for all. The virtues perfect the human person precisely as a human being, that is, as one who possesses a specific nature. When the virtues are infused by divine grace, they perfect the Christian believer according to the instructions of the Gospel. But, as the familiar adage puts it, the infused virtues perfect nature without destroying it.

We see the principle of one nature and many persons verified in the variety of the saints. Though the grace of holiness shines through many different personalities, the saints nonetheless form a recognizable group, a communion. Why? Because they are all set upon one goal, loving God? Yes, but there is something more specific that we can see in the saints. We recognize in them the elements of a common sanctified humanity, even though these recognizable virtuous traits characterize persons as different as Aloysius Gonzaga and Thomas More, or Elizabeth of the Trinity and Pope Pius X. The Dominican artist Fra Angelico beautifully captures this theme in his *Welcome into Paradise.*

THE TWO SELVES: A DISTINCTION BETWEEN SENSE WANTING AND RATIONAL WILLING

From a theological point of view, the very Incarnation of the Son of God compels us to describe the moral life as both personalist and realist. Because he is one of the Holy Trinity, the human nature of the eternal Logos is the principal instrument of God's love in the world. Christ, then, possesses the complete and integral human nature that best manifests the nobility of our common nature. Furthermore, Christ's human nature serves as the living principle for his human activity. Thus Christ uses human language to communicate divine truth. The harmony of willing in Christ is another good example: he always does as man the will of the Father, which is one with that of the Son and the Holy Spirit. "Christ's human will 'does not resist or oppose but rather submits to his divine and almighty will.'"[41] This conformity includes not only his rational will, but extends also to his sense willing or wanting.

What is true in Christ the New Adam is, on account of the sin of the Old Adam, for us originally a promise. St. Paul has this soteriological principle in mind when he speaks about the two selves (see Rom 7:21–25). I knew someone once who held the startling view that the Church should define the Pauline doctrine of the two selves, so important is it for the practice of the Christian faith. The old self stands for what we are

41. Council of Constantinople III (DS 556) as quoted in *CCC,* §475.

outside of Christ, and the new self for what we are in Christ. I suspect that Martin Luther would have happily joined in this infallible teaching.

The distinction between rational will and sense appetite enables one to explain how choosing to abide in Christ—an action in principle open to all irrespective of emotional or psychological disposition—offers a way to grow in the obedience of Christ. Von Balthasar speaks about Christ as the universal norm for the moral life.[42] This is the case only because Christ is also a concrete and personal norm for each member of his Body the Church. The Gospel promises that all that Christ is, we can become.

FAITH AS THE CHIEF VIRTUE FOR THE MORAL LIFE

To affirm what we are inasmuch as we remain united to Christ is to speak about faith. So let us end where we began, adapting Blessed Elizabeth of the Trinity's saying "Heaven on earth means heaven in faith." If the particular requirements of the transformed life, as Aquinas understands it, seem challenging to us, then we should think about the moral life as an invitation to stay close to Jesus. This means to live by faith, above all in his love for us. When we turn again and again to Jesus, especially in the face of sin and temptation, a wonderful thing happens. Whatever our moral successes and failures, we have achieved something infinitely better than perfect morality. We have found God. For Aquinas, nothing short of such an end can make men happy.

42. "Nine Theses in Christian Ethics," in *International Theological Commission: Texts and Documents, 1969–1985* (San Francisco: Ignatius Press, 1989), 108.

CHAPTER 10

SACRAMENTAL CONFESSION AND ADDICTIONS

Here Father Cessario applies the realist and personalist emphases of Thomistic theology to the habitual moral struggles Christians suffer all too frequently in today's secular culture. He argues that, against moral realism, the "neglect of being" "can affect adversely the discussion of how persons with addictions can benefit from receiving the sacraments." Because "sinful actions corrupt the *communio personarum*," the sacrament of reconciliation affords us a means of "spiritual resurrection," in which "we embrace truth, discover goodness, and receive new life or being." But while sacramental "absolution takes away sin," it does not "remedy all the disorders sin has caused" (*CCC*, §1459). Thus the "complete remedy" to vicious habits "involves the practice of satisfaction." Penance emerges as not so much a penal "tribute paid to an angry God," but rather as an expression of the "joyful conversion that the grace of Christ accomplishes in the one who freely associates himself with the mysteries of Christ." Because of their association with Christ's atoning work, "satisfactory works possess the power to shape our soul and its powers, both rational and emotional."

Originally published as "Sacramental Confession and Addictions," in *Addiction and Compulsive Behaviors: Seventeenth Workshop for Bishops*, ed. Edward J. Furton (Boston, MA: National Catholic Bioethics Center, 2000): 125–39. Reprinted by permission.

Addiction impairs human dignity "because it introduces a neglect of being and causes a loss of touch with objective truth." Although the psychological elements of addiction within the human person may diminish moral culpability, the truth still remains: vicious actions do not and cannot engender the happy life. Thankfully, satisfactory works that are accomplished in love reestablish our conformity to the authentic good. "Satisfactory works and the use of the gift of indulgences can benefit spiritually every Christian, even those who are involved in treatment for behavior that is judged to flow from an addiction." The saving Gospel of Jesus Christ does not merely correct bad behavior. Rather, it accomplishes "the complete renewal of the human person." For this reason the sacrament of reconciliation remains a "privileged instrument" for "restoring us to God's grace and joining us with him in an intimate friendship" (CCC, §1468).

In *Fides et ratio,* Pope John Paul II established the parameters for this chapter's inquiry: "It should never be forgotten that the neglect of being inevitably leads to losing touch with objective truth and with the very ground of human dignity" (§90). Our aim, then, is to show that "neglect of being" can affect adversely discussion of how persons with addictions can benefit from receiving the sacraments. Why?

Like all the sacraments, penance supplies a way to grow in the "new being" that belongs to us because of our union with Christ. Penance and reconciliation especially help us to move away from those patterns of human action that erode the good, and therefore the dignity, of the human person. As the New Testament makes plain, in order for this "new being" to flourish, the Christian must abide in the objective truth that divine revelation ultimately identifies with God himself (see Jn 15:26). But how does this mystery of the divine piety apply to the person who suffers from an addiction?

In order to answer this question, we must proceed in three steps by looking at (1) human action and the moral good, (2) the origin of human freedom, and (3) the applicable principles of sacramental theology.

HUMAN ACTION AND THE MORAL GOOD

Catholic theology has always appealed to the transcendentals—being, one, true, good—in order to locate human action within the larger framework of creation and providence. John Paul II has made this tradition his own, and so revealed his personal preference for Christian moral realism.[1] Take for example the 1984 Post-Synodal Exhortation "On Reconciliation and Penance in the Mission of the Church Today." As the pope stressed the intrinsic connection between truth and reconciliation, he reminded us that the "Church promotes reconciliation in the truth, knowing well that neither reconciliation nor unity is possible outside of or in opposition to the truth" (§9). So, as early as the mid-1980s, John Paul II anticipated a main theme of the 1998 encyclical. Perhaps the pope first conceived *Fides et ratio* in the confessional, that sacred place where any penitent with the right disposition can come forward and, in the person of the priest, meet the reconciling Christ?[2] In this sacrament of our "spiritual resurrection" (*CCC*, §1468), we embrace truth, discover goodness, and receive new life or being.

Penance also reaches the transcendental one. Reconciliation brings about unity. Sin not only erodes the good of the individual, but it also fragments the life that we live together. Penance aims to strengthen the human communion (or solidarity) that forms the ontological foundation for the Church. Sinful actions corrupt the *communio personarum,* which is the pope's preferred way of expressing what constitutes the common unity that God ordains for every person to enjoy. In order for human persons to enter once again into a perfect *communio,* the sacrament of reconciliation offers healing and reestablishment in ecclesial communion. Everyone needs this sacrament. St. Augustine makes this clear when

1. See Jarosław Kupczak, OP, *Destined for Liberty: The Human Person in the Philosophy of Karl Wojtyła/John Paul II* (Washington, DC: Catholic University of America Press, 2000).

2. For a general account of the sacraments as places of encounter with Christ, see Colman O'Neill, OP, *Meeting Christ in the Sacraments,* rev. ed., ed. Romanus Cessario, OP (Staten Island, NY: Alba House, 1991). For an account of sacramental causality in light of contemporary theology, see my "The Sacraments of the Church," in *Vatican II: Renewal within Tradition,* ed. Matthew L. Lamb and Matthew Levering (Oxford: Oxford University Press, 2008), 129–46.

he writes that "the beginning of good works is the confession of evil works."[3]

An adequate sacramental theology must explain that each sacrament comprises two moments: the first is that of image perfection, and the second that of image restoration. The expressions date to St. Augustine and help us ponder what God accomplishes in the sacramental system. We see this teaching verified in the way that the *Catechism* describes the grace of baptism: this grace comes to us "for the forgiveness of sins" (§1263–64). In other words, it is the work of image restoration. Again, this grace accounts for the fact that the human person becomes through baptism "a new creature" (§1265–66). In other words, it is the work of image perfection. To sum up, image perfection implies the bestowal of a divine intimacy that only God can confer on the human creature, whereas image restoration reminds us that this process of divinization occurs within the sinful circumstances of this present life and so is unthinkable—in every case except one—apart from personal forgiveness. That baptism introduces us into the communion of the Church establishes a sacramental bond among all the baptized, and imparts an indelible spiritual mark (or character; see §1267–74) that follows upon the restoration and perfection of the godly image, originally bestowed on every human being at creation. A similar pattern of image restoration and image perfection can be discovered in the abiding sacrament (*res et sacramentum*) of the six other sacraments.

The sacramental system would be unintelligible apart from the call to ultimate communion with the Blessed Trinity that Christ reveals as the divinely willed destiny of every human person. This also explains why the Church teaches that only theology can provide a definitive analysis of human action and freedom. Pope John Paul II leaves no room for doubt: "Seen in any other terms, the mystery of personal existence remains an insoluble riddle."[4] This affirmation applies also to those persons suffering from addiction.

Recall that Aquinas began the second part of his *Summa Theologiae*

3. *Commentary of the Gospel of John* 12, 13 (*PL* 35, 1491), cited in *CCC*, §1458.

4. *Fides et ratio*, §12.

by appealing to the doctrine of the *imago Dei*. He thought that nothing definitive could be said about Christian life without first making clear the preethical conditions for human conduct. Appealing to the anterior tradition, Aquinas writes:

> Man is made to God's image, and since this implies, so Damascene tells us, that he is intelligent and free to judge and master of himself, so then, now that we have agreed that God is the exemplar cause of things and that they issue from his power through his will, we go on to look at this *imago*, that is to say, at man as the source of actions which are his own and fall under his responsibility and control.[5]

The pastor of the Church is obliged always to consider human freedom as an instrument of God's wise providence for his creatures. On this point, Christian realism radically differs from the perspectives of Greek tragedy and philosophy, which often promote a pessimistic view about the durability of goodness in human life and about the capacity of man to embrace the good.[6]

For the sinner, especially one whose sin is grave, the restoration of the image of God always entails a turning away from some disordered attachment to a creature and a turning toward the mercy and the love of God. This is the case because, to borrow the lapidary phrase of Aquinas, sin constitutes both an *aversio a Deo* and a *conversio ad creaturam*. The "conversion" or clinging in a disordered way to some created good produces in the sinner certain effects immediately related with having embraced a good wrongly. We call this vice. Vices principally manifest themselves in the moral character of a person, impeding the sinner's full communion with God and with his brothers and sisters.[7] Further, vicious at-

5. Introduction before q. 1 of *ST* I-II.

6. For a detailed account of this view from both the perspectives of philosophy and literature, see Martha C. Nussbaum, *The Fragility of Goodness: Luck and Ethics in Greek Tragedy and Philosophy* (Cambridge: Cambridge University Press, 1986), 419. On Nussbaum's account, a tragedy such as Euripides's *Hecuba* "shows us a case of solid character and shows us that, under certain circumstances, even this cannot escape defilement. It also [shows] us that even the good character who has not suffered any actual damage or betrayal lives always with the risk of these events: for it is the nature of political structures to change, and in the nature of personal friendship that the confident man should be indistinguishable from the trustworthy man."

7. The teaching is expressed in *CCC*, §1472, which speaks about the "double consequence" of sin. Both the eternal punishment and the so-called "temporal punishment" (*poena*)

tachments sometimes leave physical traces. Think of the younger Hans Holbein's (†1543) characterizations of the drunkard, the lecher, and the miser in Tudor England. He exhibits the disordered attachments in the person's very physical appearance.

Or consider the descriptions of the punishments for the capital sins that Dante gives in the *Purgatorio*, each one calculated to represent a suitable penalty for the nature of the fault: the slothful running furiously, shouting "Faster! Faster! To be slow in love is to lose time."[8] The poet's vision is that sin deforms, and that it possesses the power to accustom a person to the deformity. Dante's is a Christian vision.

From these considerations it is possible to propose that the classical theological analysis of sin helps us understand present-day clinical and biological descriptions of addictions. Spiritual authors always have warned that vicious *habitus* can gain the upper hand in a person's life and result in a vicious deformation of character. This state of the person explains the need for image restoration, which must be accomplished either here on earth or, according to the truth of the Catholic faith, after death. Thus the *Purgatorio*. Only those ready to love as God loves are ready to see God.

Satisfactory works, which are commonly referred to as penances, constitute the appointed means for this image restoration. The Council of Trent (in 1551) provided explicit warrant for the Catholic teaching about sacramental satisfaction: "Absolution takes away sin, but it does not [*primo et per se*] remedy all the disorders sin has caused" (*CCC*, §1459, citing *DS* 1712). The complete remedy of course involves the practice of satisfaction, or making use of the gift of indulgence.[9] Unfortunately, many theologians have accepted the argument that St. Anselm exercised a negative influence on Western theology, and so much misunderstanding exists nowadays in Catholic theology about the place and role of satisfactory works.[10]

---

due to sin are distinguished from the fault (*culpa*) of sin. It is called temporal because the effects of sin are felt in this life.

8. Dante Alighieri, *The Purgatorio*, trans. John Ciardi (New York: New American Library, 1961), canto 18, cornice 4, lines 103–4.

9. For further background discussion for this topic, see my "Christian Satisfaction and Sacramental Reconciliation," *Communio* 16 (1989): 186–96.

10. For further discussion of this topic, see my *The Godly Image: Christ and Salvation in*

It is fair to say that theological misunderstandings of satisfaction arise from Reformation debates about justification. The sixteenth-century reformers argued that justification never really changes the sinner, who therefore abides *simul iustus et peccator*.[11] By making the distinction between what absolution accomplishes and what satisfaction achieves, Trent challenged the claim that justification always remains "alien justification." On the contrary, the Council affirmed that the sacrament of baptism (and penance) changes the sinner into a justified soul, even though the lingering signs of sinful defect may still manifest themselves in the forgiven person's character. This affirmation provides a good example of the truth that the Church always judges on the basis of "what is" and not what appears to be.[12] Satisfactory works contribute toward healing this defect without involving the justified sinner in an endless rhythm of propitiation. The art of the Catholic Baroque period provides a visual witness to this truth: the ornament, the spirals, the gold all exhibit a continuity between heaven and earth into which the Christian believer is inserted through the sacraments. The message was clear to anyone with eyes to see: grace transforms.

The theological issue at stake in the justification debate is profound. Because of her commitment to sacramental realism, the Church rejected and continues to reject an unmodified version of the *simul iustus et peccator* account of justification.[13] Furthermore, the Church must insist that since the Incarnation nothing human remains alien to the work of divine grace. Once you believe that an individual human nature subsists in a divine person, there should be no difficulty believing that divine grace can heal the wounds of sin in any human nature. The Church also recognized that it would not be in keeping with the biblical revelation

---

Catholic Thought from Anselm to Aquinas, Studies in Historical Theology VI (Petersham, MA: St. Bede's, 1990).

11. For the latest developments in Roman Catholic approach to this question, see the "Joint Declaration on the Doctrine of Justification" and various official responses to it in the *Pontifical Council for Promoting Christian Unity Information Service* 98 (1998): 81–103.

12. See *Fides et ratio*, §44: "Looking unreservedly to truth, the realism of Thomas could recognize the objectivity of truth and produce not merely a philosophy of 'what seems to be' but a philosophy of 'what is.'"

13. The "Joint Declaration" (see note 11 above) confirms that this theological point is one that requires clarification to be made compatible with Catholic doctrine.

to announce a doctrine of reconciliation in which sin seemed to hold the upper hand—trumping, as it were, both the work of creation and the work of redemption. Such considerations persuade us that debates about justification are not confined to theological subtleties. They affect the practices of salvation.

Consider the notion of penance. In the Catholic tradition, penance always expresses the joyful conversion that the grace of Christ accomplishes in the one who freely associates himself with the mysteries of Christ. Penance never amounts to a tribute paid to an angry god. The *Catechism* carefully selected a text from the Tridentine decrees that makes it plain that the efficacy of all penance derives from Christ, who himself has first merited for us.[14] My own practice is to encourage young priests to use the following prayer: "May the Passion of our Lord Jesus Christ, the intercession of the Blessed Virgin Mary, and of all the saints, whatever good you do and suffering you endure, heal your sins, help you to grow in holiness, and reward you with eternal life." This prayer, found in the *Rite of Penance*, sacramentalizes the whole of a sinner's life, placing the penitent, as it were, in a permanent state of making satisfaction. Because they have been associated in the sacrament to the atoning work of Christ's Cross, our penances surpass whatever intrinsic worth for spiritual training they may possess. *Incarnationis mysterium*—the Bull of Indiction for the Great Jubilee—applies this same theological principle to the gift of the indulgence, which also purifies us.[15]

The spiritualization of penances should not lead us to forget that satisfactory works do possess their own psychological power: prayer, an offering, works of mercy, service of neighbor, and voluntary self-denial all contain the ability to form our psychological powers (see *CCC*, §1460). More precisely, satisfactory works possess the power to shape our soul

14. *Incarnationis mysterium*, §10, makes the same point: "Revelation also teaches that the Christian is not alone on the path of conversion. In Christ and through Christ, his life is linked by a mysterious bond to the lives of all other Christians in the supernatural union of the Mystical Body."

15. See *Incarnationis mysterium*, §9–13 (The Bull of Indiction of the Great Jubilee), which explains the Catholic understanding of indulgences. For further explanation of the relationship of indulgences to satisfaction, see my "St. Thomas Aquinas on Satisfaction, Indulgences, and Crusades," *Medieval Philosophy and Theology* 2 (1992): 74–96.

and its powers, both rational and emotional. Satisfaction is a work of both nature and grace, or, to be more precise, a work of uplifted nature in which the requirements of both human psychology and good theology are met. At the same time, penances are not magic and should be administered on the basis of a judgment about the spiritual maturity of the person.

A question about the utility of satisfactory works naturally arises in the case of persons who are described as suffering from an addiction. A standard 1997 dictionary used by physicians describes addiction as "the compulsive and overwhelming involvement with a specific activity which may lead to either psychologic or physical dependence or both."[16] The definition is broad but serviceable for the present discussion. The question is simple. What spiritual benefits can people who are addicted to bad behaviors obtain from receiving the sacrament of penance? To keep the discussion within a reasonable framework, I will not consider the capacity of the addicted person to conceive true contrition or to confess his or her sins. It is true that some psychologists would argue that both contrition and confession can be counterproductive activities for persons actually suffering from addiction, or who are in certain stages of recovery from addiction. The Church, however, offers another outlook.

We find evidence for this view in an apparently minor modification made in the *editio typica* of the *Catechism*. In the first modern language editions, the *Catechism* instructed confessors when dealing with the virtue of chastity to take into account "the affective immaturity, force of acquired habit, conditions of anxiety, or other psychological or social factors *that lessen or even extenuate* moral culpability" (§2352, emphasis mine). The authoritative text now reads: "other psychological or social factors that *can* lessen, if not even reduce to a minimum, moral culpability" (see *CCC*, §2352, emphasis mine). I interpret this to mean that

16. Robert Berkow, ed. *The Merck Manual of Medical Information* (Whitehouse Station, NJ: Merck Research Laboratory, 1997). Current usage extends the term "addiction" beyond its original psychophysiological meaning to include all harmful compulsive behavior. Some distinguish between substance addiction (stemming from drugs, alcohol, food, etc.) and a more general class of behavioral addictions. For a discussion, see Howard Clinebell, *Understanding Persons with Alcohol, Drug and Behavioral Addictions* (Nashville, TN: Abington, 1998). However, the psychological categories do not always serve the purposes of moral analysis.

the Church does not encourage us to place vicious actions outside of all reference to the moral capacities of the person. We can conclude, then, that the Church does not envision a category of persons—other than those who are incapable of performing a human act—who by reason of some psychological description imposed on them stand outside the need for sacramental reconciliation.

In order to discuss behavioral addiction and sacramental satisfaction, we need to consider more closely the reason why the Church made this small, but still significant, change in the *editio typica* of the *Catechism*.

What prompted making this precision in §2352? The answer lies, I submit, in the way that *Veritatis splendor* had explained moral imputability: "It is possible that the evil done as the result of invincible ignorance or a non-culpable error of judgment may not be imputable to the agent; but even in this case it does not cease to be an evil, a disorder in relation to the truth about the good" (§63).

To apply this principle to our discussion, when persons suffering from an addiction commit sins, even though their moral culpability may be reduced to a minimum, they nonetheless have made an "affective mistake" about the true goods of human perfection.[17] This mistake may be evident from the nature of the addiction, as is clear in the case of drunkenness or lechery, or not so evident, as with less demonstrative compulsions like surfing the Internet or excessive shopping. In any event, a pastor of souls is obliged to make a judgment about not only the origins of behavior but also about the harm that it causes in relation to the good ends of human flourishing.

Psychologists speak about addictions in terms of negative consequences and destructive patterns. The faith, however, enables us to make more definitive assertions. If addiction impairs human dignity, it is because it introduces a neglect of being and causes a loss of touch with objective truth. Why is this affirmation from *Fides et ratio* important for everyone? *Veritatis splendor* offers a succinct answer: "Only the act in

17. Addiction should not be confused with spiritual sloth. The same text from *Veritatis splendor* warns against "feeling easily justified in the name of our conscience" and cites Psalm 19:12, "Who can discern his errors? Clear me from hidden faults." Pastors of the Church should excuse no one from the sacrament of reconciliation.

conformity with the good can be a path that leads to life" (§72). Even granted diminished culpability, persons suffering from addictions to vicious actions do not stand on the path that leads to life. The faith teaches us that only satisfactory works accomplished in love can reestablish this conformity.

THE VOLUNTARINESS OF CHRISTIAN ACTIVITY

In order to appreciate why satisfactory works can benefit even those who suffer from addictions, we need to recall those basic elements of Christian anthropology that explain the relationship of human nature and free activity. First, just as natural law inclinations arise from the specific nature that human beings possess, so also do the voluntary wellsprings of human behavior originate in both knowledge and rational appetite. Second, as a basic feature of every human action, voluntariness signifies the self-mastery that the human person can possess over his or her activity. From this we can conclude that not only does natural law reveal the imprint of the *imago Dei*, but also that the voluntary character of human activity manifests the human person's analogical participation in that divine nature wherein knowing the good and willing the truth are necessarily coincident. Third, the more the rational creature grows in holiness, the more he or she images God, who is the cause of all voluntary movements. Anything that inhibits this kind of growth must be judged as harmful to the human person.

The Voluntary and the Free

From the foregoing, we see that Christian theology introduces a useful distinction between the voluntary and the free. Every free act is voluntary, but not every voluntary act attains the perfection of human freedom. When moral theologians discuss the voluntary, they explore the basic and indispensable conditions for human freedom, not the deliberate exercise of free choice itself. Some contemporary schools of Christian ethics prefer to adopt the dominant themes of the German *Aufklärung*, with the result that we have become accustomed to read about human freedom as a transcendental category that, for all intents and purposes, obscures the status and purposes of human nature as they pertain to the moral life. Although the poetry of modern German romanticism might lead us to conclude otherwise, transcendental freedom cannot explain those human actions that surpass the act of deliberate choice.[18] Yet the Christian tradition numbers among such voluntary though technically nonfree activities realities as foundational to human life as the profound want of the human will for happiness and the ecstatic love of God, which follows upon the beatific vision. So we are advised that impairment of the voluntary touches upon the most essential goods of human nature.

Some theologians have not understood how freedom fits into the anthropology of the *imago* and so have concluded that impediments to deliberate choice (such as arguably are present in persons suffering from addictions) leave the person in a state of moral indifference, like an automobile running in neutral. Therapeutic treatments are conceived as a means to shift the gear into drive. But such a view of choice fails to take into account the intimate relationship between human nature and human freedom. With respect to choosing, there is no state of indifference—either we are moving toward God or away from him.[19] At the same time, anything that thwarts the voluntariness of human action, including addictions, impairs a human nature whose perfection depends on achieving conformity with the good.

Consider the difference between the human being and other beings whose actions depend on knowledge. Because only human knowledge can grasp the exact nature of purposeful activity, it is characteristic of

18. "Transcendental freedom" is taken to mean one's free basic stance toward being itself, as opposed to particular individual choices that may not fully reflect this basic stance. Yet neither the embodied nature nor the teleological ordering of human freedom is sufficiently regarded by this teaching, which construes the whole providential ordering of creature to creator as a supererogatory detail surpassed by naked, overarching, and disembodied will. The human will does in certain respects transcend facticity, but remains nonetheless a creaturely reality rationally specified by the whole natural hierarchy of ends, and further elevated and perfected in grace.

19. "Freedom makes man a moral subject ... Human acts ... are either good or evil" (*CCC*, §1749).

human beings that they can properly deliberate about an end and the relationship that a means bears to it.[20] In this ability, human persons differ from brute animals, which perceive ends but remain incapable of adapting themselves to creative ways of achieving them. Likewise, but for quite different reasons, angelic persons do not reflect about means, for their intuitive knowledge eliminates the need for deliberation about circumstantial means. As a result, in both angelic nature and angelic activity, the voluntary and the free coincide, although the angels remain capable of choice.[21] Because the capacity to engage in intelligent behavior forms the basis for imputing responsibility, moral theologians ascribe praise or blame only when it is a case of fully voluntary activity.[22]

Again, the Catholic tradition acknowledges a distinction in the human being between the free and the voluntary. The importance of this distinction for our present discussion should be obvious: whatever impedes the voluntary goes against the good of human nature, and so affects immediately the spiritual well-being of the human person. We can see this claim exemplified most clearly by recalling the ways that classical moral theology dealt with impairment to the voluntary: ignorance, violence, fear, and lust.[23] A review of these classical expositions would confirm, I submit, that addiction is best understood as a metacategory for whatever factors can impede voluntary action. Our concern is not only with bad choices or, for that matter, wrong or inappropriate choices, but with the dislocations of nature that impairment of the voluntary introduces.

20. See *ST* I-II, q. 6, a. 2.

21. See, for example, the discussion in *ST* I, q. 60, a. 2, "Are the angels loving as choosing to love?," where Aquinas accounts for freedom of choice in the angels, even though the intuitive infallibility of their knowledge always shapes their prior and natural desire for only good ends.

22. So when the lamb flees from the wolf, it receives neither praise nor blame; its reward consists only in its continued existence or, if it fails to flee successfully, its "punishment" amounts to death. On the other hand, we designate angels as either good or bad on the basis of their once-and-for-all choice whether to love God as the supremely desirable good or not.

23. The *Catechism of the Catholic Church* adjusts the list: ignorance, inadvertence, duress, fear, habit, inordinate attachments, and other psychological or social factors (see §1735).

Enemies of the Voluntary

What is a voluntary action? Again, to state it briefly: a voluntary action is one that finds its principle from within the agent and proceeds with knowledge of the end.[24] When it comes to making a judgment about what affects the voluntary in a given circumstance, interiority and due knowledge serve as the criteria for evaluating a human action's voluntary character. Threats to voluntary action, such as those caused by addictions, arise from anything that can upset the psychological poise or balance in either of these areas.[25]

Established moral teaching identifies certain factors that affect voluntary activity. Violence, fear, ignorance, and lust constitute the *hostes voluntarii*, or the enemies of the voluntary.[26] These factors, when they affect a human person, either restrict the requisite knowledge for deliberate human activity or else intrude upon that interiority distinguishing authentic human conduct or "human acts" from what the tradition described as mere "acts of man." While this theory of how certain factors reduce the voluntariness of human action borrows from classical philosophy, its application belongs to the structure and the logic of the *sacra doctrina*.

24. *ST* I-II, q. 6, a. 1.

25. The pinball machine provides a helpful, albeit mechanical, metaphor for grasping the relationship of the voluntary to the free. Let the object of yesteryear's penny arcade game—namely, to score as many points as possible—represent the ultimate goal of a virtuous life. Now some intrusive factor, such as too much leaning with one's elbows, can interrupt the pinball either immediately or at some point before the game's end. As a result of such external interference, the pinball machine tilts and the game abruptly ends. Let the intrusive factors that cause the machine to tilt represent the enemies of the voluntary. To one degree or another, such intrusions tilt or upset the psychological balance or poise required for authentically free human behavior. Such factors affect the voluntariness of human activity so that the resulting actions fall into the category of either involuntary or non-voluntary actions. When this occurs, we can designate the action as authentic moral behavior only in a depreciated sense of "moral."

26. For a concise account of this material, see Ralph McInerny, *Ethica Thomistica*, rev. ed. (Washington, DC: Catholic University of America Press, 1982), 60–69. In *Aquinas on Human Action: A Theory of Practice* (Washington, DC: Catholic University of America Press, 1992), the same author gives a lucid and readable account of Aquinas's complete theory of human action. Additionally, also consult the magisterial writings of Steven A. Long on the nature of moral action: *The Teleological Grammar of the Moral Act* (Ave Maria, FL: Sapientia Press, 2007); "Natural Law, the Moral Object, and *Humanae Vitae*," in *Ressourcement Thomism: Sacred Doctrine, the Sacraments, and the Moral Life*, ed. Reinhard Hütter and Matthew Levering (Washington, DC: Catholic University of America Press, 2010), 285–311.

We are pursuing a properly theological discussion. The life sciences can aid our understanding of how such factors as collective ignorance, societal violence, personal fear, and heightened lust impair a person's ability to operate in a fully human way, but a proper analysis of these circumstances as they apply to a human person depends on theology. Only theology safeguards the relationship between being, acting, and the supernatural destiny of the human person.

Consider violence. It signifies some action imposed on a subject from the outside and against its natural bent; as such, it represents a form of coercion. Violence renders a given action involuntary—that is, an act that goes against willing—for the simple reason that an action so produced effectively results from the will of another person. Even when a person becomes an instrument of another's choice, this instrumentalization affects adversely his or her human dignity.

The second enemy, the emotion of fear, affects voluntariness in a different way.[27] Fear first arises through the contending or irascible emotions as a certain alarm of mind that shapes the way we react to some evil that is absent but likely to befall us. By contrast, those evils that already have befallen an individual generate the emotion of sorrow. The effect of fear on voluntary activity depends upon various and complex factors. The classical example of the rich merchant at sea illustrates a typical scenario. When the threatening storm arises without forewarning, the merchant on the high seas must immediately estimate the peril that presently endangers both his life and his merchandise. Once he determines that his life is actually jeopardized as long as he holds on to the merchandise in the boat, fear moves him to throw the goods overboard. While he does this freely, still throwing the goods overboard expresses voluntary action only after a fashion, for he certainly would act otherwise if not for the sure perception that his fragile bark might sink and his life would be lost. Acting under the aspect of simple voluntariness, the merchant would preserve both life and merchandise. Actions induced by fear, then, exemplify the voluntary only in a qualified sense of the term, for apart from the concrete circumstances that precipitate

27. See *ST* I-II, q. 6, a. 6.

the fear, the individual would not have acted in such a way. One only has to consider apostasy born of fear to realize that sacramental satisfaction serves the healing of the person who acts as a result of undue fear.

In the context of human voluntariness, concupiscence or lust represents the basic human desire for pleasure but does not necessarily imply a note of baseness. This emotion concerns the human response to things perceived as good but not yet possessed in joy and delight. Lust ensures that human nature remains capable of moving toward the essential goods required for individual perfection and the perfection of the species. Precisely because of its drawing-from-within function, lust always increases the voluntary character of an action.[28] In other words, lust draws the person toward a perceived good so that the interiority characteristic of the voluntary increases rather than decreases.

Because in conditions of lust the agent's interior movement follows its voluntary direction toward some object of desire, the lustful person is not said to act involuntarily. Instead, in cases where actions proceed from lust, the resultant action illustrates non-voluntary activity, that is, action proceeding from a strong interior drive while the agent lacks a keen comprehension of the object of his or her lust. Lust, it is true, can obscure the work of right reason, but even when it causes diminished culpability, there still remains the need for image restoration. Think of the person caught in the practice of autosexual behavior and what is required to reintroduce him or her into the full relational quality of sex that is required by the nuptial meaning of the body.

While such considerations obviously merit attention when it comes to evaluating a person's culpability for a particular action, emotional upset of the magnitude suggested by impaired voluntary clearly does not betoken a desirable state for human beings to foster. Consider the harm that living in a habitually disordered state brings to human happiness. For example, one who sins habitually against the virtue of temperance becomes, as it were voluntarily bound, to goods in a way that conform neither to integral human perfection and contentment nor to evangelical values and beatitudes. Some moral theologians argue that, because

28. See *ST* I-II, q. 6, a. 7.

the lustful state of a person diminishes the voluntary character of human conduct, we should reclassify certain species of disordered activity, such as adolescent masturbation and daytime unchaste reveries. Such authors, it seems, grasp only half the truth about moral culpability, for while they aim to acknowledge the factors that depreciate the voluntary in a certain persons, at the same time they risk exculpating whole classes of vicious behavior.

From these short remarks about the enemies of the voluntary, we learn that the juridical category of imputability and the psychological category of responsibility do not determine the moral status of the person whose voluntary is impaired. The standard teaching on the enemies of the voluntary persuades us that impairment of human nature at this level is neither a neutral matter nor a matter of no consequence for the moral life.[29] Human conduct that falls short of bringing a person to human perfection and Christian maturity requires forgiveness and restoration.

SACRAMENTAL SATISFACTION AND ADDICTION

Contemporary magisterial teaching provides a way to assess the effect of impaired human action on the agent. It goes without saying that we are in a better position to understand the interrelationship of physiological factors and human actions than were the theologians of yesteryear. Still, in order to maintain the radical spirituality of human freedom, it is necessary to consider any biological factor dispositive for, rather than determinative of, human action. Otherwise, psychology produces determinism. This subject introduces another discussion that is not our purpose today.

We can conclude, however, that satisfactory works and the use of the gift of indulgences can benefit spiritually every Christian, even those who are involved in treatment for behavior that is judged to flow from

29. Again, the sobering judgment found in *Veritatis splendor* is germane: "It is possible that the evil done as the result of invincible ignorance or a non-culpable error of judgment may not be imputable to the agent; but even in this case it does not cease to be an evil, a disorder in relation to the truth about the good" (§63).

an addiction. The reason is simple: anyone who is impaired from pursuing the good ends that perfect the Christian life needs to embrace the work of image restoration. The spiritual renewal complements psychological health. It does not impair it.

I recognize that associating sin with certain addictions, especially those for which the hypothesis of physical causation is largely accepted, challenges some suppositions of good counseling practices. If I were asked to begin a reply, I would begin with the Easter *praeconium*, the Exultet, where we read that it is better to have been redeemed by Christ than never to have sinned. It is a paradoxical exclamation, but warns us nonetheless not to find too much comfort in psychological strategies for easing guilt. For the Christian believer, the truth is that they are not necessary. What is more important, it would be an error only to correct bad behavior and not accomplish the complete renewal of the human person that Christian forgiveness promises.

It remains an exercise of pastoral charity to encourage those persons whose ability to choose the good in freedom is somehow impaired to seek the sacrament of reconciliation. The confessor, on the other hand, needs to be alert to the special conditions of the person. In a Christian context, both therapist and confessor aim to restore the person to freedom, so that he or she once again is able to embrace the truth. The sacrament of penance remains a privileged instrument of this renewal, one that enjoys the distinctive quality of being both sign and cause of that personal healing which consists "in restoring us to God's grace and joining us with him in an intimate friendship" (*CCC*, §1468).

CHAPTER 11

THOMISTIC MORAL GUIDANCE

An Illustration from the Maritains

In this essay, Father Cessario recounts the friendship that Jacques and Raïssa Maritain shared with a young Frenchman named Maurice Sachs. This moving narrative illustrates the application of Thomistic moral principles to a concrete moral situation and figure. From the very beginning, sound theology and an unwavering commitment to sanctity informed the Maritains' relationship with the "mysteriously dark" Sachs. Not for a moment did either Jacques or Raïssa believe that even the bleakest recesses of grave moral disorder could stand impervious to the sanctifying power of God's love. "The Maritains pursued their evangelizing efforts inspired by a confidence that the basic dynamisms of creation flow from the divine will from which all striving for perfection derives." Jacques and Raïssa knew that the truth has grace—grace that can heal, perfect, and transform any person. This narrative testifies to the mystery of divine predilection and predestination. As Raïssa herself said, "Only the Good God, in effect, is able to begin, continue, and accomplish the work of our sanctification." On the surface, the complexities present within Maurice's story may not afford us much by way of sanguine consolation. Nonetheless, the mys-

Originally published as "*Humanae Vitae* 17: *Vaticinium ex eventu?* An Illustration from the Maritains' Moral Guidance to Maurice Sachs," *Nova et Vetera* 6, no. 4 (2008): 711–30. Reprinted by permission.

tery of divine grace remains just that, a mystery, and we entrust ourselves—as Jacques and Raïssa entrusted Maurice—to God's love and mercy.

In remarks prepared for a conference that commemorated the twenty-fifth anniversary of *Humanae vitae*, Father Ernest Fortin, AA, made the following observation: "In retrospect, *Humanae vitae* can be said to have been truly prophetic. It foresaw that the use of contraceptives and the development of a contraceptive mentality would deal a severe blow to family life and therewith to society as a whole."[1] The text that Father Fortin probably had in mind is found at §17 of the 1968 encyclical letter of Pope Paul VI:

> Not much experience is needed in order to know human weakness, and to understand that men—especially the young, who are so vulnerable on this point—have need of encouragement to be faithful to the moral law, so that they must not be offered some easy means of eluding its observance. (*Humanae vitae*, §17)

In 1993 at Assumption College in Worcester, Massachusetts, Father Fortin included among the unhappy consequences of the widespread acceptance of contraceptives the fact that "homosexual partnerships are being granted both family status in law and the right to adopt children."[2] He wondered about future "nightmarish choices." He was right to wonder out loud. In 2014, eighteen states recognize civil unions or marriages between persons of the same sex.

This chapter reports on the distinctively Catholic moral guidance that Jacques and Raïssa Maritain gave to a certain young Frenchman named Maurice Sachs. We know of course that Jacques Maritain and Pope Paul VI were friends. It remains speculation whether the following story of Maurice Sachs may have contributed to that warning—the one Father Fortin calls "prophetic"—that is contained in §17 of *Humanae vi-*

1. Ernest Fortin, "*Humanae Vitae*'s Silver Jubilee: Twenty-Five Years Later," in *Ernest L. Fortin: Collected Essays*, vol. 4, *Ever Ancient, Ever New: Ruminations on the City, the Soul, and the Church*, ed. Michael P. Foley (New York: Rowman & Littlefield, 2007), 164.

2. Ibid.

tae. In other terms, whether this text does in fact constitute a *vaticinium ex eventu*.

SOME BACKGROUND TO SEXUAL MORES *ENTRE LES DEUX GUERRES*

Taking a broad view, the English philosopher Roger Scruton has observed that the situation of French intellectuals during the early twentieth century was not unlike that of English intellectuals. Writers and artists were drawn in three directions—toward a kind of iconized vision of France and her Catholic faith, toward a flamboyant bohemianism that defied bourgeois conventions, and toward the new universal faith of the Communist church.[3] The Maritains became acquainted with representative figures from each class. The early decades of the twentieth century also witnessed a marked increase in the number of homosexual liaisons that occurred among *les vedettes* of the Paris literary and artistic salons. These ephemeral gay relationships were countenanced for the most part by the fashionable elite that inhabited *le beau monde*. What one may describe as a sociological phenomenon, this "world" forms some of the background for the exercise of that divine mission to evangelize that Jacques and Raïssa Maritain undertook with passion during *les Années Folles*.

THE FIGURE OF MAURICE SACHS, 1906–45

To explore the Maritains as spiritual guides for the perplexed, I have chosen one figure from the period, Maurice Sachs, a man whose biography is subtitled *Les travaux forcés de la frivolité*.[4] If we follow the standard accounts of this Frenchman's topsy-turvy life, he comes out looking like the poster boy for French-style bohemianism. Truth to tell, however, Maurice Sachs at various times and at other times perhaps simultaneously followed all three of the directions that Roger Scruton sketches

3. In private research that Roger Scruton has contributed to a research project on the natural law at the Institute for the Psychological Sciences in Arlington, Virginia.

4. Henri Raczymow, *Maurice Sachs, ou Les travaux forcés de la frivolité* (Paris: Gallimard, 1988), 423. Sachs himself coined the expression.

out to describe the paths taken by early twentieth-century French intellectuals.

It should be noted first of all that the second path, that of flamboyant bohemianism, was not explicitly or exclusively homosexual. It was, again on Roger Scruton's account, a path of wit, satire, bohemianism, and cosmopolitanism, a thousand miles from the patriotic fervor of Charles Péguy. It owed much, however, to Péguy's contemporary Guillaume Apollinaire, illegitimate son of a Polish mother. Apollinaire coined the term "surrealism" and revived interest in the works of the Marquis de Sade. He wrote erotic novels as well as verses (for example, *Alcools*) that made him famous, and was perhaps the first apostle of transgression.[5] Among his friends were Jean Cocteau, Erik Satie, Marc Chagall, and Max Jacob, all of whom belonged after World War I (at the end of which Apollinaire died of influenza, weakened by a head wound received at the front) to the circle that frequented *Le boeuf sur le toit*.[6] This celebrated eighth-

5. "*Alcools* (1913) was a selection of poems written over the previous fifteen years. It combined classical verse forms with modern imagery, involving transcriptions of street conversations overheard by chance and the absence of punctuation. It opened with the poem 'Zone,' in which the tormented poet wanders through streets after the loss of his mistress. Among its other famous lyrical pieces is 'Le pont Mirabeau.' Some of its poems were inspired by Jacqueline Kolb. Annie Playden, an English governess, inspired the Rhineland piece, 'La chanson du mal aimé.'" For further information, see www.kirjasto.sci.fi/apollina.htm.

And of course one notes the unmistakable and almost overbearing Christian symbolism of "Zone," which intimates something of the intensely Catholic milieu of early twentieth-century France. It seems that no matter what the position (from nihilistic transgression to apostolic exhortation) an intellectual or artist adopted in those days, Catholicism was inevitably close at hand. Also noteworthy is the temptations of paganism and its connection with eroticism, which would preoccupy Georges Bataille (another failed Catholic) for the rest of his life. Bataille was at first deeply involved in surrealism until his break with André Breton. The scene at the end of *Histoire de l'oeil* involving the mutilation and murder of a Catholic priest is perhaps the most ugly expression of the rage some of these men felt at being not only tied to a Catholic past, but also involved in a Catholic present. No wonder so much of this work in transgression is taken up in the search for new gods, in the form of idols and concepts.

6. *Le Boeuf sur le Toit* [*The Ox on the Roof: The Nothing-Doing Bar*], op. 58, is a surrealist ballet. It is based on a score composed by Darius Milhaud that is strongly influenced by Brazilian popular music (the title is that of an old Brazilian tango, one of close to thirty Brazilian tunes quoted in the composition). Originally, the piece was to have been the score of a silent Charlie Chaplin film (*Cinéma-fantaisie* for violin and piano). Its transformation into a ballet was the making of the piece, with a scenario by Jean Cocteau, stage designs by Raoul Dufy, and costumes by Guy-Pierre Fauconnet. The choreography was deliberately very slow, in marked contrast to the lively and joyful spirit of the music. The premiere was given in February 1920 at the Théâtre des Champs Élysées and comprised, besides the ballet, *Adieu, New York* by Georges Auric, *Cocardes* by Francis Poulenc, and *Trois petites pièces montées* by Erik

arrondissement cabaret was the place at which Stravinsky and Diaghilev could be seen along with the surrealists, the fauves, poets like Jacob and Paul Claudel—and just about anybody who was anybody among the bohemians of the day.[7] It played a great role in the "education" of the unattached adolescents of the period—or so we are told by one prominent individual among those who frequented *Le boeuf*.[8]

The person in question was the abovementioned teenager Maurice Sachs, a budding novelist who seduced and betrayed in endless succession, and who finished life as a prisoner of the Gestapo, having first worked for them as an agent happy to betray even his friends. On the surface, Sachs was the epitome of the serial double-dealer whose predatory homosexuality began in adolescence, when he was educated in a Parisian English-style boys' school, and later led to promiscuous affairs with everyone who mattered—including Gide, Coceatu, and Jacob—as well as with many who did not.[9] Persuaded by Cocteau in 1925 to embrace Catholicism, Sachs shortly thereafter entered a seminary with a view to becoming a priest. But he shortly left on account of a relapse into promiscuous homosexuality, and seems thereafter to have drifted away from the practice of the Catholic faith, though not from his Catholic friends.[10] Nor did his Catholic friends abandon him. In his acclaimed biography of Jacques and Raïssa Maritain, Jean-Luc Barré reports that Jacques Maritain as late as 1949 plaintively wondered out loud, "Poor Maurice Sachs, is he dead, is he alive?"[11]

Satie. The version for chamber orchestra was followed by another for piano duet, subtitled *Cinema Symphony* on South American Airs. Its performance lasts about a quarter of an hour. The ballet gave its name to a well-known Parisian bar and restaurant that opened in 1922. For further information, see www.boeufsurletoit.com.

7. Sergei Pavlovich Diaghilev, also referred to as Serge (March 31, 1872, to August 19, 1929), was a Russian art critic, patron, ballet impresario, and founder of the Ballets Russes, from which many famous dancers and choreographers would later arise.

8. Maurice Sachs, *Witches' Sabbath*, trans. Richard Howard (New York: Stein and Day, 1964), 72.

9. The school was L'École de l'Isle-de-France, to which Sachs referred in *The Sabbath* as *le college de Luza*.

10. "Il parlait beaucoup, beaucoup de Paris et en particulier de la Maison Maritain à Meudon . . . À la fin, nous avions decidé de nous rencontrer à Meudon apres la guerre." Maurice Sachs and Jacques and Raïssa Maritain, "Letter of Richard Hitzler to Raïssa Maritain," in *Correspondance (1925–1939)*, ed. Michel Bressolette and René Mougel (Paris: Gallimard, 2003), 323.

11. Jean Luc Barré, *Jacques & Raïssa Maritain: Beggars for Heaven*, trans. Bernard E. Doer-

As will become evident in what follows, Maurice Sachs affords a good example of the second of Scruton's directions—the bohemian. Thanks to his association with André Gide, Sachs also briefly followed the third—the Communist—direction.[12] And his attachment to the first, or Christian, direction may not be as short-lived as many commentators assume. We know, for instance, that from his prison cell at Fuhlsbüttel, a Nazi concentration camp located near Hamburg, Sachs recalled his early association with the Maritains, which led to his baptism.[13] Richard Hitzler, a fellow prisoner at Fuhlsbüttel who, unlike Sachs, survived his internment, reports that, during his final days, Sachs repeatedly expressed the ardent wish that he would be able to return after the war to the Maritains' home at Meudon, which since the spring of 1923 had provided a spiritual gravitational center for the poets, painters, and musicians whom they had met in the company of their own evangelist, Léon Bloy.[14]

To appreciate the Maritains' influence on Maurice Sachs, we must examine closely the evolution of their friendship with him. Abandoned by his father at the age of five, Maurice Sachs was brought up in straightened circumstances. "From the time of his teens," writes one author,

> the physically unappealing yet highly seductive Sachs, whom [Jean] Cocteau has depicted in his memoirs stuffing his pockets with toilet paper he pretended was money, followed an essentially theatrical calling, an endless getting into character. Sachs has hastily been labeled "the Jean

---

ing (Notre Dame, IN: University of Notre Dame Press, 2005), 405. The book has been favorably reviewed by John F. X. Knasas in *Catholic Historical Review* 93 (2007): 435–36.

12. His biographer includes a chapter on "Maurice 'communiste.'" See Raczymow, *Maurice Sachs*, 249–56.

13. The prison, originally built as a regular prison in 1879, was converted to a satellite concentration camp after the Nazis' takeover of Germany in 1933, when it was placed under the control of the SS and SA. Most of the inmates were anti-Nazi sympathizers, Jews, Jehovah Witnesses, Roma, gays, and others whom the regime wanted to lock up. Over seven hundred people were interned in the camp following Kristallnacht in 1938. "Konzentrationslager Fuhlsbüttel" (Fuhlsbüttel concentration camp) was referred to as "KolaFu" in common parlance and became a synonym for oppression and death through hard labor. Fuhlsbüttel was often an initial point of incarceration for prisoners who were sent on to other camps such as Buchenwald, Neuengamme, Ravensbrück, or Sachsenhausen. The camp was liberated in May 1945, by which time over 250 people had been murdered there. A camp memorial has been constructed nearby.

14. Sachs, *Correspondance*, 23. See also, Barré, *Jacques & Raïssa Maritain*, 149ff.

Genet of the twenties," but the resemblance is superficial, based on their shared combination of homosexuality, thieving, black marketeering, and later fascination with Nazi Germany.[15]

This sketch published in *Yale French Studies* represents the standard unsympathetic account of the teenager that the Maritains welcomed into their affections. At the same time, this short description helps us to appreciate Raïssa Maritain's first reaction to Maurice Sachs: "something mysteriously dark," she opined.[16]

What follows touches only the high points of the interaction between the Maritains and Maurice Sachs, whose true personal dispositions and intentions, it should become evident, are not always easy to judge. We begin in July 1924, when, at Meudon, Jacques the evangelist first receives Jean Cocteau and eventually welcomes his friends, including the eighteen-year-old Maurice Sachs, who in February of the same year had become one of Cocteau's "secretaries."[17] Twelve months later, on August 2, 1925, to be precise, and urged on by Cocteau, Maurice Sachs visits Jacques Maritain in order to pursue instructions in the Catholic faith. Jacques begins with the Trinity.[18] By the end of the month, Maurice receives baptism with Raïssa Maritain as godmother and Jean Cocteau as godfather by proxy, with Jacques standing in. The place was the private chapel of the Maritains' at 10 rue du Parc, Meudon. It is on the same day, August 29, 1925, that we read in Raïssa's *Journal*, "Baptism of Maurice. Still, I am not reassured. This lad has something mysteriously dark about him that makes me ill at ease." Maurice's first communion and confirmation by the Bishop of Versailles follow appropriately.[19]

His biographer, Henri Raczymow, describes the young Maurice Sachs as an all or nothing man.[20] Soon the new convert is thinking

15. David J. Jacobson, "Jews for Genius: The Unholy Disorders of Maurice Sachs," *Yale French Studies* 85 (1994): 183.

16. Barré, *Jacques & Raïssa Maritain*, 216. See also Raczymow, *Maurice Sachs*, 58, citing Jacques Maritain, *Journal de Raïssa* (Paris: Desclée de Brouwer, 1963): "Ce garçon, écrira-t-elle dans son Journal, a quelque chose de obscur qui m'inquiète."

17. Barré, *Jacques & Raïssa Maritain*, 180–226, devotes a chapter to the meeting of Maritain and Jean Cocteau titled "God or Jean Cocteau?" See also Sachs, *Correspondance*, 33n1.

18. Raczymow, *Maurice Sachs*, 101.

19. Ibid., 106.

20. "Sachs, c'est toujours tout ou rien" (ibid., 108).

about pursuing a priestly vocation and in the meantime about taking up temporary residence with the Maritains. Raïssa holds out the advantages of his living with them: the presence of the most blessed sacrament and *la douce influence de Jacques*.[21] On January 2, 1926, Maurice enters the Séminaire des Carmes, 21 rue d'Assas, which in 1792 had been the scene of the martyrdom of 115 priests and three bishops.[22] The Maritains, Jean Cocteau, Max Jacob, and his peer friend, Jean Bourgoint, support him variously and variously.[23] Maurice perseveres in his vocational resolution for about six and a half months.

With certain allowances, Maurice adapted to the rigorous schedule of the seminary. Jacques Maritain, it is said, helped him to obtain permission to wear the clerical soutane in advance of the usual time. Maurice argued that the cassock would help him sustain the moral requirements of his new vocation, although he later confessed a perverse fascination with the dress style of the soutane. At the same time, for six months, he made his daily morning meditation, mostly while reading Pascal, and assisted, kneeling, at Mass, even though he later reported in his diary that he suffered from spontaneous movements of the flesh. "But still," Sachs further recalled, "it is a futile and merely nervous erection when the imagination does not sustain it with any incongruous image; there is no harm in it, at most a certain surprise and embarrassment."[24] Sachs nonetheless goes on to admit that these occurrences caused him "to feel remorse," and that they led him to ask for permission to serve the Mass, an activity that he imagined would ease his discomfort.

All in all, Maurice's first days in the seminary were not without peace, especially when at the end of the day he came before the Blessed Virgin Mary. "There was no occasion to forget her," writes Sachs.

21. Letter of Raïssa Maritain to Maurice Sachs, November 19, 1925, Archives Madeleine Castaing, cited in Raczymow, *Maurice Sachs*, 110.

22. The website reports: "L'accueil du séminaire des Carmes: Durant la Première Guerre mondiale, des séminaristes venus du nord et de l'est de la France sont hébergés dans l'ancien couvent. En 1919, Mgr Verdier y fonde un séminaire universitaire, toujours en fonctionnement aujourd'hui."

23. Max Jacob (July 12, 1876, to March 5, 1944) was a French poet, painter, writer, and critic. He, too, was a convert to Catholicism.

24. Maurice Sachs, *Witches' Sabbath*, 128–29.

> It was here that I prayed best, it was here that I believed best. Perhaps because it is easier to believe in the Holy Virgin than in God; for she created neither heaven nor earth, but a man in our image; because everything in us believes in her, as all that we are has grown within her, nine months from the day of conception.[25]

Not bad for a young convert burdened with past disorders and present temptations.

Seminary discipline soon taxed the immature virtuous dispositions of the young Maurice. After two months of presumably good-willed endeavor, he began to think of his cell as a "chamber of horrors and demons."[26] Old deep-seated habits, including losing struggles with masturbation, recurred: "I groaned in my solitude; I ran to the chapel, the garden, returned, knelt, got up again, fell back, started up, and finally sank down, beaten, into my lacerating pleasures."[27] Neither the ascetical practices of the period, which included using the discipline and other instruments of physical penance, nor the more humane suggestion of Jacques Maritain that he take up a minimum amount of apostolic activity—which Maritain, one assumes, rightly considered would put the still-teenager "M. Le Cure Maurice Sachs" into living contact with other persons—was sufficient to calm his unholy desires.

Then came the summer vacation months of 1926, when the diocesan seminarians were allowed to return to their families. Maurice left with his maternal grandmother Alice Bizet—sometime daughter-in-law of the composer Georges—for the French Riviera. The devil was waiting for him, as Jacques Maritain, who took the time to escort grandmother and grandson to the Gare de Lyon, may have instinctually anticipated.

"I had come in utter innocence of heart," Maurice later pleaded with his reader to believe in faith.[28] Still, the highly charged atmosphere of the beachside resort Juan-les-Pins quickly overpowered this all too recently converted habitué of *le beau monde*. The young American writer Glenway Wescott, who would later become a familiar figure in the New York artistic and gay community, introduced Maurice to a teenage boy

25. Ibid., 132, original emphasis.
26. Ibid., 135.
27. Ibid.
28. Ibid., 140–41.

named Tom Pinkerton, who was then vacationing with his high-strung mother on the Côte d'Azur.[29] Infatuation developed first, followed by what may have been a mutual seduction. "We succumbed to the exhaustion of our forces of resistance but took no pleasure in doing so," Maurice later wrote, perhaps tendentiously.[30] The public scandal caused by Maurice's sudden preoccupation with the sixteen-year-old Tom was enough to make the recently repentant Cocteau react strongly, and to insist that Maurice return immediately to Paris. Once back at the seminary, the priest who had baptized him the year before counseled: "Better make a good Christian than a bad priest."[31] In November 1926, Maurice left the seminary to fulfill his military service. From his military barracks, he wrote to Jacques on November 23, 1926, recounting his religious practices: "The only thing is that there is no Mass, but I make my stations of the cross while walking up to the stables which are two kilometers away, and I make my meditation while combing my horse."[32]

After finishing his military service in April 1928, Maurice took on literary projects, eventually left for the United States, where he opened an art gallery, married the daughter of a New York Presbyterian minister (whom he thereafter shortly abandoned), and subsequently took up a relationship with a young man, Henry Wibbels, in California. In March 1933, he encountered Jacques Maritain in Chicago. Later that same year, Maurice returned to France. In 1939, Sachs was assigned to the commander of the British troops in Caen, and then in 1942 he impulsively volunteered for service in Germany, where he briefly worked in 1943 for

29. As a writer, Glenway Wescott (1901–87) left behind a series of novels, including *The Grandmothers* and *The Pilgrim Hawk*, noted for their remarkable lyricism. As a literary figure, Wescott also became a symbol of his times. Born on a Wisconsin farm in 1901, he associated as a young writer with Hemingway, Stein, and Fitzgerald in 1920s Paris and subsequently was a central figure in New York's artistic and gay communities. Though he did not finish a novel after the age of forty-five, he was just as famous as an arts impresario, as a diarist, and for the company he kept: W. H. Auden, Christopher Isherwood, Marianne Moore, Somerset Maugham, E. M. Forster, Joseph Campbell, and scores of other luminaries. See Jerry Rosco, *Glenway Wescott Personally: A Biography* (Madison: University of Wisconsin Press, 2002).

30. Sachs, *Witches' Sabbath*, 142.

31. Ibid.

32. "Seulement pas de messe, mais je fais mon chemin de croix en montant à pied aux écuries qui sont à deux km. et ma méditation en étrillant mon cheval." See Sachs, *Correspondance*, 183.

the Gestapo—that is, before he was arrested and sent to the Fuhlsbüttel concentration camp.[33] Even his work as an informer betrayed his conflicted state of soul: "Though willing," reports one authority, "to turn in other resistance workers, he refused for example, to hand over a Jesuit priest."[34] Maurice perished toward the end of the war, perhaps on a forced march. His death certificate is dated April 14, 1945.

THE MARITAINS' "INTEMPERATE ZEAL"

The above account of Maurice Sachs's life largely follows the account of his biographer, Henri Raczymow, complemented with excerpts from Sach's own "illusionist" autobiographical essay, *Le Sabbat*, translated as *Witches' Sabbath*.[35] In 2003, Michel Bressolette and René Mougel published an edition of the known correspondence between Sachs and the Maritains. The letters, cards, and telegrams date from 1925 to 1939, the year that Maurice disappears into the fog of the Second World War. So we have a privileged vantage point from which to inquire about what transpired between the Maritains and this young Jewish convert who today some would say suffered from deep-seated same-sex tendencies. Secular studies of Sachs take for granted his dominant sexual preferences; they have a more difficult time granting the authenticity of his conversion to Catholicism, still less of accepting it as something permanent. The *Correspondance*, on the other hand, raises questions about these assumptions. Maurice after all had fallen under the sway of the Maritains' "intemperate zeal."[36]

In his first letter to Jacques, dated July 28, 1925, the nineteen-year-old Maurice states things clearly: "Nothing concerns me more than Baptism. I regret the years empty of faith that are behind me."[37] As the days

33. His biographer speculates that the decision to go to Hamburg may have been made for no reason more profound than the *l'impatience de changer d'air*. See Raczymow, *Maurice Sachs*, 410.

34. Jacobson, "Jews for Genius,"198.

35. See Barré, *Jacques & Raïssa Maritain*, 208ff.

36. Ibid., 205. The conversions for which the Maritains were instrumental did not win the admiration of all, even of the ecclesiastical authorities.

37. Sachs, *Correspondance*, 33.

pass, the exchanges between Maurice and each of the Maritains intensify both in rhythm and spiritual density. On August 13, 1925, Raïssa quotes to him large chunks of the Liturgy for the feast of the Assumption—"les Anges se réjouissent de son Assomption et ils en louent le Fils de Dieu."[38] Maurice replies appreciatively, although it is clear that he has not yet completed his mystagogy: "I am accustoming myself," he writes, "to fear no longer the Church in her exterior rituals."[39] Again, Maurice acknowledges the satisfaction he found in reading the copy of the *Imitation of Christ* that the Maritains sent him. Though, at the same time, he writes revealingly:

> I do not have to confess the sins of the catechism, but I must fortify my heart against the human affections that suddenly surge into my heart like gushing water. They upset the calm blood that passes tranquilly through our arteries when we love only God and those who are like us in this love.[40]

Certain of Maurice's human affections center on, among others, Jacques Maritain, who reminds him of images of Christ, and on Jean Cocteau, whose initials are the same as those of Christ's—J. C.[41] Then there is the figure of Jean Bourgoint, who on March 11, 1966, would die a Cistercian monk, caring for lepers in the Cameroon.[42] He was Maurice's peer and one of Cocteau's ephebes, whom Maurice later introduced to Le Père Pressoir, the seminary priest who would soon baptize Maurice and later serve as his spiritual guide.

From the day of Maurice's baptism through the rest of 1925, the exchange of letters between Maurice and the Maritains continues steadily. Even the editor of their correspondence is constrained to remark, "Mystère des lettres et leur rapidité, 29 sept. 7 h moins ¼."[43] All in all, these

38. Ibid., 39.

39. Ibid., 44.

40. Ibid., 49, 50; my translation.

41. Maurice to the Maritains, "Letter of 6 August 1925," in Sachs, *Correspondance*, 35.

42. For further information on Jean Bourgoint, see Jean Bourgoint (Frère Pascal), *Le Retour de l'enfant terrible: Lettres, 1923–1966*, ed. Jean Hugo and Jean Mouton (Paris: Desclée de Brouwer, 1975), and Georges Lauris, *Itinéraire d'un enfant terrible: De Cocteau à Cîteaux* (Paris: Presses de la Renaissance, 1998).

43. Letter 23, in Sachs, *Correspondance*, 62.

accelerated communications reflect the struggles of a young man exposed suddenly to the highest forms of Catholic spiritual doctrine, including a compendium of the entire mystical doctrine of St. John of the Cross, and at the same time trying to understand how the baptism that gave him every grace of the Christian life still leaves him uncertain of himself. "My spirit is weak, distracted, and sometimes tepid," he writes to his *très chers et doux amis,* "and my body is sometimes shaken up by the demon."[44] Maurice also writes individually to Raïssa and Jacques. Each in turn replies, sometimes on the same day; for instance, on October 20, 1925, when Jacques briefly reminds Maurice of his prayerful sentiments and suggests that he send a letter to Fribourg, Switzerland.

After hearing High Mass at Notre Dame, Maurice exclaims, "It's the only possible environment. One must be either a poet or a priest. Jacques is both, but he is a miracle."[45] A Catholic comprehension develops in Maurice. On November 2, 1925, he asks his godmother to pray for his grandfather, Jacques Bizet, whose anniversary of death falls on the next day. As November draws to a close, Maurice, who has decided to move in with the Maritains, cries out, "My God, I can't wait to live at Meudon. What better preparation than to sleep under your chapel and to pray for long times in your house which is the House of God."[46] December interrupts the rhythm of letters. Maurice is living with Jacques and Raïssa. By January 4, 1926, Maurice again takes up his correspondence with the Maritains. Now from the seminary, *des Carmes.*

During the first month, the letters from the seminary reveal the interests of Maurice's life; his personal relationships—including Raïssa's sister Vera and their mother, who of course live with the Maritains—his efforts to begin a spiritual life, especially of prayer; and his concern to settle affairs left over from his former life, such as the payment of debts. Something of the emotionally immature and of the mawkishly sentimental inform these letters—such as the hand-drawn sketch that depicts his friends on a field of roses and stars.[47] At the same time, Maurice reports on his careful reading of Jacques's books as they appear; for exam-

44. Sachs, *Correspondance,* 66.
45. Ibid., 80.
46. Ibid., 84.
47. Ibid., 103.

ple, on February 13, 1926, *Élements de philosophie (Premier Fasicule)*. On March 7, the old feast of St. Thomas Aquinas, Maurice sends a poem on a homemade card decorated with religious symbols. By the end of the month, however, he writes to his dear friends: "I am very weak. What now! God gave me a little of his Cross and I let it down."[48]

On the Monday of Holy Week, Maurice writes in order to borrow 660 francs from Jacques. Maurice was in the habit of visiting the Maritains and his other Paris friends when his seminary schedule allowed, and he did so on the following Easter Sunday. By June 6, Raïssa is constrained to remind him: "It is not without cruel struggles that nature cedes to grace." By the middle of July 1926, after passing some days of retreat at Solesmes, "where he cried for the first time in six years," Maurice is moved to consider a Benedictine vocation as the only way to ensure his perseverance.[49] The Maritains continue to support the young seminarian by giving sound spiritual advice, by assuring him of their personal support, and, on the part of his godmother Raïssa, by offering a womanly expression of understanding and consolation.

Even while on vacation, Maurice still writes "home." The first letter from Juan-les-Pins is written on the feast of St. Mary Magdalene. Three days later, on the feast of St. James, Maurice writes to Jacques: "Thank you, thank you for all that you have done for me. My heart is full of gratitude for you, for you James the Apostle."[50] On July 31, the feast of St. Ignatius, "How beautiful will be the day of my ordination; I will be able to bless you as my heart blesses you."[51] On the Vigil of the Assumption, Maurice sends a postcard from Lerins. Next, on August 22, he writes, "I prayed this morning to ask God for all the graces of conversion that we hope for, by the intercession of our Mother."[52] From these external signs, Maurice's Marian and liturgical spirituality appears in order. He expresses himself as one would expect from a seminarian of the period, even while on vacation.

Then arises the storm. On August 29, 1926, Maurice writes to Jacques as to a secular father confessor, and he tells him that for four days he has

48. Ibid., 121.
49. Ibid., 149.
50. Ibid., 151.
51. Ibid., 153.
52. Ibid., 155.

lived in horrible disarray and deception: "I am taking the only remedy. I am leaving here tomorrow for Solesmes. There, I hope to gain my composure."[53] Maurice had met Tom Pinkerton. "Pray Jesus that he will humble me and that he will bend me. I belong to Him, and still all of me wants to be elsewhere . . . Write!"[54] It would be difficult to overlook the conflicted state of Maurice's soul. The rational in Maurice reaches out for truthful counsel from the "apostle" who had guided him to Catholic faith. But his emotional powers are captivated by other, less reliable, forces.

Things did not improve for Maurice. After he had both finished another stay at Solesmes and spent some time at Meudon, Jacques is obliged to write on October 1, 1926, a sharp letter of admonition: "The Maurice of before, we did not know. This time, during the few days that you spent at Meudon, we met him. He and the Christian Maurice were at the same time before us, creating together an unhappy peace."[55] This exercise in fraternal correction displays a masterful expression of both spiritual paternity and spiritual direction. Jacques spared no effort to curb the waywardness that he rightly recognized as recapturing the soul of Maurice Sachs. Like a father, Jacques explained the classical teaching on repentance: "Your life from before has left profound marks in you that only a long practice of the most strict Christian life is able to erase."[56] Later the same month, Maurice writes confidentially to Jacques, informing him that he has seen "the young American," though without committing a carnal sin. But this *affaire* is not finished. "For two months now, my heart has been aching," admits Maurice.

Maurice spends time at another French Benedictine monastery, Saint-Benoît-sur-Loire, along with his old friend Max Jacobs (†1944), whose religious conversion achieved stability with his retirement to Benedictine life.[57] "Jacques," Maurice writes, "I am not doing well."[58] Again, on No-

53. Ibid., 156–57.
54. Ibid., 157.
55. Ibid., 165.
56. Ibid., 167.
57. "Jacob converted to Christianity in 1909 and became a Roman Catholic in 1915, but he nevertheless continued to oscillate between extravagant penitence and wild bohemianism until 1921, at which time he retired into semi-monastic seclusion at Saint-Benoît-sur-Loire. He lived there most of the time, supporting himself by painting, until World War II, when he was interned in the concentration camp at Drancy, near Paris, where he died." See http://www.britannica.com/EBchecked/topic/298950/Max-Jacob.
58. Sachs, *Correspondance*, 172.

vember 5, Maurice tells Jacques that he vows not to have sexual relations with Tom Pinkerton, who is not homosexual, but at the same time allows that he cannot live without his friendship altogether. Maurice sends Tom the *Imitation*, and he encourages him to return to the practice of the faith. He also warns Tom to escape the "constant torment that homosexuality is."[59] This long letter written from Saint-Benoît-sur-Loire expresses clearly Maurice's at least unconscious identification with what St. Paul writes in the Letter to the Romans: "For I take delight in the law of God, in my inner self, but I see in my members another principle at war with the law of my mind, taking me captive to the law of sin that dwells in my members" (Rom 7:22–23).[60] Or, to cite a text of the Second Vatican Council that may apply to Maurice, "And being weak and sinful, they frequently do what they would rather not, and fail to do what they would."[61]

THEOLOGICAL ANALYSIS

It is possible to interpret the personal and epistolary exchanges between the Maritains and Maurice Sachs within the context of the "vocational teleology" that dominates the first chapter of the 1993 encyclical letter, *Veritatis splendor*. Pope John Paul II there appeals to the dialogue of Jesus with the rich young man as related in the nineteenth chapter of St. Matthew's Gospel. "Teacher, what good must I do to gain eternal life" (Mt 9:16)? "Because God is there," Raïssa wrote early on to a young Maurice worried about his conversion, "you have nothing to fear. I do not say, you have nothing to do, that would be to miss what is apparent. 'If you love me, keep my commandments.'"[62] Maurice, it seems difficult to deny, was an earnest searcher, at least for a time.

The Maritains embraced him and their other "guests" from the perspective of the overarching participation of the rational creature in the divine goodness: *L'infinie Bonté de Notre Seigneur*.[63] They acted toward

59. Ibid., 174.

60. Ibid., 173–77, no. 119.

61. See Vatican Council II, "Pastoral Constitution on the Church in the Modern World," *Gaudium et spes*, §10.

62. Sachs, *Correspondance*, 45.

63. Ibid.

Maurice on the basis of their conviction that, as St. Thomas teaches, "each creature is stretched out toward the attainment of its own perfection, which is a likeness of the divine perfection and goodness."[64] In other words, the Maritains pursued their evangelizing efforts inspired by a confidence that the basic dynamisms of creation flow from the divine will from which all striving for perfection derives. *Veritatis splendor* repeats this key interpretative principle of Thomist moral theology:

> The moral life has an essential "teleological" character, since it consists in the deliberate ordering of human acts to God, the supreme Good and ultimate end (*telos*) of man. This is attested to once more by the question posed by the young man to Jesus: "What good must I do to have eternal life?"[65]

The encyclical further reminds us that "only God can answer the question about what is good, because he is the Good itself."[66] Or, as Raïssa wrote in 1925 to Maurice, "Only the Good God, in effect, is able to begin, continue, and accomplish the work of our sanctification."[67]

Maurice received instruction in both nature and grace. Adoptive sonship is prefigured by a more limited likeness of God in the created nature, which, as St. Thomas also teaches, becomes fuller as it approaches the absolute expression of the divine sonship.[68] The adoptive sonship of the Christian is not a sonship that is simply and univocally natural as is that of Christ who is the eternal Word. Rather, there exists within human nature—which is specifically different from the divine nature—an analogical likeness to God that is able to undergo transfiguration. This may be expressed in an analogy of proper proportionality: Christ the natural Son is to the Father as the adoptive son is to the Trinity. Love for the full truth of man's divine good can surmount the difficulties that human weakness and a fallen world create. Only the man whose operational

64. See *ST* I, q. 44, a. 4: "Et unaquaeque creatura intendit consequi suam perfectionem, quae est similitudo perfectionis et bonitatis divinae."

65. *Veritatis splendor*, §73.

66. Ibid., §9.

67. Sachs, *Correspondance*, 45.

68. See *ST* I, q. 33, a. 3. Also, my "Sonship, Sacrifice, and Satisfaction: The Divine Friendship in Aquinas and the Renewal of Christian Anthropology," *Letter and Spirit* 3 (2007): 71–93 (chap. 4, this volume).

capacities are conformed to Christ through the infused theological and moral virtues will love as does Christ. Maurice had come to understand that the goal of life is to become like Christ. As late as August 1927, he tells Jacques that he wants to include an image of the Shroud of Turin in a book of poems that he intends to publish, with the title "Miraculous Sketch of Jesus."[69] And, of course, he found in Jacques himself a living resemblance of how Maurice envisaged the Savior. His personal embrace of Christ raises other questions. While trying to rationalize an acceptable relationship with Tom Pinkerton, Maurice wrote to Jacques: "I think about God with fear and revolt."[70]

If Maurice Sachs today were to seek entrance into a Catholic seminary, he would have to confront the directives for persons with same-sex tendencies set down by the 2005 "Instruction" of the Congregation for Catholic Education.[71] Grace is called to stand before the psychological tribunal. It is useless to engage in historical psychoanalysis. At the same time, it is evident from the *Correspondance* that the Maritains did not hesitate to regard Maurice's baptism as the start of a new life. In doing this, they clearly drew on classical Catholic teaching about the "rich reality" that baptismal grace bestows.[72] How, then, did they regard what in Maurice today would be called "deep-seated homosexual tendencies"? Three points emerge:

1. First, the Maritains refused to hypostasize homosexuality. Note in the 2005 "Instruction" that the use of the word "tendency" to describe homosexual leanings is meant to signal that, although the Church considers "homosexual tendencies" distelic and therefore incapable of perfecting human nature, such tendencies are not as close to the appetites as natural inclinations. In Catholic moral thought, there exists only one sexual inclination, only one sexual orientation. It should be noted that

69. Sachs, *Correspondance*, 215.

70. Ibid., 176.

71. Congregation for Catholic Education, "Instruction Concerning the Criteria for the Discernment of Vocations with Regard to Persons with Homosexual Tendencies in View of Their Admission to the Seminary and to Holy Orders," 2005.

72. See *CCC*, §1279: "that includes forgiveness of original sin and all personal sins, birth into the new life by which man becomes and adoptive son of the father, a member of Christ and a temple of the Holy Spirit."

the "Instruction" of 2005 speaks of *tendencies* that are "objectively disordered."[73] The terminology is that of the *Catechism of the Catholic Church.*[74] On the other hand, when discussing the moral anthropology of Catholic life, *Veritatis splendor* employs the word "inclination" seven times. The word "tendency" appears only once, however, and then to describe a trend of thought not a psychological state. The Maritains read correctly Maurice's human and religious inclinations. They were less successful, it seems, in comprehending his disordered and predominately homosexual tendencies.

Veritatis splendor employs twice the adjective "disordered" to describe sinful actions. The *Catechism* cites the 1976 "Persona Humana" document of the Congregation for the Doctrine of the Faith (issued during the height of the sexual revolution in North America). It defines homosexual acts as intrinsically disordered.[75] Disordered tendencies to commit such acts describe psychological dispositions toward sin. The theological word would be "temptation."[76] In any case, the Church does not locate homosexual lust at the level of being.

The Maritains obviously viewed Maurice's past profligacy as something altogether remediable. They believed in the forgiveness of all personal sins that baptism brings. They knew what Aquinas teaches about the *fomes peccati*. In short, temptations after baptism should be overcome by manfully resisting them by the grace of Jesus Christ.[77] We can infer the gist of their spiritual counsel from what Maurice plaintively says when his struggles with presumably sexual temptations had led to discouragement. In a 1927 letter, Maurice complains to Jacques: "You tell me that God wants me to play the hero. But what thanks should I give God who permitted that my heart and my body be perverted at an

73. Congregation for Catholic Education, "Instruction," §2.

74. *CCC*, §2358: "Virorum et mulierum numerus non exiguus *tendentias homosexuales praesentat profunde radicatas*" (emphasis added).

75. *CCC*, §2357, citing *Persona humana*, §8: "actus homosexualitatis suapte intrinseca natura esse inordinatos."

76. For an interesting essay that mentions classical outlooks on sexual temptations, see John Joseph Williams, "Ordered and Disordered Friendships: Some Classic Distinctions," *Faith and Reason* 29 (2004): 33–47.

77. *CCC*, §1264.

age when one is ignorant, and who ten years later requires heroism of me?"[78] "Manfully resist." "Play the hero."

2. The Maritains brooked no sympathy for any chosen expression of homosexual lust. Aquinas never discusses explicitly homosexual tendencies. He alludes to what since the late nineteenth century we call homosexuality in the treatise on the old law where he notes that the sixth commandment forbids the "vices against nature" and cites Leviticus 19:16: "You shall not lie with a male as with a woman; it is an abomination."[79] He mentions the same "vice against nature" in the reply to an objection in the treatise on the natural law.[80] Again, "homosexuality" appears in the treatise on intemperance, where Aquinas discusses the shamefulness of homosexual coitus.[81] And again, when he is discussing the sins of lust.[82] All sins of lechery go against reason, but some—what Mary Ann Glendon likes to call the filthy five—also go against nature; they are not only against reason but also *contra naturam*: masturbation, bestiality, sodomy, contraception, and fetishes.

The first mention of sodomy in the *Summa Theologiae* comes, however, when Aquinas discusses pleasure. In this article, the Common Doctor offers what may be the closest thing to clinical psychology in the *Summa*, namely, that some men are sick of soul and so take pleasure in cannibalism, bestiality, homosexual congress, and other things not in accord with their nature.[83] Do such persons act from an innate inclination to find pleasure in practicing the vices against nature? It would come as a surprise to discover that the Maritains thought so. There is no evidence to think that Aquinas did. There are persons who take pleasure habitually in bad sex. Maurice seems to have been one of them. He shared his bed with men up until his arrest in 1943. Does the word "tendency" adequately describe his condition? Perhaps. Then there is the testimony of Maurice himself: "My life is impossible because I love *equally* virtue and sin, God and the devil."[84] In other words, he explains himself in terms of a choice.

78. Sachs, *Correspondance*, 228.
79. *ST* I-II, q. 100, a. 11.
80. *ST* I-II, q. 94, a. 3.
81. *ST* II-II, q. 142, a. 4.
82. *ST* II-II, q. 154, a. 11.
83. *ST* I-II, q. 31, a. 8.
84. Sachs, *Correspondance*, 267. This reminds one of an aphorism from *The Way* of St.

3. The Maritains believed in the power of contemplation to pacify the lower powers of the soul. What distinguishes deep-seated homosexual tendencies from, as the "Instruction" puts it, "homosexual tendencies that were only the expression of a transitory problem"?[85] It is important to determine criteria to answer this question. Those who experience the latter may be admitted today into seminaries. Others may not. It seems to me that if we follow the lead of Aquinas, then we will find ourselves obliged to discover a way to evaluate the pleasure that an individual takes in the prospects or realization of sexual congress with a person of the same sex. The *Catechism* tells us that many of them find their situations a trial—*pro maiore eorum parte constituit probationem.*[86] We find ourselves back to Maurice Sachs and his advice to Tom Pinkerton: at all costs, escape the "constant torment that homosexuality is."[87] For their part, the Maritains proceeded on a premise that Aquinas enunciates in *Summa Theologiae* I-II, question 38: "The contemplation of truth is the greatest of all pleasures. We have seen that every pleasure assuages pain. The contemplation of truth therefore assuages pain; and it does so the more, the more perfectly one loves wisdom."[88] How else may one interpret the words of Raïssa? "God will make known to you interiorly and little by little what he desires of you. And little by little, and sweetly, he will teach you how to remain strong by his love."[89]

POSTSCRIPT

Maurice continued to exchange letters with the Maritains during his period of military service. He also continued for a time to practice the Catholic faith. He reported back to the Maritains on conversations with his confessor, who advised him to marry. And so one assumes that "the torment of homosexuality" remained an issue for Maurice. On Novem-

Josemaría Escrivá (§24): "You tell me that in your heart you have fire and water, cold and heat, empty passions and God: one candle lit to St. Michael and another to the devil. Calm yourself. As long as you are willing to fight there are not two candles burning in your heart. There is only one: the archangel's."

85. Congregation for Catholic Education, "Instruction," §2.

86. *CCC*, §2358.

87. Sachs, *Correspondance*, 174.

88. *ST* I-II, q. 38, a. 5.

89. Sachs, *Correspondance*, 45.

ber 20, 1927, he writes to Jacques and confesses to some form of relationship with a certain Jean Mangüe that had the same effect on Maurice's desire to marry as what had happened at Juan-les-Pins had on his desire for the priesthood. "A brutal warning," he tells Jacques.[90]

Marry, we know, however, Maurice did. But his struggles with homosexual impulses continued. They eventually took a toll on his religious practice. "But you know better than I," he writes to Jacques in April 1934, "how essential is the Eucharist, which I cannot receive without a firm purpose of not living in a manner that St. Paul condemns."[91] Jacques agrees, and the next month tells him that if a firm purpose is impossible, there is nothing else to do except to wait, while still doing all that is in one's power.[92] The last letter that Maurice writes is addressed to Raïssa Maritain, shortly before Christmas 1939. Sin appears to have worked its sad effect. "I am born, it seems to me, without the sense of the eternal . . . I remain indifferent toward life eternal. *Mille et mille affections.* Maurice."[93]

On November 16, 1943, Maurice Sachs was arrested by the Gestapo under the pretext of article 175, the section of criminal law that condemned the practice of acts "against nature." Ordinarily, those who, like Maurice Sachs, served as agents for the Nazi government were exempt from this law, except when the Gestapo found reason to lose confidence in them. This they did in the case of Maurice when they discovered that he had alerted a Jesuit priest, le Père Jean Nicot, who was working undercover in Hamburg with the help of the Swiss consulate. Illusionist accounts of his death circulated after the end of World War II. On February 4, 1951, Karl-Ludwig Schneider published an article in the Berlin magazine *Welt am Sonntag* proving that Maurice Ettinghausen (Sachs's real family name) had been killed by a Flemish SS officer while trying to escape a prison march. On April 21, 1951, his mother had a funeral Mass celebrated for him at Saint-Philippe-du-Roule in Paris.

90. Ibid., 226.
91. Ibid., 291.
92. Ibid., 292.
93. Ibid., 312.

CHAPTER 12

PREMOTION, HOLINESS, AND POPE BENEDICT XIII, 1724–30

Some Historical Retrospects on *Veritatis splendor*

Following upon his account of the Maritains' relationship with Maurice Sachs, Father Cessario explains that "the worst thing that can happen in the Christian life is for a Christian to become convinced that virtue is impossible." Conversely, the best thing that can happen in the Christian life is for the Christian to remember the truth of divine love: "God can save us. God does forgive." And "the divine goodness governs the bestowal of the divine help."

This chapter considers the spiritual implications of the traditional Thomistic doctrine of physical premotion. Otherwise put, it examines the theology of sanctity, or "how God makes us saints." The "'spirituality' of physical premotion" gives us a glimpse into God's "blueprint for salvation." Physical premotion attests to the intrinsically salvific dynamics of grace: God moves each creature according to its nature, and thus he moves the human creature freely from within. The reality of premoved human freedom and "premotive holiness" is essential to

Originally published as "Premotion, Holiness, and Pope Benedict XIII (1724–30)," *Nova et Vetera* 11, no. 4 (2013): 1115–35. Reprinted by permission.

the Thomistic teaching on moral theology and human sanctity. "The cardinal principle of Aquinas's blueprint for holiness is that God loves us because he is good, not because we are." Moreover, this truth about God's loving initiative bears vital implications for Catholic renewal in the twenty-first century. "Until Catholics discover how the dynamics between divine grace and human freedom work both according to God's plan and unto the sanctification of the human person, one may not ... expect a worldwide renewal of Catholic theology." The Thomistic doctrine of physical premotion enables all individual Catholics—in spite of any and all obstacles—to rest in the interior peace and recollection that only the truth of God's love can provide.

> Christian morality consists, in the simplicity of the Gospel, in *following Jesus Christ*, in abandoning oneself to him, in letting oneself be transformed by his grace and renewed by his mercy, gifts which come to us in the living communion of his Church.
>
> —*Veritatis splendor*, §119

Doing theology, as Father Matthew Lamb never tires of reminding us, requires conversion of life. The "conversion principle" (to give it a name) finds verification within the pages of the New Testament. St. Paul identifies mature Christian witness as "speaking the truth in love" (Eph 4:15). More proximately, we find the principle brilliantly illuminated in the life of St. Bernard of Clairvaux (†1153). One of his best-known modern interpreters, Dom Jean Leclercq, describes succinctly how St. Bernard envisioned the conversion principle at work in those who take up the burden of theology: "Just as there is no theology without moral life and asceticism, so there is no theology without prayer."[1] One indeed may inquire why so many theologians today ignore the time-honored conversion principle. After all, the practice it stipulates has guided theologians from Justin Martyr (†165) to Father Garrigou-Lagrange (†1964).[2] No

1. Jean Leclercq, OSB, *The Love of Learning and the Desire for God: A Study of Monastic Culture*, trans. Catherine Misrahi (New York: Fordham University Press, 1974), 7.

2. For information on Reginald Garrigou-Lagrange, OP, see his *The One God: A Commentary on the First Part of St. Thomas' Theological Summa* (St. Louis, MO: B. Herder, 1943), 26–37:

easy answer to this question exists. One clue to the answer runs something like this: theologians no longer observe the conversion principle because they have grown tired of seeking conversion. Why would someone grow tired of prayer, asceticism, and in some cases aspects of the moral life?[3] The answer may lie in the manner in which such persons attempt prayer, asceticism (which may include the discipline of study), and a life of virtue.[4] Those who seek to sustain themselves spiritually by relying on their own energies always grow weary of conversion. Sound Catholic theology, such as one finds set forth in the 1993 encyclical letter of St. John Paul II, *Veritatis splendor*, holds out a quite different approach to persevering in conversion of life.[5] I discuss this approach to holiness by talking about premotion, holiness, and Pope Benedict XIII.

Put simply, this essay to mark the twentieth anniversary of the abovementioned encyclical discusses how God makes us saints. In other

---

"When the priest's interior life is one of great and solid piety, his theology is always more rigorous. After this theologian has made the descent from faith for the purpose of acquiring theological knowledge by the discussion of particular questions, he desires to return to the source, namely, to ascend from the theological knowledge thus acquired by the discussion of particular questions to the lofty peak of faith. The theologian is like a man who is born on the top of a mountain, for instance, Monte Cassino, and who afterward descends into the valley to acquire an accurate knowledge of individual things. Finally this man wishes to return to his lofty abode, that he may contemplate the whole valley from on high and in a single glance" (35). No doubt the life and example of St. Thomas Aquinas inspired this beautiful image to describe the theologian. Garrigou-Lagrange earlier notes, "There is often too great a separation between study and the interior life; we do not find sufficiently observed, that beautiful gradation spoken of by St. Benedict which consists in: reading, cogitation, study, meditation, prayer and contemplation. St. Thomas, who received his first education from the Benedictines, retained this wonderful gradation when speaking of the contemplative life" (31). The author's comparison of the theologian on the mountain, who descends into the valley and returns to the mountain, puts one in mind of Aquinas's comparison in *ST* I, q. 14, a. 13, ad 3, regarding God's eternity versus time.

3. See my "Scholarship and Sanctity: A Lesson Aquinas Teaches the Priest and Seminarian," *Nova et Vetera* 8, no. 2 (2010): 233–49 (chap. 8, this volume).

4. For the ascetical character of study, see Garrigou-Lagrange, *The One God*: "Our interior life is in many ways benefitted by good study; and the choicest fruit of penance is to be found in the arduousness of study. It is a fruit much more precious than the natural pleasure to be found in study that may consist in intellectual labor not sufficiently sanctified or directed to God. In diligent study that is commanded by charity, we find pre-eminently verified the common saying: If the roots of knowledge are bitter, its fruits are the sweetest and best. We are not considering here the knowledge that inflates, but that which, under the influence of charity and of the virtue of studiousness, is truly upbuilding" (33).

5. See the 1993 encyclical letter of the Supreme Pontiff Pope John Paul II, "*Veritatis Splendor* Regarding Certain Fundamental Questions of the Church's Moral Teaching."

words, I explicate how we can sustain the demands of Christian life and witness, and so, whether we do theology or not, merit the reward of everlasting life. The mention of the eighteenth-century Pope Benedict, Pietro Francesco Orsini (1649–1730), signals that I take up the discussion of premotive holiness within the context of the post-Reformation debates on human freedom and divine grace, whose written records fill volumes. This Dominican pope's reign (May 29, 1724, to February 21, 1730) witnessed in 1728 the submission by the Archbishop of Paris to the last of the major anti-Jansenist papal condemnations, the 1713 bull *Unigenitus*. This prelate, Cardinal Louis-Antoine de Noailles (1651–1729), remained deeply attached to the ancient prerogatives of the Church in France.[6] Benedict XIII's reign was important for another reason. Throughout the high period of the Jansenist struggles, Dominicans were on guard to ensure that the papal condemnations of Jansenist distortions were not interpreted as extending to Thomist theses about grace and freedom. Benedict XIII approved these efforts of his Dominican brethren. The precious clarifications that the defenders of Thomist orthodoxy produced also shaped what—for lack of a better expression—I refer to as the "spirituality" of physical premotion. We are talking about the blueprint for salvation.

Father Robert Barron and Professor Ralph Martin recently exchanged views about the divine plan for salvation.[7] The different viewpoints of these two Catholic thinkers reveal that theologians and priests still struggle to discover the right way to encourage people toward conversion. The present essay does not address directly whether many will be saved. Rather, I hope to indicate how the Thomist doctrine of physical premotion works in conjunction with a teleology of beatitude, which supplies the theoretical backbone for *Veritatis splendor*.[8] At the same time, it goes without saying that those who observe the "spirituality" of physical premotion

6. Jansenism and *Unigenitus* in particular have been the object of many books by the renowned scholar Lucien Ceyssens, OFM. For further information on the life and work of Ceyssens, see Jörgen Vijgen, "Lucien Ceyssens OFM," *Biographisch-Bibliographisch Kirchenlexikon* 24 (2005), 443–45.

7. See the following websites for details: http://www.catholicnewsagency.com/column.php?n=2383; http://www.renewalministries.net/wordpress/?p=348.

8. For an introduction to "premotion," see note 44, infra.

discover that the question of whether many will be saved need not trouble them. To be sure, the question of who will be saved vexed the Jansenists. One of their number described Father Matteo Ricci, the Jesuit missionary to China, as a "faithful servant of the Devil, who fortified his dominion over the infidels instead of destroying it."[9] Today, few Christians, I suppose, would locate the *massa damnata* in China. Getting salvation right, however, remains important. Until Catholics discover how the dynamics between divine grace and human freedom work both according to God's plan and unto the sanctification of the human person, one may not, I submit, expect a worldwide renewal of Catholic theology. Father Lamb is correct: doing theology requires conversion of life or, as *Veritatis splendor* puts it, "a continuous conversion to what is true and to what is good."[10]

PREMOTION

The late Dominican historian Father Guy Bedouelle published, among his last books in English, a small volume titled *The Reform of Catholicism, 1480–1620.*[11] With some approximation, the dates point, respectively, to the coming-of-age of Girolamo Savanarola (1452–98) and to the death of St. Francis de Sales (1622). As the title indicates, Father Bedouelle prefers to describe the events that surround the Council of Trent as exercises in reform instead of reaction. He eases away from presenting the post-Tridentine period as a time of counterreformation. What is more important, Bedouelle argues that the unquestionable success of the Tridentine reforms derives not from the Council's dogmatic definitions and decrees alone, but from "the joint, complementary consideration and articulation of the dogmatic and disciplinary decrees."[12] In other words, the sixteenth-century Council's defense of Catholic doctrine, drawn mainly from the works of St. Thomas Aquinas, proceeded both to inform and to

9. See J. H. Crehan, "Jansenism," in *A Catholic Dictionary of* Theology, vol. 3, *Hegel—Paradise*, ed. H. F. Davis, Ivo Thomas, OP, and J. H. Crehan (London: Nelson, 1971), 147.

10. *Veritatis splendor*, §64.

11. Guy Bedouelle, OP, *The Reform of Catholicism, 1480–1620*, trans. James K. Farge (Toronto: PIMS, 2008).

12. Ibid., 12.

shape the Catholic world. This renewal occurred under the impulsion of the disciplinary reforms, however, which themselves found enthusiastic supporters in saintly figures like Charles Borromeo (†1584), Pope Pius V (†1572), Teresa of Avila (†1582), Robert Bellarmine (†1621), and Francis de Sales (†1622).

Make no mistake. Father Bedouelle does not undervalue the theological achievement of the Council of Trent. "If the humanists—beginning with Erasmus," he writes, "had had their way, the different Churches would have been able to be reconciled and to agree on a minimalist Credo, a *via media* independent of the subtleties of scholastic theology."[13] Anyone who casts a glance onto the dogmatic decrees of the Council of Trent realizes that the Fathers do not choose the path of compromise, accommodation, and false irenicism. Trent rather enacted *ante nomen* the principle of reform and continuity that, in our own day, Pope Benedict XVI stipulated for the Church's proper reading of the documents of the Second Vatican Council.[14] Still, as Bedouelle goes on to observe, "despite its will and its attempts to be prudent, the Council of Trent issued many rather dense texts which, inevitably open to interpretation, already contained, from the very time they were approved, the seeds of future quarrels."[15]

Within twenty years of the close of the Council of Trent, one such quarrel arose in Spain when, in the school year 1581–82 at Salamanca, a now-celebrated Dominican, Domingo Bañez (1528–1604), took issue with certain theses on grace and freedom advanced by a Jesuit theologian, Father Prudencio de Montemaior (†1599). As the name of the papal commission established to resolve the disputes that subsequently developed suggests, the *Congregatio de Auxiliis* debate turns on the question of how to interpret human freedom within the context of the divine helps (*auxilia*) that make choosing unto salvation possible. Father Bedouelle observes that "the quarrel *de auxiliis* between Dominicans and Jesuits, which was not resolved but only postponed by a 1607 papal order that chose neither side, was only the prelude to the even greater

13. Ibid., 135.

14. For further explanation, see *Vatican II: Renewal within Tradition*, ed. Matthew L. Lamb and Matthew Levering (Oxford: Oxford University Press, 2008).

15. Bedouelle, *Reform of Catholicism*, 135.

theological debates between Catholics of the seventeenth century."[16] He points of course to the Jansenist controversies that found their most eminent expressions in the elegant, controlled aesthetic developed by certain great figures of French classicism: Blaise Pascal (1623–62), Jean-Baptiste Molière (1622–77), Jean Racine (1639–99), Jacques-Bénigne Bossuet (1627–1704), and François de Salignac de la Mothe-Fénelon (1651–1715). As the diverse métiers of these eminent personages suggest, "Jansenism was a complex phenomenon with a long gestation."[17]

No attempt to analyze completely the "complex phenomenon" can be undertaken at this juncture in the exposition. Suffice it to remark that Jansenism arose in reaction to the ethos that the Jesuit thinker and writer Luis de Molina (1535–1600) established by his innovative accounts of the interplay between human freedom and divine grace. Molina's *Concordia,* first published in Lisbon in 1588—three years after the birth of Cornelius Jansen (1585–1638), from whom Jansenism takes its name—supplied the anthropological and psychological supports for the moral theology that Molina's Jesuit confrères had been developing since the middle of the sixteenth century.[18] Emblematic of the new moral theology is the Jesuit father whom St. Alphonsus Ligouri praised as a "moderate Probabiliorist," Juan Azor (1535–1603), who started his teaching in 1568.[19] Azor's three-volume manual of moral theology was published in Rome from 1600 to 1611 under the title *Institutiones Moralium, in quibus universae quaestiones ad conscientiam recte aut prave factorum pertinentes breviter tractantur.* Juan Azor's professional career as a moral theologian represents the start of the innovative moral systems that dominated the post-Tridentine period. The importance of the period of post-Tridentine

16. Ibid., 136.

17. Thomas O'Connor, *Irish Jansenists, 1600–70: Religion and Politics in Flanders, France, Ireland, and Rome* (Dublin: Four Courts Press, 2008), 20.

18. Elsewhere I argue that Molinism flows naturally, if one will, from the form of life that the Jesuits undertook, and from the way in which they separated religious and professional occupations. See my "Molina and Aquinas," in *A Companion to Molina,* ed. Matthias Kaufmann and Alexander Aichele (Leiden: Brill, 2013), 291–323.

19. See Arthur McCaffray, "Juan Azor," in *The Catholic Encyclopedia,* vol. 2 (New York: Robert Appleton, 1907). For further background information on the Jesuit moralist, see A. F. Dziuba, "Juan Azor, S.J., teólogo moralista del siglo XVI–XVII," *Archivo Teológico Granadino* 59 (1996): 145–55.

casuistry that directed Catholic life for nearly four hundred years is easy to summarize.[20] First, the practice of this case-based moral analysis came to a screeching (though unpublicized) end about fifty years ago. Second, one finds the replacement model for the casuist categories in *Veritatis splendor*, whose twentieth anniversary we commemorated in 2013 on the feast of the Transfiguration (August 6).[21]

When I refer to a Molinist ethos, I mean the typically modern temptation to safeguard the autonomy of human freedom by detaching it from the divine motion that "moves" all created things that exist.[22] As the Book of Wisdom sets it forth: "For Wisdom is mobile beyond all motion, and she penetrates and pervades all things by reason of her purity" (Wis 7:24). In his *Summa Theologiae*, St. Thomas Aquinas explains how the divine wisdom "is mobile" without compromising God's unchangeableness: "To call wisdom mobile," he writes, "is a metaphorical way of saying that wisdom spreads its own likeness throughout the length and breadth of things. For nothing can exist except it be a sort of reflection (*imitationem*) deriving from God's wisdom as from its primary operative and formal cause; just as works of handicraft derive from craftsmanship ... It is as though we talked of the sun sallying forth on the earth when light-rays touched earth."[23] To adapt this "sun metaphor" to the Jesuit-sponsored ethos, Luis de Molina considered it necessary to introduce an eclipse of the sun when rendering an account of the concordance between the divine motion and the human will. The position represents a typically modern ethos inasmuch as his followers, when giving an account of the interplay between divine grace and human freedom, deem this eclipse of the divine sun's rays a nonnegotiable element in the equation. How else to preserve, they ask, what moderns construe as the autonomy of human

20. One may conveniently mark the span from 1568 to 1968, the publication of the encyclical letter *Humanae Vitae*, as the years of casuist moral theology.

21. For my remarks on the tenth anniversary, see "Walk According to the Light: An Illustration from North America," in *Camminare nella Luce: Prospettive della teologia morale a partire da 'Veritatis splendor,'* ed. Livio Melina and José Noriega (Rome: Lateran University Press, 2004), 401–7.

22. *Veritatis splendor* observes: "The modern concern for the claims of autonomy has not failed to exercise an influence also in the sphere of Catholic moral theology" (§36).

23. *ST* I, q. 9, a. 1, ad 2.

freedom? Molina's critics—at the start, mainly Dominicans—made another analysis. They found Molina's schema to embody a recrudescence of ancient errors about divine grace and human freedom that imposed the burden of growing holy squarely on the putative good will of the human creature. Leszek Kolakowski, in his book *God Owes Us Nothing*, provides a more precise identification. Molina's critics found his position a form of "brazen, modern Pelagianism."[24] Pope Paul V forbade Jesuits and Dominicans from speaking "more severe words" about each other,[25] so I leave things with Kolakowski's analysis.

Veritatis splendor addresses mistakes that moderns still make about human freedom. The encyclical puts it simply: "*the autonomy of reason cannot mean* that reason itself *creates values and moral norms*. Were this autonomy to imply a denial of the participation of the practical reason in the wisdom of the divine Creator and Lawgiver, or were it to suggest a freedom which creates moral norms, on the basis of historical contingencies or the diversity of societies and cultures, this sort of alleged autonomy would contradict the Church's teaching on the truth about man."[26] The pope says that a wrong understanding of autonomy results from separating the human creature from the divine wisdom. The participation of the practical reason in the divine wisdom, which participation does not suffer rupture even in the sinner, forms the basis for premotive holiness. For the reason I mentioned above, a Dominican may not claim that this papal text puts the final nail in the coffin of sixteenth-century Molinism. Still, this twentieth-century magisterial text makes it clear that the sun of the divine wisdom suffers no eclipse when it informs the human conscience about how to act. The encyclical, moreover, expresses its pleasure with the theological practice of referring to human freedom as a "*participated theonomy*," because, as the pope insists, "man's free obedience to God's law effectively implies that human reason and human will participate in God's wisdom and provi-

24. Leszek Kolakowski, *God Owes Us Nothing: A Brief Remark on Pascal's Religion and on the Spirit of Jansenism* (Chicago: University of Chicago Press, 1995), 7.

25. Denzinger-Schönmetzer, *Enchiridion Symbolorum Definitionum et Declarationum de rebus fidei et morum*, ed. XXXVI (*DS*), 1997: "Quin optat etiam, ut verbis asperioribus amaritiem animi significantibus, invicem abstineant."

26. *Veritatis splendor*, §40. Emphasis original.

dence."[27] The post–Vatican II papal magisterium differs in its expression from that of the early modern period. As Father Bedouelle has reminded us, the post-Tridentine popes ruled largely through disciplinary canons, which for the most part, as *Denzinger-Schönmetzer* amply illustrates, were confined to correcting errors. Recent popes have provided constructive teaching to support their condemnations.[28]

Ronald Knox places Jansenism among the expressions of "enthusiasm" that from time to time crystallize into movements among Christian believers.[29] This episode of enthusiasm was occasioned by the publication (posthumously) in 1640 of Cornelius Jansen's *Augustinus,* a book that aimed to counter Molinist theology by appeal mainly to patristic

27. *Veritatis splendor,* no. 41. For a more extended examination of the importance of theonomy in Christian life and thought, see Steven A. Long, "On the Loss, and the Recovery, of Nature as a Theonomic Principle: Reflections on the Nature/Grace Controversy," in *Natura Pura: On the Recovery of Nature in the Doctrine of Grace* (New York: Fordham University Press, 2010), chap. 1, 10–51. This is a theme I also explore in my *Introduction to Moral Theology,* rev. ed. (Washington, DC: Catholic University of America Press, 2013), 206–8.

28. For this constructive teaching, popes often relied on St. Thomas Aquinas. See Pope John Paul II, who cites the eighteenth-century Pope Benedict XIV, to the participants in the 9th International Thomistic Conference on September 29, 1990: "Quanto alla sua funzione di guida negli studi, la Chiesa, nel ribadirla, ha preferito far leva, più che su direttive di indole giuridica, sulla maturità e saggezza di coloro che intendono accostarsi alla parola di Dio con sincero desiderio di scoprire e conoscere sempre più a fondo il suo contenuto, comunicarlo agli altri, specialmente ai giovani affidati al loro insegnamento. A questo proposito, è bene ricordare un aspetto del metodo e del comportamento di san Tommaso, messo in risalto dal mio predecessore Benedetto XIV, quando, nella costituzione apostolica *Sollicita ac provida* del 10 luglio 1753, scriveva che 'il Principe Angelico delle Scuole ... ha necessariamente urtato le opinioni dei filosofi e dei teologi, che egli era spinto a confutare in nome della verità, ma ciò che completa mirabilmente i meriti di un sì grande dottore è che non lo si è mai visto disprezzare, ferire o umiliare alcun avversario, ma al contrario li ha trattati tutti con molta bontà e rispetto. In effetti, se le loro parole contenevano qualcosa di duro, di ambiguo, di oscuro, egli l'addolciva e spiegava con una interpretazione indulgente e benevola. Che se la causa della religione e della fede gli imponeva di respingere le loro idee, egli lo faceva con una tale modestia che lo rendeva non meno degno di elogio nel separarsi da essi che nell'affermare la verità cattolica. Coloro che si gloriano di ricorrere a un maestro così eminente—e noi ci rallegriamo che siano molto numerosi, a causa del nostro interesse e della nostra particolarissima venerazione per lui—si propongano come modello la moderazione di espressione di un tale dottore e il suo modo caritatevole di comportarsi nelle discussioni con gli avversari. Quanto a coloro che non appartengono alla sua scuola, si sforzino di conformarsi anch'essi a questo metodo ...' (Benedetto XIV, *Sollicita ac provida,* 24)." See *Insegnamenti di Giovanni Paolo II,* XIII/2 (1990): 768–74. For a related discussion, see Russell Hittinger, "*Pascendi Dominici Gregis* at 100: Two Modernisms, Two Thomisms: Reflections on the Centenary of Pius X's Letter Against the Modernists," *Nova et Vetera* 5, no. 4 (2007): 843–80.

29. Ronald A. Knox, *Enthusiasm: A Chapter in the History of Religion, with Special Reference to the XVII and XVIII Centuries* (Westminster, MD: Christian Classics, 1983), chaps. 9–10.

citations, especially, as the book's name indicates, from St. Augustine. The theological, social, and political dimensions of the Jansenist movement defy, as Jacques Gres-Gayer affirms, "a compact definition because of a conflict-filled history that spans two centuries of major change in European society."[30] At this juncture, then, the present discussion takes up a restricted consideration of the Jansenist debates and intrigues. I refer to the perils that the Jansenist outlook on salvation posed to Thomist orthodoxy and its teaching on how God premotively sanctifies the human creature.

HOLINESS

We can conclude from what has been said up to this point, at least, that respectable Christian people strongly object to accounts of human autonomy that, shall we say, make the "free" in free choice dependent upon an eclipse of the divine light: Bishop Cornelius Jansen, certain French classicists, many Dominicans—to name a few. Does this mean that in order to embrace an orthodox doctrine of grace and freedom one must adopt the five condemned propositions excerpted or paraphrased from the *Augustinus*? The answer, of course, to this question is clear. Whatever the political wrangling over the papal condemnation of the propositions ascribed to Cornelius Jansen, the fact remains that the five theses over which the May 31, 1653, bull *Cum occasione* of Pope Innocent X first cast a shadow do not express Catholic truth.[31] Molinism continued on its merry way. Even saints of the period, like St. Francis de Sales, found themselves "molinised," to borrow a term.[32] The Dominicans, on the other hand,

30. J. M. Gres-Gayer, *New Catholic Encyclopedia*, 2nd ed., s.v. "Jansenism."

31. See *DS* 2001–2007. Nos. 2006 and 2007 list the notes levied against the five propositions.

32. Francis Vincent, "The Spirituality of Saint Francis of Sales," http://www.ewtn.com/library/spirit/salespir.txt. See also A. Schmidt, "Tirez-moi, nous courrons nous deux: Göttliche Gnade und menschliche Mitwirkung in der Theologie des hl. Franz von Sales," *Jahrbuch für salesianische Studien* 33 (2001): 7–79. However, see Aidan Nichols, *The Latin Clerk: The Life, Work, and Travels of Adrian Fortescue* (Cambridge: Lutterworth Press, 2011), 169: "He [Adrian Fortescue] spent the day before going into the hospital with the Dominicans at Haverstock Hill ('no Molinism for me, thank you', he told Myers in what turned out to be the farewell letter—the Jesuit theology of grace was too humanistic for what he called 'a soul that has no hope but in the mercy of God')."

faced a different challenge. They had to show that Thomism was not infected with the same fatal errors as Jansenism. Right-thinking theologians accordingly set themselves the task of separating orthodox Thomists from card-carrying Jansenists. The task proved challenging.

Though what today one may call a ressourcement theologian, Cornelius Jansen did not exhibit the anti-Thomist outlook that motivated certain theologians of the pre–Vatican II period.[33] "If one wishes," writes Jansen, "to call the help of Christ 'physical predetermination,' though Augustine would not have heard of the expression, that wouldn't bother me at all. It suffices that the substance of the Doctor of Grace gets handed on."[34] One may hope that what St. Augustine himself means by the "help of Christ" does in fact correspond to what Thomists understand by physical premotion.[35] Whether what Jansen and the Jansenists took to be the doctrine of St. Augustine may be identified with the Thomist doctrine on the bestowal of divine grace, however, raises another question. Pope Benedict XIII surely did not think so. Earlier in 1656, however, Antoine Arnauld (1612–94) argued in a theological treatise for the conformity of Jansenist views on grace and freedom with those of the Thomist Schools.[36] Additionally, there arises a methodological question. The *Augustinus* contains a section devoted to the limitations of human

33. Jean-Louis Quantin, *Le catholicisme classique et les Pères de l'Église: Un retour aux sources (1669–1713)* (Paris: Institut d'Études Augustiniennes, 1999), chap. 11, examines the relationship between positive theology and Jansenism under the heading "Nourrir La Ferveur: La Patristique des Dévots." Gemma Simmonds, "Jansenism: An Early *Ressourcement* Movement?," in *Ressourcement: A Movement for Renewal in Twentieth-Century Catholic Theology*, ed. Gabriel Flynn and Paul D. Murray (Oxford: Oxford University Press, 2012), 23–35, tries favorably to compare Jansenists and the liberal reformers of the pre- and postconciliar periods. For a different approach to the place of ressourcement in contemporary theology, see my "On the Place of Servais Pinckaers (†7 April 2008) in the Renewal of Catholic Theology," *Thomist* 73 (2009): 1–27.

34. Jansenius, *Augustinus, seu Doctrina S. Augustini de humanae naturae sanitate, aegritudine, medicina, adversus Pelagianos et Massiliensis*, 3 vol. (Louvain, 1640), t. iii, l. viii, c. ii, coll 818.

35. Although a nineteenth-century work, J. B. Mozley's *A Treatise on the Augustinian Doctrine of Predestination* (London: John Murray, 1883) offers an interesting analysis of the Augustinian account of predestination and its role in later scholastic engagements with the question.

36. See Antoine Arnauld, *Dissertatio theologica in qua Augustiana proposito* Defuit Petro gratia sine qua nihil possumus *totius Traditionis auctoritate confirmatur, cum variis Thomisticae Scholae sententiis conciliatur, et a peruulgata de praeceptorum impossibilitate calumnia purgatur* (s.l., 1656). *Le Grand* Arnauld (to distinguish him from his Jansenist relatives) reveals something of what is noble in the Jansenist character, and he is said later to have developed an authentic appreciation for the Thomist doctrine of efficacious grace.

reason. Did the difficulties occasioned by the *Augustinus* arise as a result of its author's heavy reliance on what today we would call a "return-to-the-sources" approach?[37] "Jansen claimed"—interestingly—"that in order to write the book he had read the entire works of Augustine ten times, and the treatise against the Pelagians thirty times."[38] One may be permitted to wonder, however, how much he had read of Aristotle. In any case, Jansen was not a man given to appreciation of the scholastic mode of doing theology.

Bishop Jansen died in 1638, before the movement that bears his name coalesced. Antoine Arnauld's retirement to Port Royal around 1640 may be thought to mark the start of Jansenism as an organized front, whereas the death of Louis XIV in 1715 marks its end, at least as a theological quarrel. The election in 1724 of Pope Benedict XIII, a Dominican, signals a surcease of the decades-long struggle, mainly in France, when many of the Jansenists tried to present themselves as real Thomists. I will not burden the reader with the perpetual back and forth of these maneuverings. Suffice it to remark that this eighteenth-century pope, in his June 28, 1727, bull *Pretiosus*, "declared that the teaching of St Thomas and the Thomist school had nothing to do with the errors of Cornelius Jansen (1585–1638) and Pasquier Quesnel (1634–1719)."[39] Quesnel was the last standard-

37. For background, see Crehan, "Jansenism," 147: "Between 1580 and 1620 there had been a great increase in the editing of patristic works; men like Henry Savile and Peltan were followed by Sirmond, Petau . . . It was therefore in fashion for a theologian to desire a return to the Fathers, while by a reciprocal causality the Jansenist controversy itself stimulated still further research into the Fathers."

38. Cited in *New World Encyclopedia*, s.v. "Cornelius Jansen"; available at http://www.newworldencyclopedia.org/p/index.php?title=Cornelius_Jansen&oldid=685560. Crehan, "Jansenism," 146, claims that this "boast" was made originally by the Irish Archbishop, Florence Conroy, OFM (1560–1629), about his own study of Augustine. Conroy, while living in Louvain, was influential on Jansen. Antoine Arnauld, *Apologie de Monsieur Jansenius evesque d'Ipre. & de la doctrine de S. Augustin, expliquée dans son livre, intitulé, Augustinus. Contre trois sermons de Monsieur Habert, theologal de Paris, prononcez dans Nostre-Dame, le premier & le dernier dimanche de l'advent 1642. & le dimanche de la septuagesime 1643*, [S.l.] M.DC.XLIV, 8: "Il a leu Saint Augustin dix fois d'un bout à l'autre, & plus de trente fois tous ses ouurages sur la Grace, & a esclaircy auec vn trauail infatigable."

39. J. N. D. Kelly, *Oxford Dictionary of Popes* (Oxford: Oxford University Press, 1986), 295. See also *The Papacy: An Encyclopedia*, ed. Philippe Levillain, 3 vols. (New York: Routledge, 2002), which is a translation of *Dictionnaire historique de la papauté* (Paris: Fayard, 1994). The article on Benedict XIII (1:165–67) by Luigi Fiorani of the Vatican Library opines: "In fact, the bull *Pretiosus*, drafted by the Inquisition and published in 1727, brought about a stiffening in

bearer for the Jansenist movement. The twentieth century is not the first time that seemingly well-meaning people have mistreated the doctrine of St. Thomas.[40] Standard histories of the period do not offer great detail about how the Jansenist theological positions risked compromising the doctrine of St. Thomas. So one welcomes the 2011 publication of an erudite 555-page work by Sylvio Hermann de Franceschi titled *La Puissance et la Gloire. L'orthodoxie thomiste au péril du jansénisme (1663–1724): Le zénith français de la querelle de la grâce.*[41] It would surprise me to discover that the least detail has escaped this meticulous author's attention.

But one need not wait until the publication of De Franceschi's scholarly historical study in order to realize that Thomist views of predestination and freedom do not cast dark shadows over the human creature or make a tyrant of the world's Creator. Thomism gives no quarter to "Sinners in the Hands of an Angry God."[42] Professor Steven A. Long achieved considerable recognition when the Dominican editor of the venerable *Revue Thomiste* invited him to submit for publication in French a paper delivered at an early symposium sponsored by Ave Maria University.[43] After a suitable interstice, the essay appeared in the author's original and challenging English prose as "Providence, Freedom, and Natural Law."[44]

favor of the positions of the Molinists and a fresh confirmation of the bulls *Unigenitus* and *Pastoralis officii*. With this document, which clearly did not take the pope's thinking into account, the traditional line of the Curia was reaffirmed, one close to the Molinist positions" (Levillain, *The Papacy*, 1:167). For a late nineteenth-century take on the topic, see J. Brucker, "Le Bref «Démissas Preces» de Benoit XIII et le Molinisme," *Études* 50 (1890): 28–53.

40. For discussion of the twentieth-century disruption, see Ralph McInerny, *Praeambula Fidei: Thomism and the God of the Philosophers* (Washington, DC: Catholic University of America Press, 2006), and my review of his book: "Neo-Neo-Thomism," *First Things* (May 2007): 48–51.

41. Sylvio Hermann de Franceschi, *La Puissance et la Gloire. L'orthodoxie thomiste au péril du jansénisme (1663–1724): Le zénith français de la querelle de la grâce* (Paris: Nolin, 2011).

42. "Sinners in the Hands of an Angry God," a sermon preached by Jonathan Edwards (1703–58) at Enfield, Massachusetts (later Connecticut), July 8, 1741. For the text, see *Jonathan Edwards's "Sinners in the Hands of an Angry God": A Casebook*, ed. Wilson H. Kimnach, Caleb J. D. Maskell, and Kenneth P. Minkema (New Haven, CT: Yale University Press, 2010), 33–50

43. See Steven A. Long, "Providence, Liberté et Loi Naturelle," trans. Hyacinthe Defos du Rau, OP, and Serge-Thomas Bonino, OP, *Revue Thomiste* 3 (2002): 355–406.

44. Steven A. Long, "Providence, Freedom, and Natural Law," *Nova et Vetera* 4, no. 3 (2006): 1–55. The author gives a short account of physical premotion: "There is a motion bestowed by God without which the rational creature cannot proceed to its act of self-determination. This motion is 'prior'—hence 'pre' motion—not in a temporal sense, but in the sense in which the cause is prior to that which is caused: apart from this moving of the rational

Two texts supply the epigraph. The first comes from the *Catechism of the Council of Trent*: "Not only does God protect and govern all things by His Providence, but He also by an internal power impels to motion and action whatever moves and acts, and this in such a manner that, although He excludes not, He yet precedes the agency of secondary causes."[45] The second comes from the catechism published after the Second Vatican Council:

> The truth that God is at work in all the actions of his creatures is inseparable from faith in God the Creator. God is the first cause who operates in and through secondary causes: "For God is at work in you, both to will and to work for his good pleasure." Far from diminishing the creature's dignity, this truth enhances it. Drawn from nothingness by God's power, wisdom and goodness, it can do nothing if it is cut off from its origin, for "without a Creator the creature vanishes." Still less can a creature attain its ultimate end without the help of God's grace.[46]

The two texts rely on the philosophical notion of secondary causes. One may only infer that it is impossible to understand the relationship of divine action and human freedom without recognizing that the omnipotent God and the free human creature stand in a relationship that is best conceived as one of first cause to secondary cause. Given a moment's reflection, we see that no other arrangement is possible. God cannot act in half measures. This is the mistake that Luis de Molina had made and that launched the thousand ships of Jansenism, whose captains in fact set out to squelch secondary causes in a vain effort to leave untouched the dreadful sovereignty of God. Molina's divinity acts partially. For, in order to safeguard human freedom, Molina had to introduce a phase—the eclipse—wherein the human will is left unencumbered, so to speak, to take some initiative. This view of the cooperation between God and man results in thinking about God and man as

---

creature from potency to act with respect to its act of self-determination there can be no such act. But of course, in time, the motion is simultaneous with the activation of the power of self-determination. It is 'physical' not in the sense of being a material thing, but in the sense of being real. And of course its character as a motion has been noted" (11).

45. *Catechism of the Council of Trent*, article one.

46. *CCC*, §308.

two partial co-causes, like—to use Molina's own pellucid image—"two men rowing a boat."[47] It is not difficult to sympathize with those devout Christians who recoiled from the conception of Christian life that such imagery evokes. Given the challenges that confront us throughout a lifetime of living according to all that God commands of his holy ones—remember prayer, asceticism (which may include study), and the virtuous life—who would relish the thought of responding to the gift of grace on one's own naked initiative? Consider any temptation that may occur in our lives. Which among us would cry out, "Thank you God for eclipsing your sun's ray so that I may experience myself as truly free"? The more parlous question concerns what happens to those who do espouse this brand of "spirituality."

The Molinist duel ended, as Father Bedouelle has observed, in a draw. Jansenism drew condemnation. Mostly in France, Dominicans toiled to produce treatises that explained why the accepted theses of the Thomist school on predestination, grace, freedom, and the overall salvific purpose of Christ's death on the Cross should not be confused with Jansenist distortions of Catholic doctrine. The Provençal Dominican Jean Baptiste Gonet (†1681) illustrates the battle that the Thomists of the period mounted in order to distinguish the teaching of St. Thomas Aquinas from the teaching of Calvin and that of Jansen.[48] The best illustration of his copious efforts occupies the pages of his celebrated *Clypeus theologiae thomisticae contra novos ejus impugnatores*, which saw many editions after its *princeps* edition published at Bordeaux between the years 1659 and 1669. Gonet takes up the theological style of the Thomist tradition that one of his Provençal confreres, John Capreolus (ca. 1380–1444), had initiated two centuries earlier. Capreolus and Gonet, in a word, were about argument, not catenae. Gonet requires only two half-page columns of his *Clypeus* to ex-

47. See Molina, *Concordia*, q. 14, a. 13, d. 25, ed. Rabeneck: "Ordo agentium respondet ordini finium. Sed unius rei non possunt esse duo fines immediati et perfecti. Ergo neque esse possunt duo agentia, nisi forte supplerent vicem unius agentis perfecti; quo pacto duo trahentes navim efficiunt unum agens integrum ac sufficiens et perfectum; et eodem modo ejusdem rei possunt etiam esse plures fines partiales."

48. For background information, see B. Peyrous, "Un grand centre de thomisme au XVIIe siècle: Le couvent des Frères Prêcheurs de Bordeaux et l'enseignement de J.-B. Gonet," *Divus Thomas* (Pl.) 77 (1974): 452–73.

plain why the Jansenist theses condemned in 1653 by Innocent X do not represent the teaching of St. Thomas Aquinas.[49]

The first condemned proposition (which is the only one taken verbatim from the *Augustinus*) expresses a pessimistic view of human nature and its capacities. The proposition holds that some divine precepts are impossible for men to keep. The spirituality of premotive holiness does not proceed under promise of failure. The cardinal principle of Aquinas's blueprint for holiness is that God loves us because he is good, not because we are.[50] In other words, the divine goodness governs the bestowal of the divine help. In fact, when Aquinas explains why despair is a vice, he points out that the person who despairs of doing God's will fails to embrace the divine omnipotence and the divine mercy. God can save us. God does forgive. The worst thing that can happen in the Christian life is for a Christian to become convinced that virtue is impossible. This persuasion leads not to holiness but to sin, specifically a sin against hope, whose motivating force comes from the propriety of seeking divine goodness.[51] *Mihi sed non propter me*, underscores Cardinal Cajetan.[52] I refer the divine goodness to myself, but I do not subordinate God to my own purposes. The Jansenists ignored this distinction, and so they concluded that despair, not hope, supplies the default position for the human being. But one does not require espousing Jansenist rigorism to conclude that divine help is not forthcoming and that the divine mercy does not embrace me. Many moral laxists secretly succumb to the same despair, although they usually disguise it with rationalization and bravado.

The second condemned proposition privileges "interior grace" to the point of making this grace irresistible to fallen human nature. This thesis describes the physical demolition, not premotion, of the will. Aquinas, on the other hand, recognizes both that we can resist the gift of divine grace and that the grace of the new dispensation does not confirm a

49. See Jean Baptiste Gonet, OP, *Clypeus Theologiae Thomisticae*, vol. 1 (Paris: Vivès, 1875), tract. 3, disp. 6, a. 10.

50. For one reference from Aquinas, see *ST* I, q. 20, a. 2.

51. See *ST* II-II, q. 20, a. 3.

52. Thomas de Vio, Cardinal Cajetan (1469–1534), *In IIam-IIae*, q. 17, a. 5, no. 8.

man in holiness: "The grace of the New Covenant," he writes, "although it helps man not to sin, does not confirm him in good in such a way that he cannot sin: this belongs to the state of glory."[53] Justification, in other words, does not imply impeccability.[54] The spirituality of premotion finds its underpinnings and pinnacles in the practice of the theological virtues—what the French call *la vie théologale*.[55] The life of grace and the virtues establishes the Christian in a right tension that avoids, on the one hand, the uptight rigidness generated by lofty moralism enforced by servile fear and, on the other hand, the callous nonchalance inculcated by disregard of the divine law and by presumption on God's mercy. Within the constellation of virtues that premotive holiness encourages, theological hope ensures that Christian life proceeds within the proper dynamism of grace and freedom.

The third proposition takes the freedom out of merit, and so reduces the Christian believer to a mechanical robot programmed for heaven or hell: "In order to merit or demerit in the state of fallen nature," so Jansenists held, "freedom from necessity is not required in man, but freedom from external compulsion is sufficient."[56] The Jansenists fail to distinguish between freedom with respect to exercise (*quoad exercitium*) and the freedom of specification. With what the whole Christian tradition teaches about everyday holiness, Aquinas places freedom of specification (*quoad specificationem*)—freedom with respect to a sort of action—at the heart of our meriting and demeriting. That the good actions Christians perform reflect the spirituality of premotion holds more interest for Christian theology than a merely human consideration of the freedom with which

53. *ST* I-II, q. 106, a. 2, ad 2.

54. Steven A. Long in a personal communication in January 2013 offers this observation: "It is also difficult [to explain] in that the divine permission does not imply merely libertarian indifference but the non-upholding in good (i.e., for God to permit the defect is for Him not to cause the contrary; granted, He does not owe it to the creature in justice to cause the contrary, a point missed by virtually all the customary naysayers of the tradition, who always suppose that God owes the defectible creature to preserve it from all defect). Greater good is given to all than they can possibly merit absolutely speaking; and lesser penalty is bestowed to those penalized than they actually deserve. But it is a very profound mystery."

55. For further information, see my *Christian Faith and the Theological Life* (Washington, DC: Catholic University of America Press, 1996).

56. *DS* 2003, trans. Denzinger, *The Sources of Catholic Dogma* (St. Louis: Herder, 1957).

they perform them. To relate this element of Thomist doctrine to what is taught explicitly in *Veritatis splendor*, premotive spirituality focuses on teleology: "The primary and decisive element for moral judgment is the object of the human act, which establishes whether it is *capable of being ordered to the good and to the ultimate end, which is God* ... These are the goods safeguarded by the commandments, which, according to Saint Thomas, contain the whole natural law (see *ST* I-II, q. 100, a. 1)."[57] Thomists do not fuss over freedom. They, with the Church, focus on distinguishing the good from the bad. That is, on what perfects and on what detracts from the truth about the good of the human person. Herein lies the nub of the reason for the conflicts, mainly carried on between Dominican and Jesuit moralists, that were issued in the two casuist schools of Probabilism and Probabiliorism. Probabilism favored maximizing freedom of choice within the law. Probabiliorists kept their focus on the choice of the perfective good. Within the casuist systems, Probabilists were content to follow the advice of a few, whereas Probabiliorists—committed to the "more probable" course of action—sought a broad consensus about what (to use the parlance of the period) is permitted or forbidden.[58] Jesuits mainly leaned toward Probabilism, whereas Dominicans, for the most part, held to Probabiliorism.[59]

The fourth proposition concerns the freedom of the will before the grace called sufficient. Jansenists regard talk of sufficient grace as Semipelagian. As Pascal observes in *The Provincial Letters*, Thomists speak in a qualified way about sufficient grace.[60] Grace, because it comes from an omnipotent God, they correctly prefer to stress as efficacious. After the Jansenist condemnations, however, Thomists honed their view of sufficient grace.[61] Gonet offers an insightful reply to the fourth proposition

57. *Veritatis splendor*, §79. Emphasis original.

58. See Romanus Cessario, OP, "Casuistry and Revisionism: Structural Similarities in Method and Content," in *"Humanae Vitae": 20 Anni Dopo. Atti del II Congresso Internazionale di Theologia Morale*, vol. 3 (Milan: Edizioni Ares, 1990): 385–409.

59. As the above reference to St. Alphonsus makes clear, no hard-and-fast rule can be applied.

60. Blaise Pascal, *The Provincial Letters*, trans. A. J. Krailsheimer (Baltimore: Penguin, 1967), 49: "'We [Dominicans] would all sooner suffer martyrdom,' said the Father, 'than consent to the establishment of *sufficient grace in the Jesuits' sense*, for St. Thomas, whom we vow to follow to the death, is directly opposed to it.'"

61. Steven A. Long explains the divine movement in the sinner in this way: "The issue

by citing Aquinas's first Quodlibetal Question: "God moves everything according to its manner. So divine motion is imparted to some things with necessity; however, it is imparted to the rational creature with liberty because the rational power is related to opposites. God so moves the human mind to the good, however, that a man can resist this motion."[62] Garrigou-Lagrange summarizes the accepted teaching with help from the "Eagle of Meaux," Jacques-Bénigne Bossuet:

> In sufficient grace, efficacious grace is offered to us, as the fruit is in the flower; but if resistance is made on account of our defectibility, then we deserve not to receive efficacious grace. For this reason Bossuet declares: "Our intellect must be held captive before the obscurity of the divine mystery and admit two graces (sufficient and efficacious) of which the former leaves our will without any excuse before God, and the latter does not permit the will to glory in itself" (*Œuvres complètes*, Paris, 1845, I, 644).[63]

When one ponders the divine omnipotence and the divine mercy, it becomes evident that the Thomist double insistencies on the efficaciousness of the divine gift and the creature's potential sinful refusal of it create an optimistic view of salvation. The questions "How many are saved?" or "Am I saved?" never trouble the practitioner of premotive holiness. Only one question remains for the person who lives by the divine premotion: "At this moment, do I unite myself with the saving grace that God efficaciously offers me?" If so, whether the grace comes as an operative or a

---

wholly reposes on what is meant by 'resistance to' or 'refusal of' grace. Insofar as the sinful act has any being or good, these derive from and are caused by God (as Thomas makes clear in *De malo*); but the resistance to grace itself is a function of the defectibility of the creature, and if we mean full blown resistance/refusal, this is not a simple negation, but a deprivation, i.e., a privation of something that is owing or due or necessary for the perfection of the subject. It is true that such deprivation presupposes some prior negation, but it is only when the moral agent does not advert to, and conform his action to, the rule of reason and charity, that an action is subject to deprivation and moral evil. By contrast, the simple negation of consideration is consistent with there being no act whatsoever ... Lastly, of course, God must permit such resistance if it occurs, but He is not bound or obligated in justice to preserve the defectible creature from all defect."

62. Gonet cites the text "quod lib.1. art. 7. ad 2." Modern editions make it *Quodlibetal Question* 1, q. 4, art. 2, ad 2, trans. Sandra Edwards (Toronto: PIMS, 1983), 46.

63. Reginald Garrigou-Lagrange, OP, *Grace: Commentary on the Summa Theologica of St. Thomas*, trans. Dominican Nuns, Corpus Christi Monastery (St. Louis, MO: Herder, 1952), chap. 5; also available at http://www.ewtn.com/library/Theology/grace5.htm#_ftn8.

cooperative one, at that moment my salvation is assured.[64] Only the delusional try to travel north and south at the same time.

The fifth proposition considers it heretical to say that Christ died for all men. In reply, Gonet cites the *Summa contra Gentiles*: "As far as He is concerned, God is ready to give grace to all; 'indeed He wills all men to be saved, and to come to the knowledge of the truth,' as is said in 1 Timothy (2:4)." Aquinas continues, "But those alone are deprived of grace who offer an obstacle within themselves to grace; just as, while the sun is shining on the world, the man who keeps his eyes closed is held responsible for his fault, if as a result some evil follows, even though he could not see unless he were provided in advance with light from the sun."[65] This text, which affirms Catholic teaching that "God freely wills to communicate the glory of his blessed life," brings us back to the metaphor of the sun and its rays.[66] For, according to the premotive holiness that follows upon the principles of St. Thomas Aquinas, the sun represents the warmth of the divine love that preveniently anticipates our every need. How differently emerges the portrayal of the sun in the French classical tragedy *Phaedra*, whose author, Jean Racine, also wrote a history of Port Royal, the Parisian Jansenist convent. Racine put these words on the lips of Phaedra: "Do I yet live, wretch that I am, and dare / To face this holy Sun from whom I spring? / My father's sire was king of all the gods; / My ancestors fill all the universe. / Where can I hide? In the dark realms of Pluto?"[67] Pluto, of course, holds sway in a place of perpetual eclipse.[68]

64. The doctrine of St. Thérèse of Lisieux (1873–97) offers a practical application of this Thomist principle. See, for instance, Vernon Johnson, *Spiritual Childhood: The Spirituality of St. Thérèse of Lisieux* (San Francisco: Ignatius Press, 2001).

65. *ScG* III, c. 159, trans. Vernon J. Bourke (Notre Dame, IN: University of Notre Dame Press, 1975), 261.

66. See *CCC*, §257.

67. Jean-Baptiste Racine, "Phaedra," Act IV, vi, trans. Robert Bruce Boswell; available at http://www.gutenberg.org/cache/epub/1977/pg1977.txt.

68. Thanks to the Laurence McGrath, Jörgen Vijgen, and Cajetan Cuddy, OP, for their invaluable assistance in developing this chapter.

CHAPTER 13

CULTURE AND CONTEMPLATION

Catholicism in the Twenty-First Century

In this final chapter, Father Cessario offers us a reflection on Catholicism as we enter into the twenty-first century. Originally delivered on November 11, 2013, as his inaugural lecture after receiving the degree *Sacrae Theologiae Magister*—the highest intellectual award of the Dominican Order—this chapter is uniquely personal in nature. He provides an autobiographical sketch of his life in the Order of Preachers and remembers the figures who were instrumental in his own theological and spiritual formation. Most importantly, Father Cessario shares the fundamental conviction that has shaped the whole of his life's work: *Only the truth has grace*. In many ways, this statement stands as the single most encompassing theological theme of this book, and the most important truth for all of those pursuing a life of sanctity.

Pope Paul VI addressed the closing session of the Second Vatican Council on December 7, 1965, with these words:

> With the help of this council, by a doctrine of human nature and the world which is theological and theocentric, as they say, the

Originally published as "Culture and Contemplation: Catholicism in the 21st Century," *Thomist* 77, no. 3 (2013): 453–71. Reprinted by permission.

> Church has turned the minds of men to herself . . . She embraces what the world at first considers absurd—the claim that God exists, But we are strongly confident that the age will later of its own accord acknowledge this belief as humane, wise and beneficial. For God is: He actually exists; He lives; He is a person; He is providential, endowed with infinite goodness, and He is not only good in himself, but especially good in regards to us; He is our creator, our truth, our happiness; so much so that when a man tries to fix his mind and heart on God through contemplation he elicits an act of his own spirit which is the most fine and perfect of all; thus even in the modern world, in all fields of human endeavor, we can and should aspire to this contemplative act so that all human activity is raised and perfected in its own order from within.[1]

Together with this explicit avowal of the excellence that persons and culture derive from contemplation, the Holy Father also proffered an evaluation of mid-twentieth-century moral outlooks. In December 1965—as members of that year's profession class for the Province of Saint Joseph were taking up the study of philosophy at Dover, Massachusetts, under Dominican masters such as Raymond Smith (†1990) and William A. Wallace—Paul VI drew a stark picture of the ethos that dominated his generation. Blessed Pope John XXIII had convoked the Council, so his immediate successor reported, at a time when men preferred terrestrial kingdoms to heavenly ones at a time when men habitually forgot about God, at a time when men displaced God's law in order to proclaim their own autonomy, at a time when *il laicismo* (rendered in English as "secularism") trumped the highest wisdom, at a time when men's souls experienced the desolation to which acting outside of reason leads, and, finally, at a time when all organized religion experienced a general decline.[2] The religious significance of the Second Vatican Council, so Paul VI added confidently, would help Catholics and persons of good will to address these challenging cultural circumstances.[3]

1. Paul VI, "On the Religious Significance of Vatican II: Discourse at the Last General Session of Vatican II (7 December 1965)," *Acta Apostolicae Sedis* 58 (1966): 57–59; also in *Readdressing the Liberal State: Reading Maritain's "Man and the State,"* ed. Timothy Fuller and John P. Hittinger, trans. Michael Woodward and John P. Hittinger (Washington, DC: American Maritain Association, 2001), 248.

2. Ibid., 248.

3. Ibid., 247: "What is the religious importance of our council? By the term 'religious' we

I would like to report that the pope's message rallied the Dominican students at Dover. To the best of my recollection, however, the Council's termination did not alter the focus of their daily regime. The student brothers went about assiduously studying cosmology and the philosophy of science, metaphysics and the history of philosophy, while at the same time faithfully observing the rhythms of conventual life. Of course, there were the occasional breaks for canoeing or skating on the Charles River as the seasons allowed or for walking along the paths that crisscrossed like a giant, disorganized maze the tall pines that flourished on the priory grounds. In other words, these future priests went on preparing to fulfill their Dominican vocation: *Contemplari et contemplata aliis tradere.*[4] Those who found this task too challenging left.

Saint Stephen's Priory and College stood a short twenty miles from Kenmore Square and nearby Fenway Park. Because they lived close to Boston, the Dominican philosophers of the mid-1960s were not completely oblivious to the big events happening within the world and the Church. They in fact profited much from dwelling so close to the "Hub of the Universe"—an expression that Oliver Wendell Holmes thought apt to describe nineteenth-century Boston.[5] In late 1965, the Dover Dominicans, even if papal discourses did not distract them, were in fact quite attuned to the papacy. Earlier the same year, in October, Paul VI became the first Roman Pontiff to set foot on American soil.

Strictly speaking, the pope came to visit the United Nations in order to mark the organization's twentieth anniversary. His poignant cry for peace delivered in French before the General Assembly introduced most Americans, including the philosophers at Dover, to the second pope of

---

mean to signify our relationship to God, which is, after all, why the Church exists, what she believes, what she hopes for, what she loves; this personal relationship to God defines what she is and what she does."

4. Adapted from *ST* II-II, q. 188, a. 6: "Sicut enim majus est illuminare quam lucere solum, ita majus est contemplata aliis tradere quam solum contemplari." In *ST* III, q. 40, a. 1, ad 2, Aquinas identifies the Dominican life as that form of Christian living that Christ himself chose.

5. See Oliver Wendell Holmes, *The Autocrat of the Breakfast-Table* (Boston: Houghton, Mifflin and Company, 1891), 172: "A jaunty-looking person . . . said there was one more wise man's saying that he had heard; it was about our place—but he didn't know who said it . . . 'Boston State-House is the Hub of the Solar System.'"

the Council: Never again. Never again, war, he declaimed. This papal *Jamais plus*—pronounced with such insistence—moved many American Catholics, especially the young, to hope that the pope's appearance in our country would confirm a new era of optimism for the Church, to believe that the pope had absolved our nation, as it were, of the Kennedy assassination in November 1963.[6] When the pope celebrated Mass in Yankee Stadium, American Catholics witnessed firsthand the new program of papal outreach. Prior to the pontificates of the second half of the twentieth century, a pope sojourning outside of the papal domains could only be in exile, coerced, or deported. In October 1965, the City of New York's welcome of the bishop of Rome was a triumphal occasion, one crowned at the Waldorf Astoria, where the pope conferred with President Lyndon Baines Johnson.

Back in autumnal New England, Father Dominic Rover, OP, preached that year the traditional October 4th homily at the Franciscan Friary in Rye Beach, New Hampshire. He encouraged his listeners with an eloquent account of the pope's "walk in the world." Now that the pope had visited the United States, Father Rover assured both Franciscans and Dominicans, nothing would be the same. As things turned out, he was right. In 1965, however, this Dominican preacher *par excellence*, on a crisp, colorful fall day along the Atlantic coast, envisioned a renewal within the Church that would proceed in continuity with classical Catholic doctrine. He announced a forthcoming period when a retrieval of the Church's rich spiritual heritage would complement the solid doctrinal instruction given during the postwar period. Others who had come of spiritual age during those buoyant years for American Catholicism received different messages. For instance, Jesuit Father Walter Abbott's hastily produced and, as later became evident, seriously defective edition of the Council documents witnessed brisk sales at $10 for a hardbound copy—a handsome price in those days.[7] It did not take long for popular presentations

6. "Discours du Pape Paul VI à l'Organisation des Nations Unies à l'Occasion du 20ème Anniversaire de l'Organisation, Lundi 4 octobre 1965," *Acta Apostolicae Sedis* 57 (1965): 877–85. The pope actually quoted the late President Kennedy.

7. Walter M. Abbott, SJ, ed. *The Documents of Vatican II* (New York: Herder and Herder, 1966).

of the Council to adopt the language of revolution. "Change" became a new word, indeed commonplace, in the vocabulary of American Catholics, even among those who opposed the notion. For instance, before his departure for the Council, the archbishop of New York, who would have been informed of Roman rumors, announced that "no change" would get past the Statue of Liberty.[8] Despite Cardinal Spellman's best precautions, however, most Catholics subsequently came to learn the meaning of the Italian word *aggiornamento* before they encountered the French *ressourcement.*

Dominican students of the Province of Saint Joseph, in retrospect, were fortunate. They were dissuaded from adopting the hermeneutic of rupture, *ante nomen.* As I have said, Father Rover interpreted the pope's "walk in the world"—his phrase—as an occasion to reinvigorate the Order's commitment to contemplation, not to alter or discard it. The student brothers found nothing revolutionary in this counsel. Their Dominican mentors had always set forth the image of St. Dominic, of whom a liturgical text says, "Documentis artium eruditus satis, transiit ad studium summae veritatis."[9] Having mastered the arts and sciences, Dominic Guzman passed over to the study of the Highest Truth. Who better than Holy Father Dominic—that *être de feu,* that man on fire—who passed a whole night converting one Albigensian innkeeper, demonstrates that only the truth has grace?[10] Seven hundred and fifty years later, in leafy Dover, Massachusetts, his spiritual sons were being prepared to face the world with faith and recollection, the indispensable spiritual conditions for advancing toward contemplation. Without fully realizing that a theory explained their good fortune, the Dover Dominicans found themselves committed to pursuing an authentic *ressourcement.* As the second half of the 1960s unfolded, however, the world outside the cloister began rapidly to fulfill Father Rover's prediction, though not as he had intended

8. See John Cooney, *The American Pope: The Life and Times of Francis Cardinal Spellman* (New York: Times Books, 1984), 276.

9. From a Latin antiphon once used at the first nocturne of Matins on the Feast of Saint Dominic.

10. See Guy Thomas Bedouelle, OP, "Saint Dominique, ou la grâce de la prédication," *Sources* 8, no. 5 (1982): 193–201. Father Bedouelle delivered this conference at Notre Dame de Paris on October 25, 1981.

it. Nothing was as it had been. Change happened, and not only in the Church.

"HERE COMES EVERYBODY"

The word "contemplation" does not appear on many pages of the conciliar documents.[11] Indeed, the Council's emphases, as the pope in his closing address identified them, centered on the Church and the virtue of charity.[12] The diligent student may enquire: Why did Paul VI include a paragraph on contemplation in his short summation of the Council's achievements? To answer this question, one should recall the Holy Father's intellectual preferences. As his communications with Jean Guitton suggest, Giovanni Battista Montini (1897–1978) trusted French Catholic intellectuals of the early twentieth century.[13] In addition to the well-known thinkers of that era, there were also many French spiritual authors who initiated Christian believers into the art of contemplation.

As practitioners of *haute-vulgarisation*, as the French say, their influence was both immediate and widespread. Take for example the French Dominican Pierre-Thomas Dehau (1870–1956), who guided, among his other disciples, the Maritains and their broad circle of friends.[14] Notable among these latter were refugees from the beau monde like Max Jacob, Jean Cocteau, Maurice Sachs, Erik Satie, the Claudel convert, and, later,

11. There are approximately eight references to "contemplation," of which half refer to those who practice a contemplative life.

12. Paul VI, "Religious Significance of Vatican II," 249: "Someone might say that the council focused less on the elaboration of divine truths than on its principal theme—the consideration of the Church, her nature, her composition, her ecumenical task, and her apostolic and missionary work." See also ibid., 250: "We prefer to notice that our council's spirituality was chiefly one of love, on account of which express purpose no one will be able to treat the council as though it were irreligious or deviating from the holy Gospel."

13. See Jean Guitton, *The Pope Speaks: Dialogues of Paul VI with Jean Guitton* (New York: Meredith Press, 1968); Jacques Maritain, *The Peasant of the Garonne: An Old Layman Questions Himself about the Present Time*, trans. Michael Cuddihy and Elizabeth Hughes (New York: Holt, Rinehart and Winston, 1968), 4. For the text that Maritain produced at the request of Pope Paul VI, "The Spiritual Mission of the Laity," see *Communio* 14 (Summer 1987): 183–202, which includes a section on those laity who can offer *le témoignage intellectuellement manifesté*.

14. For an introduction to this early figure of the twentieth century, see Rémi Pelon, *Invitation à la contemplation: Vie et choix de textes du père Pierre-Thomas Dehau, dominicain* (Paris: Les Éditions du Cerf, 2006), esp. 70–76.

de Foucauld disciple Charles Henrion. The last, while a First World War prisoner at Fribourg, encountered the anti-Molinist Dominican scholar Norbert del Prado (1852–1918).[15] To those who sought willy-nilly to escape continental nihilism, Father Dehau and others offered a path toward the contemplation of the highest truth.

Father Dehau spoke directly from the heart. "Contemplation," he wrote, "stands above all things and constitutes the ultimate end of creation." To those who struggled to escape spiritual lethargy and cruder ailments, like opium addictions and disordered lusts, Father Dehau provided a distinctively Dominican instruction about how to approach contemplation: "For the Father seeks such [contemplative persons]," this holy priest recalled from John 4:23, which records the encounter with the Samaritan Woman. He went on to explain, "God, in fact cannot be passive in any of His acts; when therefore, we are told that He searches for adorers, this means that He is fashioning them, and He fashions them by His very searching." To which our Dominican author adds innocently, "This is a very mysterious and very lofty truth."[16] Père Dehau illustrates well the twentieth-century Catholic focus on contemplation, if not on the divine premotion, that one assumes attracted *Papa* Montini. This Dominican priest—and others that could be mentioned, especially the Carmelite Marie-Eugène de l'Enfant-Jésus (1894–1967)—helped Catholics from all spiritual backgrounds to envisage contemplation as a perfection of their Christian existence.[17] What is more surprising, Father Dehau's influence, like that of other French spiritual authors, expanded beyond the francophone world.

French panegyrics for contemplation, as we have seen, did not appeal only to cloistered nuns and pure saints. The American-born novelist Julien Green, one of the Maritains' diverse friends, considered that

15. For further information about the Maritains' evangelical outreach at Meudon, see Romanus Cessario, OP, "*Humanae Vitae* 17: *Vaticinium ex eventu*? An Illustration from the Maritains' Moral Guidance to Maurice Sachs," *Nova et Vetera*, 6, no. 4 (2008): 711–30 (chap. 11, this volume). For more on Charles Hernion, see René Voillaume, *Charles de Foucauld et ses premiers disciples: Du désert arabe au monde des cités* (Paris: Bayard Éditions, 1998), 78–82.

16. Pierre-Thomas Dehau, OP, *The Living Water*, trans. Dominic Ross, OP (Westminster, MD: Newman Press, 1957), 131. Translation slightly altered.

17. Marie-Eugène de l'Enfant-Jésus's *Je veux voir Dieu* (2005) was first published in 1949 by Éditions du Carmel, Venasque.

Father Dehau's writings contained what Ralph Waldo Emerson had called the "accent of the Holy Spirit."[18] On November 22, 1951, Green wrote to Maritain, "Has anybody thought of translating Father Dehau into English? Who knows whether in America he may not find an echo in many souls."[19] As it providentially followed, two Dehau books were published in English before the end of the decade. One of these books, *Eve and Mary*, was translated by the Dominican Nuns of the Perpetual Rosary at La Crosse, Wisconsin.[20] (This monastery is now located in Linden, Virginia.) The other, *The Living Water*, was translated by a member of the Province of Saint Joseph, Father Dominic Ross, who taught French at Providence College.[21] One may safely suppose, then, that in 1965 far-flung regions of the Catholic world were prepared to welcome Paul VI's reminder that contemplation remains the most noble and most perfect of all human acts.

Père Dehau offers one example of the allure that contemplation exercised on Catholic believers before 1962, when Good Pope John opened the Second Vatican Council. The dramatic biographies of some converts of this period, such as the French fashion model Jean Bourgoint, should not incline us to think that Catholic contemplation emerges in the early twentieth century only as cheap palliative care for Eliot's Hollow Men.[22] Spiritual masters, as is well known, have preached the practice of contemplation from the very beginning of the Christian era. Each age affords its own witnesses to contemplation: From the patristic Cassian († after 430), whose *Conferences* St. Dominic so much admired; to the Renaissance scholar Thomas de Vio, Cardinal Cajetan (1469–1534), whose definition likens contemplation to seeing the face of a friend; to

18. "The word by seers or sibyls told, / In groves of oak, or fanes of gold, / Still floats upon the morning wind, / Still whispers to the willing mind. / One accent of the Holy Ghost / The heedless world hath never lost." Ralph Waldo Emerson (1803–82), "The Problem," in *Poems* (Boston: J. Monroe, 1847).

19. See Pelon, *Invitation à la contemplation*, 90n2.

20. Peter Thomas Dehau, *Eve and Mary*, trans. Dominican Nuns of the Perpetual Rosary, La Crosse, Wisconsin (St. Louis, MO: Herder, 1956).

21. See Dehau, *Living Water*, i.

22. For a glimpse at his remarkable life, see Jean Bourgoint (Frère Pascal), *Le retour de l'Enfant Terrible: Lettres 1923–1966*, ed. Jean Hugo and Jean Mouton (Paris: Desclée De Brouwer, 1975). For T. S. Eliot's 1925 poem "The Hollow Men," see *The Complete Poems and Plays of T. S. Eliot* (London: Faber and Faber, 1969), 83–86.

the twentieth-century author Thomas Merton (1915–68), whose book *The Seeds of Contemplation* underwent multiple editions throughout the spiritually buoyant 1950s.[23] These and many other witnesses convey the central place contemplation occupies within the Christian life.

In the 1950s, French authors A. J. Festugière and R.-A. Gauthier had produced classical studies on contemplation in Plato and Aristotle, respectively, that supported Pope Paul's confidence that contemplation perfects culture.[24] The best of Greek antiquity acknowledged the exigency of contemplation for the human creature.[25] Shorter essays on philosophical contemplation, like the one published after the Council by the Swiss Dominican Pierre-Marie Emonet, *Dieu contemplé dans le miroir des choses*, illustrated that the Christian contemplative act does not destroy our human capacities but, like other divine gifts of grace, perfects them.[26] Père Emonet quotes the French *litterateur*, poet, and occasional scoundrel Charles Baudelaire, "Happy the one who can vigorously soar toward the shining serene fields," in order to stress that contemplation remains an aspiration of the human heart even among those who do not display public attachment to religion.[27] At the same time, as Father Festugière pointed out as early as 1932, the attainment of the Greek contemplative ideal engaged only an exclusive elite among the Hellenic gentry.[28]

For a period of his apostolic life, Père Emonet served as chaplain to Swiss contemplative nuns at Estavayet-le-Lac in the Canton of Fri-

23. For the influence of John Cassian on the formation of St. Dominic at Osma, see M.-H. Vicaire, OP, *Histoire de Saint Dominique*, vol. 1, *Un Homme Évangélique* (Paris: Les Éditions du Cerf, 1982), 118–20. For the views of Cardinal Cajetan, see his commentary on *Summa Theologiae* II-II, q. 180, a. 1, which provides a remarkably succinct account of the essentials. See Thomas Merton, *Seeds of Contemplation* (New York: Dell, 1949).

24. See A. J. Festugière, *Contemplation et vie contemplative selon Platon* (Paris: Vrin, 1950); R.-A. Gauthier and J.-Y. Jolif, *L'Ethique à Nicomaque: Introduction, traduction et commentaire*, 2 vols. (Louvain: Nauwelaerts, 1958, 1959).

25. See M.-D. Philippe, *L'Être*, vol. 1 (Paris: Éditions P. Téqui, 1972), 99–109: "Philosophie de l'être, de l'un, du bien, recherche de la verité, la philosophie greque a proclamé avec force l'exigence de la contemplation."

26. Pierre-Marie Emonet, *Dieu contemplé dans le mirroir des choses* (Chambray-lès-Tours: Éditions C.L.D., 1997).

27. Charles Baudelaire, "Élevations," in *Les Fleurs du mal* (Genève: Ambilly, 1968): "Heureux celui qui peut d'une aile vigoureuse / S'élancer vers les champs lumineux et sereins." For the translation, see Pierre-Marie Emonet, *God Seen in the Mirror of the World: An Introduction to the Philosophy of God*, trans. Robert R. Barr (New York: Crossroad, 2000), 15.

28. See A. J. Festugière, *L'idéal religieux des Grecs et l'Éuangile* (Paris: Gabalda, 1932).

bourg, where he succeed the well-known Polish aristocrat Alex-Ceslas Rzewuski, OP (1892–1983). This latter, even when he had heavy duties in Fribourg, maintained close ties with the Parisian glitterati. He served as a spiritual guide to Misia Sert (née Marie Sophie Olga Zénaïde Godebska), Coco Chanel, and their sparkling entourage of the rich and gifted.[29] In 1946, this Toulouse Dominican also played an influential role in drawing *l'enfant terrible*, Jean Bourgoint—sometime intimate of Jean Cocteau—to the contemplative life of Citeaux.[30] Like the call to holiness, Christian contemplation, as another Dominican has observed, can overpower even those persons who appear least disposed to assume the obligations of a contemplative life.[31] Count and fashion model, couturier and priest, princess and apprentice, harlot and nun: God excludes none from the call to holiness. What is more, those who were habitués of twentieth-century pastimes like intrigue, drugs, and concubinage required more than intellectual satisfaction as a motive for seeking contemplation; they wanted to be loved. Spiritual persons commonly borrow the words of the Song of Songs, "I belong to my lover, and my lover belongs to me" (Song 6:3), to describe their union with Jesus, the heavenly Bridegroom who chooses them before they seek him. This immediacy of the divine embrace can overpower lost souls even as it sustains faithful ones.

Father Garrigou-Lagrange has observed that "infused contemplation . . . remains, through docility to the Holy Spirit, the prayer and the cross accessible to everyone."[32] What has sustained a holy inclusivism among Dominicans? One reply to this "Here Comes Everybody" question returns us to France.[33] Since 1295, the Order has maintained the sanctu-

29. See Alex-Ceslas Rzewuski, *La Double tagédie de Misia Sert* (Paris: Les Éditions du Cerf, 2006).

30. Bourgoint, *Le retour de l'Enfant Terrible*, 9–12. See also Ceslas Rzewuski, OP, *À travers l'invisible cristal* (Paris: Plon, 1976), as well as the biography of Bourgoint by Georges Lavis, *Itinéraire d'un Enfant Terrible: De Cocteau à Cîteaux* (Paris: Presses de la Renaissance, 1998). In 1950, Jean-Pierre Melville produced a film, *Les enfants terribles*, adapted from Jean Cocteau's novel of the same title, that is based on Bourgoint's early life.

31. See Jean-Hervé Nicolas, OP, *Contemplation et vie contemplative en christianisme* (Fribourg: Édition, Universitaire, 1980), 23–26.

32. P. Réginald Garrigou-Lagrange, OP, *Perfection chrétienne et contemplation selon S. Thomas d'Aquin et S. Jean de la croix*, vol. l (Saint-Maximin [Var]: Éditions de La Vie Spirituelle, 1923), i.

33. The phrase comes from James Joyce, *Finnegans Wake* (London: Faber and Faber, 1939).

ary of La Sainte-Baume, a grotto located in a craggy stretch of mountains in southern Provence.[34] There, according to an ancient tradition, Mary Magdalene ended her days in contemplation. Though the Dominican Order enjoys no exclusive patent on mystical theology, its nearly eight-hundred-year record of sustaining Christian contemplation offers hope for Catholicism in the twenty-first century. The *spes Ordinis* face a daunting challenge, however, one that requires their maintaining a holy exclusivism. The mystical movement within the Order that begins in the thirteenth-century Rhineland district and continues into eighteenth-century France, before the Revolution, suggests that contemplation flourishes during those times when Dominicans maintain the rhythm of life that the Order stipulates or blesses.[35] The witness of reformers, like Blessed Constantius of Fabriano (1410–81) and Blessed Sebastian Maggi (1414–96), further illustrates that when the ambient culture—the early Italian Renaissance for these fifteenth-century contemporaries of Jerome Savonarola—lacks stability and virtue, the pursuit of the contemplative life requires a deadly seriousness of purpose.

In *Fides et ratio*, St. Pope John Paul II has encouraged Catholic intellectuals to practice philosophy in Mary: *philosophari in Maria*.[36] Charles De Koninck, in the 1940s, taught his students that the philosophical enterprise properly conducted leads almost serendipitously to the Blessed Virgin Mary. He invited them to ponder what the Old Testament says about Holy Wisdom: "For she is an aura of the might of God / and a pure effusion of the glory of the Almighty; / therefore nought that is sullied enters into her ... And she, who is one, can do all things, / and renews everything while herself perduring; / And passing into holy souls

34. Jean Paul Cassagnères, *Marie-Madeleine et la Sainte-Baume* (Saint Zacharie: 1978).

35. Guy Bedouelle, OP, *In the Image of Saint Dominic: Nine Portraits of Dominican Life*, trans. Sr. Mary Thomas Noble, OP (San Francisco; Ignatius Press, 1994), 103–4, gives a brief overview: "There was the Rhineland school of the thirteenth century, with Meister Eckhart and his disciples among both friars and sisters. There was an Italian school deriving from St. Catherine of Siena, which through Savonarola continued its influence to the end of the sixteenth century. There was a Spanish school, also with Savonarolian influence, which became eremitical in the sixteenth and seventeenth centuries with Louis of Granada and had effect in South America, in St. Rose of Lima (†1617) for example, and later in France in Louis Chardon (†1651) and Alexander Pliny (†1709)."

36. Pope John Paul II, 1998 encyclical letter, *Fides et ratio*, "On the Relationship Between Faith and Reason," §108.

from age to age, / she produces friends of God and prophets" (Wis 7:25, 7:27). As a principle of the sapiential order, De Koninck pointed out that Mary "is at once an emanation and an indwelling."[37] When the late Father Guy Bedouelle (†2012)—a Dominican master in many senses—preached a retreat at the Priory of the Immaculate Conception in Washington, DC, he reminded the community that the Incarnation of the Son of God makes Christian contemplation possible. "Fra Angelico," so Father Guy reported, "had a predilection for depicting the Annunciation, which is the scenario for the *Sacra Conversatio*, the holy dialogue between the Angel Gabriel and the Virgin Mary."[38] In another of John Paul II's encyclical letters, *Redemptoris Mater*, the pope also proclaimed Mary the "prototype of contemplation," a title that invites imitation.[39] Those prepared to receive the truth and to abide in the truth (see Jn 15:1–10) will discover themselves rightly disposed both to recognize Mary's place in salvation and to imitate her *sacra conversatio*. Blessed Alan de la Roche (1428–75) and his Rosary Confraternity show that this imitation may begin as easily as saying "Hail, Mary!"

SAINTS SHAPE CULTURE

About a third of those who made first profession in August of 1965 advanced toward holy orders. The Province of Saint Joseph's ordination class of 1971 left the Washington *studium* without much formal classroom instruction in ascetical and mystical theology. This somewhat modern addition to the theological curriculum had been relegated to the novitiate program. Father Garrigou-Lagrange says that the specialized treatises gained prominence in the seventeenth and eighteenth centuries.[40] A revered novice master at Saint Joseph's Priory near Somerset,

37. Charles De Koninck, *Ego Sapientia: The Wisdom That Is Mary (1943)*, vol. 2, *The Writings of Charles De Koninck*, ed. Ralph McInerny (Notre Dame, IN: University of Notre Dame Press, 2009), 15.

38. Bedouelle, *Image of Saint Dominic*, 80.

39. Pope John Paul II, 1987 encyclical letter, *Redemptoris Mater*, "On the Blessed Virgin Mary in the Life of the Pilgrim Church," §33.

40. For background, see Garrigou-Lagrange, *Perfection chrétienne et contemplation*, vol. 1, a. 2, "La distinction de l'ascétique et de la mystique et l'unité de la doctrine spirituelle," 16–40.

Ohio, Father Ferrer Cassidy made use of *The Spiritual Life*, a French treatise by the Sulpician Adolphe Tanquerey (1854–1932), which had been published in English in 1930.[41] Tanquerey includes a section on fragrant mystical odors, which amused those Easterners who found it difficult to abide the late summer manured fields of Ohio's Perry County.[42] All things considered, liturgy more than manuals initiated Dominicans into contemplative prayer.

Paul VI's endorsement of contemplation was lost in the confusion that erupted in July 1968, when many theologians chose to cavil with *Humanae vitae*. By the 1970s, the dynamics of the mystical life had become the subject matter of academic specialization, and one might have expected to pursue such study with the Carmelites. Academic specialists, however, began to treat even the greats of Carmel, Teresa of Ávila and John of the Cross, more as subjects for scientific investigation than as guides for contemplative life. Other saints would have found this evolution surprising. Recall what St. Catherine de Ricci (1522–90)—herself favored with mystical experiences—wrote to a contemporary, St. Philip Neri: "Live in joy, despite the thought of your last end."[43] This injunction, addressed to a man known for his cheerfulness, came during a period when men anguished over predestination in addition to studying about it!

One may recall that the Council's teachings reached the United States at about the same time that the civil rights movement of the 1960s won widespread recognition. As a result, theologians attached enormous importance to social action. *Engagement* became the preferred form of enacting *aggiornamento*. In 1976, the erudite Jean-Hervé Nicolas, OP, did not

Students of Father Servais Pinckaers recall that the separation of mystical theology from moral theology represents an unhappy legacy of the casuist period. See Romanus Cessario, OP, "Hommage au Père Servais-Théodore Pinckaers, OP: The Significance of His Work," *Nova et Vetera* 5, no. 1 (2007): 1–16.

41. Adolphe Tanquerey, *The Spiritual Life: A Treatise on Ascetical and Mystical Theology*, 2nd and rev. ed., trans. H. Branderis (Tournai: Descleé, 1932).

42. Ibid., 712: "At times God permits the bodies of the Saints to give forth during their lifetime or after their death a fragrant odor, a symbol, so to speak, of the perfume of virtues they have practiced."

43. Cited in Bedouelle, *Image of Saint Dominic*, 110. See also the critical edition of the saint's correspondence, Santa Caterina de' Ricci, *Epistolario*, 5 vols., ed. G. Di Agresti (Florence: Leo S. Olschki, 1973–75).

mince words: "Never as today," he wrote, "have Christians contested the contemplative ideal by appeal to the Gospel, which they conceive as an ideal of action in the world and for the world."[44] Few US Catholics at that time knew much about liberal Protestantism. Fewer were acquainted with the criticisms that the best Protestant divines had mounted against it. As H. Richard Niebuhr famously put it in 1937, "This liberalism was indeed naively optimistic. A God without wrath brought men without sin into a kingdom without judgment through the ministrations of a Christ without a cross."[45] The wag adds, "in the neighborhood of Boston." Catholics, then, especially young priests and religious, found themselves affected by ideologies that drew more from a discarded liberalism than from the authentic Catholic social movements started by people like Dorothy Day.

Good works were accomplished in the turbulent 1970s. But many Catholics, both clerics and lay folk, forgot that the best human endeavors spring up from a contemplative spirit. In a word, activists overlooked the important New Testament lesson taught by Martha and Mary (see Lk 10:38–42). Recently, in preparation for the 2016 Dominican Jubilee, the Master of the Order evoked Meister Eckhart's interpretation of this Gospel text, which allows the busy Martha a contemplative life.[46] Earlier, Swiss Cardinal Charles Journet appealed to the witness of St. Nicholas of Flüe, who, while remaining in his hermitage, reconciled in 1481 warring Swiss cantons at the Diet of Stans. Bruder Klaus, a contemplative, ensured the future of the Swiss Confederation, and he managed to do it by a letter.[47] Lessons like these, however, were neglected among the enthusiasms generated by the allure of the social gospel. Instead, many religious institutes began those nettlesome discussions that pitted contemplation against apostolic mission. In retrospect, even those

44. Nicolas, *Contemplation et vie contemplative*, 7 (translation mine).

45. See H. Richard Niebuhr, *The Kingdom of God in America* (New York: Harper & Row, 1937), 193.

46. Bruno Cadoré, OP, "Mary: Contemplation and Preaching of the Word," Yearly Jubilee Theme, February 2013: "This evocation [of Blessed John-Joseph Lataste] clearly illustrates that contemplation and preaching of the Word together constitute the heart of the life and of the mission of the Order of Preachers . . . We also recall the enlightened comment of Master Eckhart about the Gospel of Martha and Mary." For "Sermon Nine," see Maurice O'C. Walshe, trans., *The Complete Mystical Works of Meister Eckhart* (New York: Crossroad, 2009), 83–90.

47. Charles Journet, *Saint Nicholas de Flue* (Neuchâtel: Éditions de la Baconnière, 1947), 77.

committed to the works of justice must admit that some mistakes were made. In any event, not a few religious found the regular form of life too restrictive for their social commitments, and they left. Although this pattern emerged mainly within religious communities, some diocesan priests also found themselves diverted from exercising their *munera*, especially in places like Boston, where major theoreticians of engagement have lectured since 1936 at the Harvard Kennedy School, and Chicago, where social activism had become a standard feature of daily life since the relief efforts following the Chicago fire of 1871.[48]

Happily, those ordained at New York's Saint Vincent Ferrer Church on May 27, 1971, had received unshakeable support for living out their Dominican vocations. These young priests were instructed that no Dominican can sustain his ministry without following the example set down by our saintly forbears like St. Catherine of Siena. Accordingly, they rejoiced the year before when Paul VI proclaimed her a doctor of the Church (on October 3, 1970). Throughout the twentieth century, the English-speaking world enjoyed access to St. Catherine's seraphic instruction. In 1905, Vida Dutton Scudder (1861–1954) published Catherine's letters in translation.[49] In 1907, Algar Thorold (1866–1936) published "a new and abridged edition" of *The Dialogue of the Seraphic Virgin, Catherine of Siena.*[50] Later in the 1960s, there was the made-for-television script "Catherine, My Mother" by the St. Francis Day preacher Father Dominic Rover. This dramatic production appeared on the *Catholic Hour*, a regular program produced by NBC, and whose earlier radio run had been made famous by the voices of Catholic stars like Fulton Sheen.[51]

The *Catholic Hour* drama turns on recollections from those who knew Catherine and whom Catherine helped to love her Sweet Jesus. One of these witnesses is her confessor and guide, Raymond of Capua:

48. For example, see Maureen A. Flanagan, *Seeing with Their Hearts: Women and the Vision of the Good City, 1871–1933* (Princeton, NJ: Princeton University Press, 2002).

49. Vida D. Scutter, trans., *Saint Catherine of Siena as Seen in Her Letters* (New York: E. P. Dutton, 1905).

50. Algar Labouchere Thorold, trans., *The Dialogue of the Seraphic Virgin, Catherine of Siena: Dictated by Her, while in a State of Ecstasy, to Her Secretaries, and Completed in the Year of Our Lord 1370* (London: Kegan Paul, Trench, Trübner, 1907).

51. For the script, see Dominic Rover, OP, "'Catherine, My Mother' (a Television Play)," *Torch* April (1962): 23–31.

> I remember once in the convent of Montepulciano. She was sick with a great fever and had asked me to come . . . Then the flood of words about God's Blood and the Bridegroom and the need for a holy hatred of self, so strong this time that it stung me. It was, perhaps, the fear and guilt in my own soul, or else the devil himself got into my heart, but I began to wonder whether it was truly the Spirit of God who moved her or only the fever, and whether some mad fever of the soul had not always possessed her, from the beginning.

Capua continues:

> It struck me that these holy words were all lies, lies of a wretched woman possessed of demons, or simply mad! Then I looked again at the virgin and suddenly, it was not Catherine! It was the face . . . the face of a man . . . looking up at me, with strong eyes and short fair beard. Majestic—like the Byzantine Christ in the church of Monreale. It was terror held me there, a great terror, but I had to speak, "Who art thou? Who?" And the voice answered: "He Who is." At that very moment the face vanished and it was Catherine lay there, cooled of her fever now, sleeping like a babe, or caught up in that prayer which for her was like a long sleep and the end of pain.[52]

Today, many people would find it hard to believe that in the 1960s NBC used such highly charged religious material to attract television viewers. "Catherine, My Mother," however, must have struck a chord in the hearts of American Catholics. Who would not rejoice to discover the seraphic virgin Catherine and to practice "that prayer which for her was like a long sleep and the end of pain"? What is more important, teachers like Father Dominic Rover helped many priests to discover how to make contemplation user-friendly amid the uncertainties of the last quarter of the twentieth century. One starts by preaching—to borrow St. Catherine's favorite themes—about "God's Blood and the Bridegroom and the need for a holy hatred of self." Then the priest moves into the confessional. The nun enters her cloister. Husbands and wives teach their children how to live in faith and recollection.

Dominic Rover was acquainted with another doctor of the Church,

52. Ibid., 26.

a woman who helped many young Dominicans to discover the dynamics of spiritual generation. The Little Flower of Lisieux described a pattern of contemplative life without extended reference to the stages and distinctions that mystical theology had accumulated over the centuries: beginners, proficients, perfects; purgative, illuminative, mystical—the levels of ascent to Mount Carmel; the mansions of St. Teresa.[53] For her part, Thérèse preferred a little way. She expressed this preference, moreover, without knowing that, a few decades after her death in 1897, the Jesuit editors of the *Dictionnaire de spiritualité, Ascétique et mystique, Doctrine et histoire* would require 551 columns to explain contemplation.[54] In other words, God sent us Thérèse just in time.

By the 1970s and 1980s, schools of contemplation gave way to encounter sessions of another kind. The sexual revolution created its own dark nights. Truth to tell, during this same period, there were not many places where earnest souls could practice highly structured programs of prayer and contemplation such as those that flourished in early modern France. Although the Woodstock generation probably shared more than they realized with seventeenth-century Quietism, the flower children from the 1960s, when they reached middle age, were not disposed to pick up something like *The Spiritual Guide, Which Dis-intangles the Soul; And Brings It by the Inward Way, to the Getting of Perfect Contemplation, and the Rich Treatise of Internal Peace*, as a 1699 English translation renders *Guía Espiritual* by the Spanish priest Michael de Molinos (ca. 1628–97).[55] Hippies and Quietists apart, Catholics worldwide rejoiced when the time came for Thérèse Martin to receive her heavenly doctorate.

Today, Catholics should take comfort from the fact that postconciliar popes have recognized saints like Catherine of Siena and Thérèse of Lisieux as doctors of the Church. These holy women encourage twenty-first century believers to take up and remain faithful to the *sacra con-*

53. Garrigou-Lagrange, *Perfection chrétienne et contemplation*, vol. 1, viii, offers a synthetic overview and description of these categories.

54. *Dictionaire de spiritualité* (Paris: Éditions Beauchesne, 1935–95). Father Garrigou-Lagrange contributed the essay on the Dominican School (*DS*, 2, c. 2074ff.).

55. For further information, see Ronald A. Knox, *Enthusiasm: A Chapter in the History of Religion* (Westminster, MD: Christian Classics, 1983), 231–318.

versatio. Thérèse's devotion to the Holy Face produced no miraculous visions. She seduces by the quotidian character of her holiness. It may strike some as strange that a young, twenty-something French girl who left behind only letters, poems, and diaries merits enrollment among the great doctors. The Church responds:

> we can rightly recognize in the Saint of Lisieux the charism of a Doctor of the Church, because of the gift of the Holy Spirit she received for living and expressing her experience of faith, and because of her particular understanding of the mystery of Christ. In her are found the gifts of the new law, that is, the grace of the Holy Spirit, who manifests himself in living faith working through charity (cf. St. Thomas Aquinas, *Summa Theol.* I-II q. 106, art. 1; q. 108, art. 1).[56]

Our blessed Sister Thérèse displays the gifts of the new law. As the twenty-first century unfolds, so must we. When we do, we discover a secret about the universe: only the Truth has grace.

56. Pope John Paul II, 1997 apostolic letter, *Divini amoris scientia*, "Saint Thérèse of the Child Jesus and the Holy Face Is Proclaimed a Doctor of the Universal Church," §7.

INDEX

Theology and Sanctity was designed in Scala Pro and Scala Sans and composed by Kachergis Book Design of Pittsboro, North Carolina. It was printed on 60-pound Sebago Cream and bound by Maple Press of York, Pennsylvania.